CAPITAL SHIPS AT WAR
1939–1945

DESPATCHES FROM THE FRONT

The Commanding Officers' Reports From the Field and At Sea.

CAPITAL SHIPS AT WAR 1939–1945

Introduced and compiled by
Martin Mace and John Grehan
With additional research by
Sara Mitchell

Pen & Sword
MARITIME

First published in Great Britain in 2014 by
Pen & Sword Maritime
an imprint of
Pen & Sword Books Ltd
47 Church Street
Barnsley
South Yorkshire
S70 2AS

ISBN 978 1 78346 204 9

Printed and bound in England by
CPI Group (UK) Ltd, Croydon, CR0 4YY

Pen & Sword Books Ltd incorporates the Imprints of Pen & Sword
Aviation, Pen & Sword Maritime, Pen & Sword Military, Wharncliffe Local
History, Pen and Sword Select, Pen and Sword Military Classics and Leo
Cooper.

For a complete list of Pen & Sword titles please contact:
PEN & SWORD BOOKS LIMITED
47 Church Street, Barnsley, South Yorkshire, S70 2AS, England
E-mail: enquiries@pen-and-sword.co.uk
Website: www.pen-and-sword.co.uk

CONTENTS

INTRODUCTION

At the outbreak of the Second World War the seas were the highways of the world. Almost all intercontinental trade around the globe was conducted by ships, great and small. Protecting Britain's maritime activities was the Royal Navy's primary role, in peace and in war, just as it was her enemies' objective to disrupt those activities.

With the commencement of hostilities in 1939, the Royal Navy sought to destroy the German Navy's ability to interfere with Britain's merchant shipping. The main threats, it was believed, came from submarines and surface raiders. In terms of the latter, it was the powerful German capital ships which were of the greatest concern to the Admiralty.

Enormous effort, in terms of time and resources, was put into neutralising these ships, and the stories of their destruction are some of the most exciting tales of the war. The first of these was the operation to sink the German Deutschland-class heavy cruiser *Admiral Graf Spee*, which culminated in the Battle of the River Plate in December 1939.

Every movement by the British and Commonwealth ships that chased and engaged *Admiral Graf Spee* is recorded in Rear Admiral H.H. Harwood's report. This culminated with these words written on Sunday, 17 December 1939, as the Royal Navy warships sailed past the burning wreck of *Admiral Graf Spee* in the estuary of the River Plate: "It was now dark, and she was ablaze from end to end, flames reaching almost as high as the top of her control tower, a magnificent and most cheering sight."

Harwood also included with his despatch a list of observations drawn from the fighting with *Admiral Graf Spee*. This had been the first battle with a capital ship that the Royal Navy had been engaged in since the end of the First World War. Possibly his most enlightening comment was on the performance of *Admiral Graf Spee*'s captain, *Kapitän zur See* Hans Langsdorff.

When the pursuing British warships were spotted by *Admiral Graf Spee*, the German cruiser immediately turned towards them at full speed. This was quite illogical. *Admiral Graf Spee*'s 11-inch guns far outranged the 8-inch and 6-inch guns of the British cruisers. With a maximum speed of almost thirty knots, *Admiral Graf Spee* was only marginally slower than the British cruisers and so could have kept out of their range for a considerable time, enabling its heavier guns to inflict serious damage on the pursuers. But by closing the distance so quickly, the guns of the British cruisers were soon brought into range. Though *Admiral Graf Spee* struck and disabled HMS *Exeter* and put HMS *Ajax*'s aft gun turrets out of action, by the time the battle was discontinued, *Admiral Graf Spee* had been hit approximately seventy times.

As is well known, the damage caused to the German cruiser induced Langsdorff to put into Montevideo, the capital city of neutral Uruguay, for repairs. It was the end of her operational career, in which she accounted for 50,089 tons of Allied shipping.

If the attack on Pearl Harbor on 7 December 1941 was a shock to the USA, the sinking of the King George V-class battleship HMS *Prince of Wales* and Renown-class battlecruiser HMS *Repulse*, was an equally devastating event to Britain. A report on this seemingly inexplicable occurrence was compiled by Vice-Admiral Sir Geoffrey Layton, Commander-in-Chief, Eastern Fleet, on 17 December 1941, but not published until 26 February 1948.

The two ships had been investigating a possible landing by the Japanese at Kuantan, Malaya, when they were attacked by Japanese aircraft as they returned to their base at Singapore. The first attack resulted in just one bomb striking HMS *Repulse*. But this was followed by an attack by seventeen torpedo bombers and one of their torpedoes hit the outer port propeller of *Prince of Wales* where it exited the hull.

Further torpedo strikes were made on both ships and, inevitably, both were sunk. The despatch by Layton is supplemented by that of Captain W.G. Tennant of *Repulse*, who was the senior officer to survive the sinking.

There are also a number of interesting appendices, one of which is a report from Flight Lieutenant Vigors, whose 453 Squadron was involved in the rescue of some of the crews: "I had the privilege to be the first aircraft to reach the crews of the PRINCE OF WALES and the REPULSE after they had been sunk. I say the privilege, for during the next hour while I flew around low over them, I witnessed a show of that indomitable spirit for which the Royal Navy is so famous. I have seen a show of spirit in this war over Dunkirk, during the 'Battle of Britain', and in the London night raids, but never before have I seen anything comparable with what I saw yesterday. I passed over thousands who had been through an ordeal the greatness of which they alone can understand, for it is impossible to pass on one's feelings in disaster to others.

"Even to an eye so inexperienced as mine it was obvious that the three destroyers were going to take hours to pick up those hundreds of men clinging to bits of wreckage, and swimming around in the filthy oily water. Above all this, the threat of another bombing and machine-gun attack was imminent. Every one of those men must have realised that. Yet as I flew around, every man waved and put his thumb up as I flew over him.

"After an hour, lack of petrol forced me to leave, but during that hour I had seen many men in dire danger waving, cheering and joking as if they were holiday-makers at Brighton waving at a low-flying aircraft. It shook me for here was something above human nature. I take off my hat to them, for in them I saw the spirit which wins wars …".

The next published despatch is that of Admiral Sir John Tovey. This provides an account of the sinking of the German battleship *Bismarck*. This famous operation requires no introduction, but what is provided in this despatch are precise details of every move by all the ships involved (and, of course, the aircraft) – details that can only be found in a report of this nature, which runs to more than 20,000 words.

With the demise of *Bismarck*, attention turned to the German capital ship *Scharnhorst*, which is variously described as a battleship and battlecruiser. Though less well known than the Battle of the River Plate and the sinking of *Bismarck*, the Battle of the North Cape was a classic capital ship engagement and the last of its kind between British and German warships.

Scharnhorst was attempting to intercept Arctic convoys but her movements were, to some extent, known by the Admiralty and plans were laid to trap the German battleship. The Royal Navy's Force 1, under the command of Vice-Admiral Robert Burnett, encountered *Scharnhorst* on 26 December 1943.

Though, as with *Admiral Graf Spee*, the German ship out-gunned the cruisers of Force 1, it was the British ships that scored decisive hits on the enemy, with *Scharnhorst*'s radar being put out of action. From that moment onwards the German ship was severely disadvantaged.

Scharnhorst turned away, followed by the British cruisers. Unable to use its radar, *Scharnhorst* unwittingly sailed into the path of the King George V-class battleship HMS *Duke of York* and its four accompanying destroyers of Force 2.

In the glare of starshells fired by HMS *Belfast* (the very same warship that is part of the Imperial War Museum and is open to visitors in London), HMS *Duke of York*'s 14-inch guns fired salvo after salvo, disabling *Scharnhorst*'s fore turrets and damaging her No.1 boiler room.

The German warship's speed fell dramatically, enabling the destroyers to close in for the kill with their torpedoes. *Scharnhorst* was hit by one of the torpedoes and then subjected to an intense barrage from Burnett's cruisers and *Duke of York*.

"Little information is forthcoming from prisoners about this part of the action as they were not unnaturally stunned by the success of our destroyer attacks and the pounding which their ship was receiving," wrote Admiral Bruce Fraser, Commander-in-Chief, Home Fleet. He went on to state that, "Prisoners state that the Captain had sent his final signal to Hitler, assuring him that SCHARNHORST would fight to the last shell, and that the Admiral and Captain had then shot themselves on the bridge."

This turned out to be not quite the case as *Scharnhorst*'s Captain, *Kapitän zur See* Fritz Hintze, and *Konteradmiral* Erich Bey, who led the German task force, were later found in the water alive but fatally wounded.

Of these two men, when Admiral Fraser briefed his officers on board HMS *Duke of York* later on the evening of 26 December 1943, he said: "Gentlemen, the battle against the *Scharnhorst* has ended in victory for us. I hope that any of you who are ever called upon to lead a ship into action against an opponent many times superior, will command your ship as gallantly as the *Scharnhorst* was commanded today."

After the big naval battles which saw the end of *Bismarck* and *Scharnhorst*, the actions against the battleship *Tirpitz*, the second of the two Bismarck-class battleships built for the *Kriegsmarine*, take on an entirely different nature.

As *Tirpitz* never fired her main armament in anger on the high seas, there was no opportunity for the warships of the Royal Navy to engage her. Instead, hidden deep within Norwegian fjords, it was only possible to attack her by aircraft or, more spectacularly, by X-Craft, or midget submarines.

Once again the story of one of these attacks, code-named Operation *Source*, is presented in minute detail. Though written in a formal manner, as would be expected of an official report, Rear Admiral C.B. Barry cannot help revealing his own sentiments on the daring operation which resulted in the awards two Victoria Crosses, three Distinguished Service Orders and a Distinguished Conduct Medal:

"In the full knowledge of the hazards they were to encounter, these gallant crews penetrated into a heavily defended fleet anchorage. There, with cool courage and determination and in spite of all the modern devices that ingenuity could devise for their detection and destruction, they pressed home their attack to the full."

The last despatch in this volume is also from Admiral Sir Bruce A. Fraser, GCB, KBE. This one concerns the contribution of the British Pacific Fleet to the assault on Okinawa in the spring of 1945. Perhaps surprisingly, this is the longest despatch in the collection.

As Fraser points out, at first the Americans were somewhat dismissive of the Royal Navy's involvement in what they considered to be their theatre of operations. However, the toll taken by Japanese suicide bombers on the more lightly armoured American aircraft carriers led to the United States becoming heavily dependent on British carriers. "We have now, I am sure, become not only welcome but necessary in Central Pacific operations," Fraser laconically remarked.

This contribution was enormous, consisting of four battleships (hence the inclusion of this despatch in this volume), as well as eleven cruisers and thirty-one submarines. The six fleet carriers, four light carriers, nine escort carriers and two aircraft maintenance carriers carried a total of more than 500 aircraft.

The Royal Navy ended the war as it had begun it, as the most powerful fighting force in the world. The loss of HMS *Prince of Wales* and the sinking of *Bismarck* and *Tirpitz* had shown, however, that large, expensive battleships could be destroyed by torpedoes and aircraft. The days of the capital ships were at an end.

*

The objective of this book is to reproduce those despatches relating to capital ships as they first appeared to the general public some seventy years ago. They have not been modified, edited or interpreted in any way and are therefore the original and unique words of the commanding officers as they saw things at the time.

Any grammatical or spelling errors have been left uncorrected to retain the authenticity of the documents. The authors of the despatches also made frequent use of abbreviations, some of which may not be immediately obvious to the reader; consequently we have included in the book an explanation of these.

IMAGES

1   A watercolour by Edward Tufnell, RN (Retd), depicting the cruisers HMS *Exeter* (foreground) and HMNZS *Achilles* (right centre background) in action with the *Admiral Graf Spee* (right background) on 13 December 1939. (US Naval Historical Center)

2   A photograph of the port bow of *Admiral Graf Spee* which was taken whilst the warship was anchored in Montevideo Harbour following the Battle of the River Plate. Note the ship's badge mounted just forward of her anchors and hause pipes, the false bow wave camouflage, and shell damage in the upper hull side (at right). (US Naval Historical Center)

3   A 15cm gun recovered from the wreck of *Admiral Graf Spee*. On display at the Uruguayan Naval Museum, the gun is trained towards the River Plate, site of the battleship's last action in December 1939. (With the kind permission of Vince Alongi)

4   The German pocket battleship *Admiral Graf Spee* after being scuttled off Montevideo, Uruguay, in the estuary of the River Plate, 17 December 1939. (HMP)

5   On 10 February 2006, the 6.6ft tall eagle figurehead from *Admiral Graf Spee*'s stern was recovered from the waters of the River Plate. It still bears the impact of a heavy calibre round through its chest, almost certainly caused during the Battle of the River Plate. (With the kind permission of Vince Alongi)

6   After *Admiral Graf Spee* was scuttled in the shallow water just outside Montevideo Harbour, much of the ship's superstructure remained above water. Over the years the wreck has subsided into the muddy seabed and today only the tip of the mast remains above the surface – as can be seen here. (With the kind permission of Anthony Papini)

7   The German battleship *Bismarck* photographed from the heavy cruiser *Prinz Eugen* on 24 May 1941, following the Battle of the Denmark Strait and shortly before the two German ships separated. This is the last photograph of *Bismarck* taken by the Germans. (US Naval Historical Center)

8   Taken from a Japanese aircraft, this poor quality image shows HMS *Prince of Wales* at far left and HMS *Repulse* beyond her. A destroyer, either HMS *Express* or HMS *Electra*, is in the foreground. One published account states that this photograph was taken "after the first torpedo attack, during which the *Prince of Wales* sustained heavy torpedo damage". (US Navy Photograph)

9   As the disaster unfolds, some of the crew of the sinking HMS *Prince of Wales* abandon ship, transferring, where they can, to the destroyer HMS *Express*. Moments later, the list on *Prince of Wales* suddenly increased and *Express* had to withdraw. The next morning after the loss of the two great warships, Winston Churchill received the news by telephone from the First Sea Lord, Sir Dudley Pound. "Prime Minister," the latter said. "I have to report to you that the *Prince of Wales* and the *Repulse* have both been sunk by the Japanese – we think by aircraft. Tom Phillips is drowned." "Are you sure it's true?" responded Churchill, to which Pound confirmed "There is no doubt at all." "In all the war," noted Churchill, "I never received a more direct shock ... As I turned over and twisted in bed the full horror of the news sank in upon me. There were no British or American ships in the Indian Ocean or the Pacific except the American survivors of Pearl Harbor, who were hastening back to California. Over all this vast expanse of waters Japan was supreme, and we everywhere were weak and naked." (HMP)

10 Also taken from a Japanese aircraft, this picture captures the early stages of the attack, the initial high-level bombing, on HMS *Prince of Wales* (top) and HMS *Repulse*. A short, thick plume of black smoke can be seen emanating from HMS *Repulse*, which has just been hit by a bomb and surrounded by at least six near misses. HMS *Prince of Wales* can be seen taking evasive action. The white smoke is from the funnels as the ships attempt to increase speed. (US Naval History and Heritage Command Photograph)

11 A remarkable image of the German battleship *Tirpitz* which was taken by Flight Lieutenant Albert Fane, of the RAF's No.1 Photographic Reconnaissance Unit, during a sortie over Norway. Taken from an altitude of just 100 feet on 28 March 1942, this low-level oblique photograph shows the central portion of the battleship aft of the bridge. This version was subsequently published in an RAF briefing document – note how the top right corner has been censored out. The original caption states that the "arrows indicate gun crews at action stations". (HMP)

12 The crews of the X-craft involved in Operation *Source*, including the passage crews, pose for a group photograph on HMS *Bonaventure* in September 1943. Soon after this image was taken, the midget submarines departed on their mission to attack *Tirptiz*, the "Beast", as Winston Churchill so famously referred to her. (HMP)

13 Four of the X-craft involved in the attack on *Tirpitz* during Operation *Source* are pictured in a floating dock at Port Bannatyne, a coastal village on the Isle of Bute

in Scotland, before their participation in the mission. The original caption states that these are "X-5 to X-10", though only four of the X-craft are visible. (HMP)

14   One of the Operation *Source* X-craft, X-6, pictured being floated alongside HMS *Bonaventure* at Port HHZ in August 1943, prior to the attack. HMS *Bonaventure* was a submarine depot ship which, having been commissioned on 26 January 1943, sailed for Loch Striven, a sea loch adjoining the west side of the Firth of Clyde just north of the Isle of Bute. It was there that HMS *Bonaventure* served as the depot ship for the X-craft crews training for Operation *Source*. Port HHZ, meanwhile, was a Royal Navy shore establishment which was based at Loch Cairnbawn on the west coast of the Scottish Highlands. The base was heavily involved in the training for the X-craft operations. (HMP)

15   A remarkable shot taken the moment that gun crews on *Tirpitz* open fire on an X-craft sighted in Kåfjord during Operation *Source*. Both X-6 and X-7 managed to drop their charges underneath *Tirpitz*, but were unable to make good their escape as they were observed and attacked. Both craft were abandoned and six crew members survived to be captured. (Courtesy of Chris Goss)

16   In 1974 divers located the missing bow and battery section of X-7, unofficially named *Pdinichthys*, at a depth of forty-nine metres. They were successfully raised and donated to the Imperial War Museum at Duxford. They can still be seen there on display alongside the post-war X-craft X-51 or HMS *Stickleback*. (Courtesy of Dr Scott Arthur, Edinburgh)

17   A vertical photographic-reconnaissance image, taken from 8,500 feet, showing *Tirpitz*, surrounded by repair vessels, whilst anchored behind double torpedo booms in Kaa Fjord on 12 July 1944. Prior to this date, the battleship had been damaged on at least two occasions – during the Royal Navy's midget submarine attack on 22 September 1943, and the Fleet Air Arm's strike on 3 April 1944. The damage inflicted by both attacks seems to have been repaired by the time this picture was taken, though it will be noted that the starboard boat and aircraft crane are both missing, replacement perhaps being necessary. The outstanding sortie which produced this photograph was flown in de Havilland Mosquito PR Mk.XVI, NS504, of 544 Squadron, temporarily detached to Leuchars, Fife. After refuelling at Sullom Voe in the Shetland Islands, Flight Lieutenant Dodd and Flight Sergeant Hill flew to Kaa Fjord and back to Leuchars, to complete one of the longest photo-reconnaissance flights ever made, having spent 7 hours 40 minutes in the air. Dodd was awarded an immediate DSO for this achievement. (HMP)

18   The man who wrote the last two despatches in this volume: Admiral Sir Bruce A. Fraser. It was Admiral Fraser who signed the Japanese surrender document for Great Britain, on board USS *Missouri* in Tokyo Bay, on 2 September 1945. (HMP)

MAPS

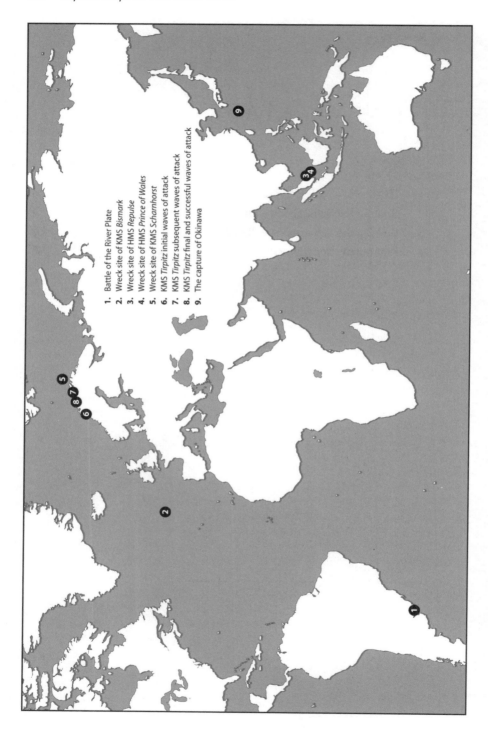

1. Battle of the River Plate
2. Wreck site of KMS *Bismark*
3. Wreck site of HMS *Repulse*
4. Wreck site of HMS *Prince of Wales*
5. Wreck site of KMS *Scharnhorst*
6. KMS *Tirpitz* initial waves of attack
7. KMS *Tirpitz* subsequent waves of attack
8. KMS *Tirpitz* final and successful waves of attack
9. The capture of Okinawa

1

THE BATTLE OF THE RIVER PLATE

13 DECEMBER 1939

The following Despatch was submitted to the Lords Commissioners of the Admiralty on the 30th December, 1939, by Rear Admiral H.H. Harwood, K.C.B., O.B.E., Rear Admiral Commanding South American Division:-

H.M.S. AJAX,
30th December, 1939.

I have the honour to submit the following report of the action between H.M. Ships AJAX* (Captain C.H.L. Woodhouse, Royal Navy), ACHILLES† (Captain W.E. Parry, Royal Navy) and EXETER (Captain F.S. Bell, Royal Navy), under my orders, and the German Armoured Ship ADMIRAL GRAF SPEE on Wednesday, 13th December, 1939, and the sequence of events leading to her self-destruction on Sunday, 17th December, 1939.

All times throughout this report are in the time of Zone plus 2, except where otherwise stated.

Wearing the Broad Pendant of the Commodore Commanding the South American Division.
† *Of the New Zealand Division of the Royal Navy.*

PRELIMINARY DISPOSITIONS

2. The British ship DORIC STAR had reported being attacked by a pocket battleship in position 19 degrees 15' south, 5 degrees 5' east during the afternoon of 2nd December, 1939, and a similar report had been sent by an unknown vessel 170 miles south-west of that position at 0500 G.M.T. on 3rd December.

From this data I estimated that at a cruising speed of 15 knots the raider could reach the Rio de Janeiro focal area a.m. 12th December, the River Plate focal area p.m. 12th December or a.m. 13th December and the Falkland Islands area 14th December.

3. I decided that the Plate, with its larger number of ships and its very valuable grain and meat trade, was the vital area to be defended. I therefore arranged to concentrate there my available forces in advance of the time at which, it was anticipated the raider might start operations in that area.

4. In order to bring this about, I made the following signal to the South American Division timed 1315 of 3rd December, 1939:-

"In view of report pocket battleship, amend previous dispositions. CUMBERLAND self-refit at Falkland Islands as previously arranged but keep at short notice on two shafts. ACHILLES leave Rio de Janeiro area so as to arrive and fuel Montevideo 0600 (Zone plus 2) 8th December, EXETER leave Falkland Islands, for Plate a.m. 9th December, covering S.S. LAFONIA with returning volunteers. AJAX, ACHILLES concentrate in position 35 degrees south, 50 degrees west at 1600 (Zone plus 2) 10th December. EXETER to pass through position 090 degrees Medanos Light 150 miles at 0700 12th December. If concentration with AJAX and ACHILLES is not effected by that time further instructions will be issued to EXETER. Oiler OLYNTHUS is to remain at sea rendezvous until situation clears instead of proceeding to Falkland Islands."

5. Strict W/T silence was kept after passing this signal.

6. Concentration of all three ships was effected by 0700 Tuesday, 12th December, and I then proceeded towards position 32 degrees south, 47 degrees west. This position was chosen from my Shipping Plot as being at that time the most congested part of the diverted shipping routes, i.e., the point where I estimated that a raider could do most damage to British shipping.

7. On concentrating I made the following signal timed 1200/12th December to my Force:-

"My policy with three cruisers in company versus one pocket battleship. Attack at once by day or night. By day act as two units, 1st Division (AJAX and ACHILLES) and EXETER diverged to permit flank marking. First Division will concentrate gunfire. By night ships will normally remain in company in open order. Be prepared for the signal ZMM* which is to have the same meaning as MM3 except that for Division read Single Ship."

8. I amplified this later in my signal 1813/12th December as follows:-

"My object in the signal ZMM is to avoid torpedoes and take the enemy by surprise and cross his stern. Without further orders ships are to clear the line of fire by hauling astern of the new leading ship. The new leading ship is to lead the line without further orders so as to maintain decisive gun range."

I exercised this manoeuvre during the evening of 12th December.

THE ACTION.
Wednesday, 13th December, 1939
0530-0623.

9. At 0520 /13th December, the Squadron was in position 34 degrees 34' south, 49 degrees 17' west. With the last of the dawn I exercised manoeuvring signals, and then re-formed the squadron on a course of 060 speed 14 knots in the order AJAX, ACHILLES, EXETER. At 0614, smoke was sighted bearing 320 and EXETER was ordered to close and investigate it. At 0616 EXETER reported "I think it is a pocket battleship" and two minutes later the enemy opened fire, one 11-in. turret at EXETER and the other at AJAX.

10. The First Division immediately altered course together by signal to 340 degrees to close the range. Captain F.S. Bell, Royal Navy, of H.M.S. EXETER, hauled out of the line and altered course to the westward in accordance with my plan, in order to attack the enemy from a widely different bearing and permit flank marking. All ships increased speed.

EXETER opened fire at 0620, ACHILLES at 0621 and AJAX at 0623.

An enemy report was immediately initiated and was broadcast at 0634. Amplifying reports were made at 0640, 0646 and 0722.

11. From this point until the action was broken off, no alter course signals were made. Captain W.E. Parry, Royal Navy, of H.M.S. ACHILLES manoeuvred his ship as necessary to clear her line of fire, remaining close to AJAX and conforming to her movements. EXETER proceeded independently, her initial course being about 280 degrees.

12. AJAX and ACHILLES opened in Single Ship firing, but Concentration was employed as soon as W/T touch had been established at about 0625.

13. It appeared at this stage as if the enemy was undecided as to her gunnery policy. Her turrets were working under different controls, and she shifted target several times before eventually concentrating both turrets on EXETER.

0623-0630.

14. EXETER was straddled by GRAF SPEE's third salvo, one shell of which burst short amidships, killed the starboard tube's crew, damaged communications and riddled the searchlights and aircraft. Preparations were being made at this time for catapulting the aircraft, but as both were by then out of action, they were manhandled over the side.

15. At 0624, after EXETER had fired eight salvos, she received a direct hit from an 11-in. direct-action shell on the front of "B" turret. This shell burst on impact, put the turret out of action, and splinters swept the bridge, killing or wounding all personnel there with the exception of the Captain and two others, and wrecked the wheelhouse communications.

16. Captain F.S. Bell, Royal Navy, then decided to fight his ship from the after conning position, but owing to communications being destroyed it was some time

before the ship could be brought under the control of that position, and then it could only be done by means of a chain of messengers to pass orders to the after steering position.

Meanwhile EXETER had swung to starboard, and was closing her "A" arcs,[†] but she was brought back to port by an order from the torpedo officer, Lieutenant-Commander C.J. Smith, Royal Navy, who succeeded in getting word through to the lower conning position.

Two more II in. hits were received in the fore part of the ship during this phase.

17. AJAX and ACHILLES were in Concentration firing and seemed to be making good shooting. They were closing the range rapidly and gaining bearing on the enemy.

0630-0638.

18. About this time, the GRAF SPEE shifted the fire of one II in. turret on to the First Division and AJAX was straddled three times at about 063I. The First Division turned slightly away to throw out the enemy's gunfire.

His secondary armament was firing alternately at AJAX and ACHILLES, but with no effect, though some salvos fell close.

I9. AJAX catapulted her aircraft with Lieutenant E.D.G. Lewin, Royal Navy, as pilot, at 0637, a very fine evolution observing that "X" and "Y" turrets were at that time firing on a forward bearing. Owing to delay in establishing W/T communication the first air spotting report was not received until 0654. This method was then employed for the rest of the action.

20. The First Division turned back to port at 0634 in order to close the range.

2I. EXETER fired her starboard torpedoes in local control at 0632 as she turned back to her westerly course, but at 0637 the GRAF SPEE altered course some I50 degrees to port, and steered to the north-westward under cover of smoke. AJAX and ACHILLES immediately hauled round, first to north, then to the west to close the range and regain bearing, accepting the temporary loss of "A" arcs. Both ships were by this time proceeding at full speed.

It appears probable that the First Division's concentration and also EXETER'S fire had up to this point been most effective and it is thought that this and the firing of EXETER'S torpedoes were the cause of the enemy making smoke and altering course away.

0638-0650.

22. At about 0638 EXETER altered course to starboard so as to fire her port torpedoes. She then steered to the north-east to close the First Division till about 0645 when she turned to a westerly course to keep within range.

23. During this period, EXETER received two more II in. hits. "A" turret was put out of action, and the second shell burst in the Chief Petty Officers' flat amidships,

started a fierce fire, and caused the 4 in. magazine to be flooded by burst water mains. All compass repeaters were now out of action, and Captain Bell, using a boat's compass, resolutely maintained EXETER in action with "Y" turret firing in local control and the gunnery officer, Lieutenant-Commander R.B. Jennings, Royal Navy, controlling the fire from the after searchlight platform.

24. At 0640 an II in. direct action shell fell short of ACHILLES in line with the bridge and burst on the water. Splinters killed four ratings in the D.C.T. and stunned the gunnery officer, Lieutenant R.E. Washbourn, Royal Navy. Captain Parry and the Chief Yeoman who were on the bridge were also slightly wounded at the time. The D.C.T. itself was undamaged and, after a few minutes, resumed control from the after control position which had temporarily taken over. The survivors of the crew of the D.C.T. took over the duties of the casualties in a most resolute and efficient manner.

About 0646 reception on ACHILLES fire control W/T set faded, and thereafter she carried on in individual control.

0650-0708.

25. During the period ACHILLES was in individual control, she had great difficulty in finding the line, and at first her salvos were falling well short. Reports of the fall of these salvos were transmitted by the aircraft of AJAX whose gun control officer, not knowing that ACHILLES was no longer in concentration firing, accepted them as referring to his own fall of shot, and corrected accordingly.

The enemy was making smoke at the time, and conditions for direct observations were very bad.

This resulted in AJAX salvos falling well over and the target was not found again until 0708.

26. AJAX and ACHILLES hauled round to the north-westward at 0656 to open their "A" arcs. GRAF SPEE made frequent alterations of course to throw out our gunfire, and from 0700 onwards she made great use of smoke; she appeared to have some form of Chloro-sulphonic apparatus aft, and used this as well as smoke floats.

27. Captain Bell, of H.M.S. EXETER, hauled round to the westward at 0650, and was still engaging the enemy, adjusting his course so as to keep "Y" turret bearing.

EXETER now had a list of 7 degrees to starboard, and had several compartments flooded forward as a result of an II in. hit under the forecastle. She was still being engaged by GRAF SPEE, but the latter's fire appeared at this time to be falling a considerable distance over EXETER.

0708-0728.

28. GRAF SPEE'S range from the First Division was still I6,000 yards at 07I0. I then decided to accept the loss of "A" arcs in order to close the range as rapidly as possible.

Course was altered to the westward, and AJAX and ACHILLES were ordered to proceed at their utmost speed.

29. At 0716, GRAF SPEE made a drastic alteration of course to port under cover of smoke, but four minutes later she turned to the north-west and opened her "A" arcs on the First Division. AJAX was immediately straddled three times by II in. at a range of II,000 yards, but the enemy's secondary armament was firing raggedly, and appeared to be going consistently over, between AJAX and ACHILLES.

30. At 0720, the First Division turned to starboard to bring all guns to bear. Our shooting appeared to be very effective, and a fire was observed amidships in GRAF SPEE.

3I. At 0725, AJAX received an II in. delay action hit on the after superstructure. The shell passed through various cabins, then "X" turret trunk, wrecking the turret machinery below the gunhouse and finally bursting in the Commodore's sleeping cabin, doing considerable damage. A portion of the base of the shell struck "Y" barbette close to the training rack and jammed the turret. It was this shell that killed four and wounded six of "X" turret's crew. This one hit therefore put both "X" and "Y" turrets of AJAX out of action.

32. It now appeared to me that GRAF SPEE intended to neglect EXETER and was determined to close the First Division on a north-westerly course. Thinking she would hold this course, it was decided to fire one broadside of torpedoes from AJAX.

At 0724 AJAX turned to starboard and fired four torpedoes at a range of 9,000 yards. GRAF SPEE probably saw these being fired, as she at once turned some I30 degrees to port, though she came back to the north-west three minutes later.

0728-0740.

33. EXETER had been dropping gradually astern, as she had to reduce speed owing to damage forward. She still continued firing "Y" turret in local control until about 0730, when power to the turret failed due to flooding. She could then no longer keep up with the action, and about 0740 steered to the southeast at slow speed, starting to repair damage and make herself seaworthy.

34. AJAX and ACHILLES hauled back to about 260 degrees at 0728 to close the range still further. At 073I, the aircraft reported "Torpedoes approaching, they will pass ahead of you." I decided, however, not to take any chances, and altered course to I80 degrees, engaging the enemy on the starboard side, with the range closing rapidly. So as to blank ACHILLES' fire for as short a time as possible, I directed her by signal to pass under the stern of AJAX.

35. At 0732 GRAF SPEE turned away to the west, making much smoke and zigzagging to throw out the First Division's gunfire, which, particularly from ACHILLES, appeared to be very accurate at this stage. AJAX was also making very good use of her three available guns. GRAF SPEE altered to the south-west at 0736, and again brought all guns to bear on the First Division.

36. By 0738 the range was down to 8,000 yards. At this time I received a report

that AJAX had only 20 per cent, of ammunition left and had only three guns in action, as one of the hoists had failed in "B" turret and "X" and "Y" turrets were both out of action.

GRAF SPEE'S shooting was still very accurate and she did not appear to have suffered much damage.

I therefore decided to break off the day action and try and close in again after dark. Accordingly at 0740 AJAX and ACHILLES turned away to the east under cover of smoke.

37. One of GRAF SPEE'S last salvos brought down AJAX'S main top mast and destroyed all her aerials. Jury aerials were, however, soon rigged.

38. It subsequently transpired that the report of shortage of ammunition in AJAX referred only to "A" turret, which had been firing continuously for 8I minutes, but this was not realised at the time.

39. GRAF SPEE made no attempt to follow, but steadied on a course of about 270 degrees, proceeding at about 22 knots on a course direct for the River Plate.

40. After opening the range under smoke for six minutes, I again turned the First Division to the westward and ordered ACHILLES to shadow in Sector "A", on the enemy's starboard quarter, and AJAX in Sector "B", on his port quarter. The range at this time being about I5 miles.

4I. The general trend of GRAF SPEE'S retreat at this stage was about 255 degrees. His very conspicuous control tower made it an easy matter to shadow him at long range in the excellent visibility prevailing.

At 0807, as AJAX'S aerials were still down, I ordered ACHILLES to broadcast GRAF SPEE'S position, course and speed to all British merchant ships. A similar message was broadcast every hour from AJAX until the end of the chase. I also passed this information to Admiralty at I0I7 and I700.

42. At 09I2, AJAX recovered her aircraft, the operation being excellently performed under difficult conditions by Captain C.H.L. Woodhouse, and the pilot of the aircraft, Lieutenant E.D.G. Lewin, Royal Navy, and shadowing was resumed.

43. At 0946 I ordered CUMBERLAND, then at the Falkland Islands, to close the Plate at full speed. She left at I200, on the initiative of her Commanding Officer, Captain W.H.G. Fallowfield, Royal Navy, who had by then only received very jumbled messages. On receipt of my signal she at once increased to full speed.

At I005 ACHILLES over-estimating the enemy's speed had closed to 23,000 yards. GRAF SPEE thereupon altered course and fired two three gun salvos at ACHILLES; the first was very short, but the second fell close alongside. She appeared to wait for the first salvo to fall before firing the second.

ACHILLES turned away at full speed under smoke and resumed shadowing at longer range.

44. At II04 a merchant ship was sighted close to GRAF SPEE. She was stopped and was blowing off steam. A few minutes later the following W/T signal was received on 500 k/cs: AJAX (pre-war call sign) from GRAF SPEE – "please pick up lifeboats of English steamer." On coming up with the merchant ship she turned out to be the British S.S. SHAKESPEARE. All her boats were hoisted, and in response

to any signals she reported that she was quite all right and did not require any assistance. By this time she was moving out to the southern flank.

At II05 I received a signal from EXETER who reported that all her turrets were out of action and that she was flooded forward up to No. I4 bulkhead but could still do I8 knots. I ordered her to proceed to the Falkland Islands at whatever speed was possible without straining her bulkheads. She later reported that one gun of "Y" turret could be fired in local control.

At I347 I informed the British Naval Attache Buenos Aires, that GRAF SPEE was heading direct for the Plate.

45. At I543 ACHILLES signalled "Enemy in sight 297", and later reported "Suspected 8 inch cruiser." However, at I559, she negatived the report, and the ship sighted was subsequently identified as S.S. DELANE, whose streamlined funnel gave her a similar appearance to a "Blucher" at very long range.

46. Shadowing continued without incident until I9I5, when GRAF SPEE altered course and fired two salvos at AJAX who immediately turned away under smoke. The first salvo fell short and in line, the second in AJAX'S wake as she turned. The range at this time was about 26,000 yards.

47. It now appeared that GRAF SPEE intended to enter the Plate, and at I902 I ordered ACHILLES to follow her if she went west of Lobos, while AJAX would proceed south of the English Bank in case she doubled back that way. I also directed ACHILLES to take every advantage of territorial waters while shadowing. My instructions were perfectly carried out by Captain W.E. Parry who took ACHILLES inside Lobos Island and close to the Uruguayan coast.

48. Just after sunset GRAF SPEE fired three salvos at ACHILLES, the third being very close. ACHILLES replied with five salvos and appeared to straddle. ACHILLES at this time was just clear of Punta Negra.

49. The Uruguayan gunboat URUGUAY closed AJAX about 2II5. She appeared to be on patrol duty, but was soon left astern.

50. GRAF SPEE also fired single salvos at ACHILLES at 2I32, 2I40 and 2I43, but the visibility to the eastward was very bad for her at these times and firing must have merely been intended to keep shadowers at a distance.

5I. Those shots, however, did not deter Captain Parry from keeping touch and by 2200 ACHILLES had closed to within five miles of GRAF SPEE. The latter was well silhouetted first against the afterglow, and then against the lights of Montevideo. GRAF SPEE proceeded north of the English Bank and anchored in Montevideo roads at 0050.

52. My chief pre-occupation at that time was how long did GRAF SPEE intend to stay there. The primary necessity was to keep to seaward of the GRAF SPEE if she came to sea again, and at the same time to avoid being caught against the dawn light. At 2350 I ordered AJAX and ACHILLES to withdraw from the Plate, ACHILLES to patrol the area from the Uruguayan coast to a line I20 degrees from English Bank, and AJAX the southern area, both ships to move back into the Plate in their respective sectors after dawn.

Thursday, 14th December.

53. I requested His Britannic Majesty's Minister, Montevideo, to use every possible means of delaying GRAF SPEE's sailing, in order to gain time for reinforcements to reach me. I suggested that he should sail British ships and invoke the 24-hour rule to prevent her leaving.

54. I learned that ARK ROYAL, RENOWN, NEPTUNE, DORSETSHIRE, SHROPSHIRE and three destroyers were all closing the Plate, but none of them could reach me for at least five days.

55. CUMBERLAND reported that she would arrive in the Plate at 2200/14th December, having made the passage from the Falkland Islands in 34 hours. I ordered her to cover the sector between Rouen and English Banks, with ACHILLES to the north of her and AJAX to the south. These dispositions were maintained during the night of the 14th/15th December. Should GRAF SPEE come out, she was to be shadowed and all ships were to concentrate sufficiently far to seaward to enable a concerted attack to be carried out.

Friday, 15th December.

56. I ordered R.F.A. OLYNTHUS, Captain L.N. Hill, to proceed to Rouen Bank to be ready to fuel H.M. ships, and proceeded there in AJAX. I ordered CUMBERLAND to close and cover AJAX, remaining at visibility distance to the northward so as to be able to give warning in case GRAF SPEE came out without her sailing being reported.

57. I made the following policy signal timed 1135/15th December:-

"My object destruction. Necessitates concentrating our forces. Increased risk of enemy escape accepted. ACHILLES is now to watch north of English Bank and CUMBERLAND to west of English Bank, latter showing herself off Montevideo in daylight. If enemy leaves before 2100, ships in touch shadow at maximum range – all units concentrate on shadower. If enemy has not left by 2100, leave patrol positions and concentrate in position 090 degrees San Antonio 15 miles by 0030; AJAX will probably join CUMBERLAND on her way south.

"If enemy leaves Montevideo after sunset, CUMBERLAND is at once to fly off one aircraft to locate and shadow enemy, if necessary landing in a lee, risking internment, and trying to find a British ship in the morning. If plan miscarries, adopt plan "B", all units concentrate in position 36 degrees south, 52 degrees west at 0600."

I also repeated my signal 1200/12th December (see paragraph 7) to CUMBERLAND at 1136/15th December, substituting CUMBERLAND for EXETER in the original.

58. AJAX took in 200 tons of fuel from OLYNTHUS, bad weather causing wires to part including the spans of two hurricane hawsers. AJAX then proceeded to join CUMBERLAND.

59. I received a report that GRAF SPEE had landed a funeral party this morning, and later, that she had been granted an extension of her stay up to 72 hours, in order

to make herself seaworthy. It appeared that she had been damaged far more extensively than I had thought likely, and had been hit 60 to 70 times in all. The British ship ASHWORTH was sailed at I900 and GRAF SPEE accepted the edict that she would not be allowed to sail for 24 hours after this. At the same time I could feel no security that she would not break out at any moment.

Saturday, 16th December.

60. CUMBERLAND, AJAX, and ACHILLES made rendezvous off San Antonio at 0030 in accordance with my plan. The squadron closed the Plate towards dawn and AJAX flew off her aircraft for a reconnaissance of the harbour. The aircraft was instructed not to fly over territorial waters.

6I. The aircraft returned at 0830 and the crew reported that they had been unable to see anything owing to bad visibility. They had been fired at while in the vicinity of the Whistle Buoy. This seemed to indicate that GRAF SPEE was taking advantage of the mist and was trying to break out. All ships went to action stations, but a report received shortly afterwards from Montevideo indicated that GRAF SPEE was still in harbour.

62. I informed H.B.M. Minister, Montevideo, of the firing on our aircraft, and suggested that an investigation into this might be a way of delaying GRAF SPEE sailing. He replied, however, that it was definitely not GRAF SPEE who fired, and that it had possibly been the Argentine Guard Gunboat at Recalada, or in some other position.

63. The Admiralty informed me in message 02I9/16th December that I was free to engage GRAF SPEE anywhere outside the three-mile limit. I decided to move my patrol into the area north and east of English Bank, as I considered that a battle in the very restricted water just outside the three-mile limit off Montevideo was impracticable, owing to lack of sea room, and possibility of "overs" landing in Uruguay and causing international complications.

64. Information from Montevideo was to the effect that GRAF SPEE was still repairing damage, having obtained assistance from the shore, and had provisioned. It was reported as unlikely that she would sail that night; on the other hand, once again I did not feel able to rely on such an optimistic report.

65. I signalled the following appreciation to ships in company timed I6I5/16th December:- "My object Destruction necessitates keeping my force together. My Appreciation. Rely on getting his time of sailing and initial course from shore. For subsequent movements rely on CUMBERLAND'S aircraft reconnaissance reports.

"Enemy's courses of Action. (*a*) North of English Bank, (*b*) Between English and Rouen Banks. (*c*) Between Rouen Bank and San Antonio. (*d*) Double back on any track. My Course of Action. I rule out righting him off Whistle Buoy as being politically impossible. Until the dawn phase I want to keep the advantage of light and from this it follows that I must keep to the east and move to intercept him from area to area depending on time and information. My Plan. To keep within reach of intercepting him north of English Bank moving south or doubling back as information comes in. Tactical. I must keep CUMBERLAND so placed that she will not have her fire masked initially, and therefore I will work in divisions 8 cables apart with ACHILLES in close order astern of AJAX.

"After action commences, divisions have complete freedom of action. CUMBERLAND'S aircraft is to be flown off as soon as news is received of enemy's sailing."

66. The British ship DUNSTER GRANGE was sailed from Montevideo at 1700 and a further period before GRAF SPEE could be allowed to sail was claimed. It was, however, reported that she had made very rapid progress with her repairs, and might break out at any moment.

67. The difficulty of intercepting GRAF SPEE who had so many courses of action open to her will, I feel sure, be realised. It was in the dog watches of this evening that I received the Naval Secretary's signal 1717/16th December informing me from the First Lord of the Admiralty of the honours so graciously bestowed by His Majesty the King on myself, Captain W.E. Parry, Captain C.H.L. Woodhouse and Captain F.S. Bell, and also that I had been promoted to Rear Admiral to date 13th December. This was a most stimulating tonic to us all and I took steps to pass it on to H.M. Ships under my command, emphasising the share of all concerned in the honours which their senior officers had received.

68. The squadron spent the night patrolling on a north and south line five miles to the east of the English Bank Light Buoy. OLYNTHUS proceeded to sea with order to be at the Rouen Bank by 1000 the next morning if GRAF SPEE had not broken out.

Sunday, 17th December.

69. I ordered ACHILLES who was getting low in fuel, to oil from OLYNTHUS off the Rouen Bank during the forenoon. AJAX and CUMBERLAND acted as look-outs at visibility distance during the operation. The squadron then cruised in company off the south-east of the English Bank, remaining concentrated throughout the afternoon and ready again to take up the same night patrol as on the previous night.

70. It was reported that GRAF SPEE had landed all her borrowed welding apparatus during this forenoon. We all expected that she would break out at any moment. I would like to place on record the fact that at this stage the most cheerful optimism pervaded all ships in spite of the fact that this was the fifth night of waiting for the enemy.

71. At 1540 I received a signal that GRAF SPEE was transferring between 300 and 400 men to the German ship TACOMA lying close to her in the ante-port. At 1720, a further report stated that over 700 men with their baggage and some provisions had now been transferred, and that there were indications that GRAF SPEE intended to scuttle herself.

Shortly after this GRAF SPEE was reported as weighing.

72. I immediately altered course to close the Whistle Buoy, and increased to 25 knots. AJAX'S aircraft was flown off and ordered to proceed towards Montevideo and report the position of GRAF SPEE and also TACOMA.

GRAF SPEE left harbour at 1815 and proceeded slowly to the westward. TACOMA also weighed, and followed her out of harbour.

73. I ordered my squadron to assume the First Degree of Readiness, in case GRAF SPEE intended re-transferring her crew from TACOMA outside the harbour, or intended to break out with or without her surplus crew.

74. AJAX aircraft reported sighting GRAF SPEE in a position in shallow water some six miles south-west of Montevideo. At 2054 the aircraft signalled: "GRAF SPEE has blown herself up."

75. The squadron carried on towards Montevideo, proceeding north of the English Bank, AJAX and ACHILLES cheering ship as they passed each other.

76. Once again Captain Woodhouse and Lieutenant Lewin made an excellent recovery of AJAX's aircraft, this time under almost dark conditions.

Navigation lights were then switched on and the squadron steamed past the Whistle Buoy within about four miles of the wreck of the GRAF SPEE. It was now dark, and she was ablaze from end to end, flames reaching almost as high as the top of her control tower, a magnificent and most cheering sight.

REMARKS BY REAR ADMIRAL COMMANDING SOUTH AMERICA DIVISION.
Appreciation of conduct of Commanding
Officers and Ships' Companies.

77. I have the greatest pleasure in informing you of the very high standard of efficiency and courage that was displayed by all officers and men throughout the five days of the operation under review.

78. Captain W.E. Parry, Royal Navy, of H.M.S. ACHILLES; Captain C.H.L. Woodhouse, Royal Navy, of H.M.S. AJAX; and Captain F.S. Bell, Royal Navy, of H.M.S. EXETER, all handled their ships in a most efficient and resolute manner.

79. In addition I would like to place on record the very great assistance that I received throughout this period from my Flag Captain and Chief Staff Officer, Captain C.H.L. Woodhouse, Royal Navy.

80. The speedy arrival of H.M.S. CUMBERLAND, Captain W.H.G. Fallowfield, Royal Navy, from the Falkland Islands, was a most creditable performance, especially as that ship was self-refitting at the time the action commenced.

81. Throughout the days of waiting off the Plate, R.F.A. OLYNTHUS, Captain L.N. Hill, arrived punctually at the various rendezvous given him and did everything possible to facilitate the refuelling of H.M. Ships.

82. Within my own knowledge, and from the reports of the Commanding Officers there are many stories of bravery, devotion to duty and of the utmost efficiency which shows that H.M. Ships have been forcefully trained and made thoroughly ready to deal with the many and various exigencies of battle. In accordance with Admiralty

message I755/I6th December, I am submitting separately a list of officers and ratings whom I consider to be especially deserving of award. I would remark, however, that the standard throughout has been so high that the preparation of this list has been very difficult.

83. I would like also to place on record the honour and pleasure I had to taking one of H.M. Ships of the New Zealand Division into action, and fully concur with the Commanding Officer of H.M.S. ACHILLES in paragraph 27 of his report where he remarks that "New Zealand has every reason to be proud of her seamen during their baptism of fire."

84. Further, it is most satisfactory for me to be able to inform you that the machinery and equipment generally of H.M. Ships proved to be of the highest efficiency and well able to stand up to the prolonged strain of battle.

Lessons learned.

85. The main impression left on my mind is of the adequacy of our peace training. Little that had not been practised occurred, particularly among the repair parties. Nevertheless, there are a very large number of points brought out in the reports by the Commanding Officers and I would recommend that they should be carefully studied.

86. As soon as the three ships were in company at the Falkland Islands I ordered committees of the Gunnery, Torpedo and Engineer Officers to be formed so as to analyse the lessons learned. Their conclusions have been forwarded direct to Admiralty.

Enemy Tactics.

87. The most salient point is that GRAF SPEE closed on sighting us, firing one turret at First Division and the other at EXETER.

This initial closing of the range by the enemy had the effect of bringing both the 8 in. and 6 in. cruisers into effective gun range at once and so avoided for us the most difficult problem of gaining range in the face of II in. gunfire.

88. It would appear that GRAF SPEE was heavily handled by the gunfire both of the First Division's concentration and also by that of EXETER in the initial phase, the culminating perhaps being the firing of torpedoes by H.M.S. EXETER. At this point GRAF SPEE turned away under smoke and from that time onwards her Commanding Officer displayed little offensive spirit and did not take advantage of the opportunity that was always present either to close the First Division or EXETER, the latter – and he must have known it – only having one turret in action. Instead GRAF SPEE retired between the two and allowed herself to be fired at from both flanks. Only at one period, i.e., at 0720, did she again open her "A" arcs and

concentrate on the First Division, and she immediately abandoned this when AJAX fired torpedoes.

89. Her frequent alterations of course under smoke were, from an avoiding action point of view, well carried out and undoubtedly threw out our gunfire. This has shown up the necessity for more frequent practice at a highly mobile target at fine angles of inclination. GRAF SPEE had an exceptionally high degree of manoeuvrability and apparently used full wheel for her turns. On many occasions this gave her an apparent list which raised our hopes, but she always came upright again on steadying.

90. At no time did GRAF SPEE steam at a higher speed than 24 knots, and generally her speed was between 19 and 22 knots. It was noticed that from the time of first sighting she was making a considerable amount of reddish-brown and occasionally white smoke.

91. Enemy smoke screens were good but not entirely effective as they did not rise high enough. A point brought out was the necessity for remote control of our smoke floats. Endeavours to light ours while the main armament was firing presented many difficulties.

Enemy Gunnery.

92. GRAF SPEE'S 11 in. fire was accurate throughout, particularly for line. The rate of fire was slow and there were short periods in which either one or the other turret did not appear to be firing, but by the evening phase both turrets were in action. They certainly did excellent shooting at AJAX and ACHILLES at a range of about 26,000 yards while these ships were shadowing. It was evident from this that shadowing ships should, available speed permitting, zigzag so as to prevent too accurate range plotting by the enemy. It was also found desirable to make drastic alterations of course when the first salvo was fired.

93. Perhaps the most interesting point was the mixing of armour-piercing delay action projectiles and direct action. AJAX'S one 11 in. hit and several of EXETER'S were of the delay action type. A delay of 42 feet was measured in AJAX and 65 feet in EXETER. It was most noticeable that at the short range at which the action was fought the 11 in. projectiles proceeded more or less on a horizontal course through the ship and did not directly affect the vitals below.

94. The direct action type produced most serious, and to a certain extent unexpected results. They burst on impact with either the ship or the water and showered splinters in all directions, causing a very large number of casualties to personnel and damage to rigging, electric cables and material generally. I would stress the necessity for more protection of bridges, fire control cables and such important parts of the offensive organisation as the 6 in. director tower. A large number of casualties on EXETER'S bridge were caused by splinters from the hit on "B" turret ricochetting off the roof of the bridge. Immediate steps should be taken to pad the under surface of bridge roofs.

95. The II in. shells that fell short made a black splash and in the vicinity of bursts a black dust like soot was found.

96. The enemy 6 in. fire was ragged and ineffective and caused little, if any, anxiety.

97. There is some evidence that GRAF SPEE fired time-fuzed H.E. possibly from her high angle guns.

Aircraft.

98. The flying off of AJAX'S aircraft with "X" and "Y" turrets firing on a forward bearing while the aircraft was waiting was a gallant and most resolute effort. The handling of both AJAX and her aircraft during subsequent recoveries was also very well carried out. During the past two months I have been most impressed with the rough weather capabilities of the Seafox type of aircraft.

99. EXETER'S Walrus aircraft had been refuelled for the dawn phase, and it was unfortunate that both were hit by splinters before either could be flown off. It was extremely fortunate that the petrol which was being sprayed all over the after part of the ship did not cause any fires. This danger must always be present when an unexpected encounter occurs. Again it emphasizes the necessity for emptying the aircraft of petrol should a night encounter be likely and for the ability to be able to fuel and defuel quickly.

I00. Another point that comes out is the need for speeding up the catapulting process.

I0I. The aircraft, once up, though extremely valuable at times, was not entirely successful.

I02. GRAF SPEE's aircraft was out of action before the battle and did not take part.

Increased Protection.

I03. There must always be a tendency for a cruiser to desire increased protection and most of the claims must, generally speaking, be resisted. Nevertheless, there are portions of the control and of the offensive armament that I feel very strongly should be protected against splinters.

(*a*) The killing or wounding of nearly the whole of EXETER'S bridge personnel is one example. The bullet-proof plating, backed up by the instrument plate was more or less successful in keeping out most of the splinters. It should, however, be made thicker and, as mentioned before, the underside of the bridge roof should be padded to prevent splinters ricochetting off it. It was this latter factor that was the main cause of the casualties.

(*b*) The hitting of ACHILLES' director control tower was most unfortunate, and I consider that, particularly in those ships with only one director tower it should be made splinter proof and also that the leads to it should be in a protected tube.

(*c*) The After Conning Position. This position was used throughout most of the action in EXETER, but its communications failed, and Captain Bell had to con the ship through a chain of messengers. In AJAX casualties from splinters occurred in this position, though it appears they were downwards from a hit on the main-topmast. I consider that the after conning position should be protected and more attention paid to the security of its communications.

(*d*) Other exposed personnel liable to attack from, splinters. I consider that the experience of this action shows that some protection should be given to torpedo tubes' crews, H.A. guns' crews and 0.5 in. machine guns' crews.

(Signed) H.H. HARWOOD,
Rear Admiral Commanding,
South America Division.

* *The signification of these signals was:*

ZMM – ships are to turn to course . . . . starting with the rear ship.

MM – Commanders of Divisions are to turn their Division to course . . . . starting with the rear Division.

†*The arcs on which all guns of a ship's main armament will bear, this allowing them to fire simultaneously at the enemy.*

2

THE SINKING OF THE GERMAN BATTLESHIP *BISMARCK*

27 MAY 1941

The following Despatch was submitted to the Lords Commissioners of the Admiralty on the 5th July, 1941, by Admiral Sir JOHN C.TOVEY, K.C.B., D.S.O., Commander-in-Chief, Home Fleet.

Home Fleet,
5th July, 1941.

Be pleased to lay before the Lords Commissioners of the Admiralty the following despatch covering the operations leading to the sinking of the German battleship BISMARCK on Tuesday, 27th May, 1941. All times are zone minus 2.

First Reports of Enemy.

2. In the second week of May an unusual amount of German air reconnaissance between Jan Mayen Island and Greenland was noticed. It seemed possible that the object of this reconnaissance was to locate the ice-limits either with a view to an attack on Jan Mayen Island, or to assist some ship to break in or out of the North Sea, through the Denmark Strait. On 14th May, accordingly, I asked the Flag Officer-in-Charge, Iceland, for a report of the ice conditions round Jan Mayen Island. The report showed that the approach was possible only from between south and south-west, with ice blocking all other directions. Reports of troop movements in Norway, a false alarm of an air invasion of Iceland and an air reconnaissance of Scapa Flow all continued to direct my attention towards the Denmark Strait; and on 18th May I

instructed SUFFOLK, who was on patrol, to keep a special watch on the passage in both directions close to the ice. The Rear-Admiral Commanding, First Cruiser Squadron, in H.M.S. NORFOLK, sailed from Hvalfiord the next day and relieved SUFFOLK, who returned to Hvalfiord to refuel.

3. Early on 21st May a report was received of 11 merchant vessels and 2 heavily-screened large warships northbound in the Kattegat the day before. Later in the day the warships were located at Bergen and identified from air photographs as one Bismarck class battleship and one Hipper class cruiser. There were indications that these two were contemplating a raid on the ocean trade routes (Admiralty message 1828/21st May) though, if this were so, it seemed unlikely that they would stop at a place so convenient for air reconnaissance as Bergen. Two other pointers were a report (unreliable) of a U-boat, north of Iceland, and an attack by a German aircraft on Thorshaven W/T station.

4. The following dispositions were made:-

(*a*) HOOD (Captain Ralph Kerr, C.B.E.), flying the flag of Vice-Admiral Lancelot E. Holland, C.B., Vice-Admiral Commanding, Battle Cruiser Squadron, and PRINCE OF WALES (Captain John C. Leach, M.V.O.), screened by ELECTRA (Commander Cecil W. May), ANTHONY (Lieutenant-Commander John M. Hodges), ECHO (Lieutenant-Commander Cecil H. de B. Newby), ICARUS (Lieutenant-Commander Colin D. Maud, D.S.C.), ACHATES (Lieutenant-Commander Viscount Jocelyn), and ANTELOPE (Lieutenant-Commander Roger B.N. Hicks, D.S.O.), were sailed from Scapa to Hvalfiord.

(*b*) BIRMINGHAM (Captain Alexander C.G. Madden) and MANCHESTER (Captain Herbert A. Packer), on patrol in the Iceland-Faeroes passage, were ordered to fuel at Skaalefjord and resume patrol.

(*c*) SUFFOLK (Captain Robert M. Ellis), who had just arrived at Hvalfiord after being relieved by NORFOLK (Captain Alfred J.L. Phillips), flying the flag of Rear-Admiral William F. Wake-Walker, C.B., O.B.E., Rear-Admiral Commanding, First Cruiser Squadron, in the Denmark Strait, was ordered to rejoin the Rear-Admiral Commanding, First Cruiser Squadron, after completing with fuel. In order to conserve fuel, this movement was deferred, SUFFOLK being sailed to arrive on patrol just before the earliest possible time of arrival of the enemy.

(*d*) ARETHUSA (Captain Alex C. Chapman), who was due at Reykjavik with the Vice-Admiral Commanding, Orkneys and Shetlands, on a visit of inspection to Iceland, was ordered to remain at Hvalfiord at the disposal of the Rear-Admiral Commanding, First Cruiser Squadron.

(*e*) KING GEORGE V (Captain Wilfrid R. Patterson, C.V.O.), flying the flag of the Commander-in-Chief, Home Fleet, GALATEA (Captain Edward W.B. Sim), flying the flag of Rear-Admiral Alban T.B. Curteis, C.B., Rear-Admiral Commanding, Second Cruiser Squadron, AURORA (Captain William G. Agnew), KENYA (Captain Michael M. Denny, C.B.), NEPTUNE (Captain Rory C. O'Conor), and the remaining three Home Fleet destroyers ACTIVE (Lieutenant-

Commander Michael W. Tomkinson), PUNJABI (Commander Stuart A. Buss, M.V.O.), and NESTOR (Commander Conrad B. Alers-Hankey, D.S.C.), were brought to short notice at Scapa. INGLEFIELD (Captain Percy Todd, D.S.O.; Captain (D), Third Destroyer Flotilla) and INTREPID (Commander Roderick C. Gordon, D.S.O.) arrived on 22nd May and joined this force, as did HERMIONE (Captain Geoffrey N. Oliver) on completing the repair of her fourth turret.

(*f*) The sailing of VICTORIOUS (Captain Henry C. Bovell) and REPULSE (Captain William G. Tennant, C.B., M.V.O.) in Convoy W.S. 8B was cancelled by the Admiralty and they were placed at the disposal of the Commander-in-Chief, Home Fleet. VICTORIOUS was already at Scapa and REPULSE was ordered to sail from the Clyde to join.

(*g*) The submarine MINERVE (Lieutenant de Vaisseau P.M. Sommeville) on patrol off South West Norway was moved to the vicinity of position 6I° 53' N. 3° I5' E.', and the P.3I (Lieutenant John B. de B. Kershaw) was sailed from Scapa to patrol west of Stadtlandet.

(*h*) A bombing attack by Royal Air Force aircraft was arranged for the dark hours and a reconnaissance of the coast from Trondheim to Kristiansand South for first light on 22nd May. Neither of these was able to establish definitely whether the enemy was still at Bergen, owing to the fog and low cloud over the Norwegian coast, but some of the bombers attacked ships, in harbour.

(*i*) The Admiralty transferred 828 Squadron of Albacores to Sumburgh, to attack the enemy at Bergen. I had hoped to embark them in VICTORIOUS in place of her Fulmars, but when it became known that the enemy had sailed, it was too late to do so.

5. The lack of further news about the enemy's movements was disturbing; and the need was felt of an air patrol similar to "Sentinel" (since established) across the route between Norwegian waters and the Northern Straits to report if the enemy left. Here, too, weather conditions were bad, with large stretches of fog, but it would have been possible with the aid of A.S.V.* to maintain some sort of watch.†

6. This state of uncertainty continued until the evening of 22nd May, when the Commanding Officer, R.N. Air Station, Hatston (Captain Henry L. St. J. Fancourt), on his own initiative, despatched an aircraft to try to break through the fog belt to the Norwegian coast. This aircraft carried Commander Geoffrey A. Rotherham, O.B.E., the executive officer of the station and a Naval observer with much experience, and was piloted by Lieutenant (A) Noel E. Goddard, R.N.V.R. Flying almost at surface level, they succeeded in penetrating to the fiords and carried out a search of the position where the enemy ships had been photographed. Finding nothing there, they examined Bergen harbour, under heavy fire, and reported that the ships had sailed. This skilful and determined reconnaissance is deserving of the highest praise, as is the initiative of Captain Fancourt in ordering it.

7. The report of the departure of the warships and convoy reached me at 2000 on 22nd May and, in view of the qualifications of the aircraft crew, I had no hesitation

in accepting it. There seemed to be four possible explanations of the enemy's intentions:-

(*a*) The convoy might contain important military stores for Northern Norway and have gone on up the Leads. Movements of troops to Kirkenes had been reported for some weeks.

(*b*) The convoy might contain a raiding force bound for Iceland, possibly with a view to capturing an aerodrome for operations against Reykjavik and Hvalfiord.

(*c*) The battleship and cruiser might be trying to break out on to the trade routes. This theory had the support of Admiralty intelligence. If it were correct, the further question arose of which passage the enemy would select. Such information as was available suggested that on all previous occasions the Denmark Strait route had been taken, and this was therefore considered the most likely; but the passages between Iceland and Scotland could not be ruled out, especially in view of the enemy's stop at Bergen.

(*d*) The battleship and cruiser might have covered an important convoy over the dangerous sea passage as far as the Inner Leads, and might now be returning to the Baltic.

8. The third possible move carried the greater menace to our interests and dispositions were therefore made to meet it. These dispositions also gave a reasonable possibility of interfering, before it was too late, with any attempted landing in Iceland.

(*a*) SUFFOLK was sailed to join the Rear-Admiral Commanding, First Cruiser Squadron, in the Denmark Strait.

(*b*) ARETHUSA was sailed to join MANCHESTER and BIRMINGHAM in the Iceland- Faeroes passage. These ships were disposed by MANCHESTER in equal areas between 6I° N. I0° 30' W., and 64° N. I5° W. Five trawlers were on their normal patrol west of these areas.

(*c*) The Vice-Admiral Commanding, Battle Cruiser Squadron, with this force then on passage to Hvalfiord, was instructed to cover the patrols in the Denmark Strait and the Iceland-Faeroes passage, operating north of 62° N.

(*d*) KING GEORGE V, VICTORIOUS, GALATEA, AURORA, KENYA, HERMIONE and seven destroyers sailed from Scapa at 2245 to cover the passages, operating south of 62° N. LANCE (Lieutenant-Commander Ralph W.F. Northcott) was compelled to return to Scapa with boiler trouble, but REPULSE and three destroyers of the Western Approaches Command joined north-west of the Butt of Lewis on the forenoon of 23rd May. I had intended to detach two cruisers to patrol the Faeroes-Shetlands passage, but I finally decided to keep all four in company with me.

(*e*) Air reconnaissance of all the passages between Greenland and the Orkneys and of the Norwegian coast was asked for, as well as reconnaissance of forces approaching Iceland. An additional air patrol line about 260 miles west of the Iceland-Faeroes passage was also established by the Admiral Commanding Western Approaches.

9. It was desirable that the cruiser patrols in the passages, and the heavy ships as well, should be as nearly complete with fuel as possible when the BISMARCK was located. The problem involved in ensuring this, during the long period between her location at Bergen and the report of her departure, was not an easy one. If the BISMARCK had chosen the Iceland- Faeroes passage, the cruisers which were sent to refuel at Skaalefjord would only just have been in time to intercept her when they resumed their patrol. The force in company with me was likewise sailed at the latest possible moment, for it was obvious that fuel would become a vital factor before the operation was completed.

I0. The battlefleet proceeded to the north-westward until reaching latitude 60° N., far enough north to be in a position to deal with an attack on Iceland or a possible break back, and then steered west. There had been an interval of 29 hours between the time the enemy was last seen at Bergen and the time they were found to have left, so no accurate estimation of their "furthest on" position could be made; but the time of their first sighting by SUFFOLK showed later that they must have sailed on the evening of 2Ist May, soon after they had been photographed at Bergen and long before their departure was discovered.

* *A.S.V. – radar equipment in aircraft.*
† *At the request of the Admiralty, Coastal Command carried out the more southerly air patrols at this time and there were insufficient A.S.V. aircraft left to fly any further patrols.*

First Sighting.

II. The air patrols arranged for 23rd May were seriously depleted by weather conditions. Two sorties were carried out in the Iceland-Faeroes gap, the more westerly one backing it up was maintained only from I300 to I700, while the Denmark Strait patrol did not fly at all, though I did not learn of this until later.

I2. The Rear-Admiral Commanding, First Cruiser Squadron, had issued the following signalled instructions to NORFOLK and SUFFOLK:-

"SUFFOLK is to patrol within R.D.F.* distance of the ice-edge on line running north-east and south-west. Southern end of 3 hour beat to be on line 3I0° from Staalbierg Huk. The time at southern end to be at 2200 and every 6 hours thereafter. When clear inshore NORFOLK will patrol about I5 miles abeam of you. When thick inshore NORFOLK will patrol to cover inshore passage. NORFOLK will make contact with you at I300B/24th May in position 66° 45' N. 26° W. to check position. Investigate ice up to minefield on parting company to-day Friday."

I3. On the afternoon of 23rd May the atmospheric conditions in the Denmark Strait were unusual, being clear over and close to the ice, and misty between the ice and the land. SUFFOLK took advantage of this to move further to the eastward across the top of the minefield than would otherwise have been prudent and kept close to the edge of the mist so as to have cover handy if the BISMARCK were sighted at close range. NORFOLK patrolled I5 miles on the beam of SUFFOLK'S patrol.

I4. Shortly after turning back to the south-westward on completing her investigation of the ice-edge, SUFFOLK at I922 sighted the BISMARCK, followed by the PRINZ EUGEN, 7 miles on the starboard quarter, steaming the same course as herself. SUFFOLK made an enemy report, increased to full speed and altered to I50° to take cover in the mist and to make for the gap in the minefield if unable to round its northern edge. She was able, however, to keep under cover and to follow the BISMARCK round the minefield, maintaining touch by R.D.F. Her alert look-out and the intelligent use made of the peculiar weather conditions enabled SUFFOLK, after this short range sighting, to avoid being engaged. At 2028 she sighted the enemy again, reported them and once more retired into the mist. At the same time, NORFOLK, who had meanwhile been closing, also made contact, this time at a range of 6 miles. The BISMARCK opened fire, but NORFOLK retired safely under a smoke screen, though some salvos fell close enough to throw splinters on board.

I5. This report from NORFOLK (2032/23rd May) was the first intimation that I received of the enemy being sighted, as none of SUFFOLK's reports up to date had been received in the battlefleet. The two cruisers proceeded to shadow with great skill in very difficult conditions. There were rain storms, snow storms, ice floes and mirage effects, which occasionally deceived SUFFOLK into thinking that the enemy had closed to very short range. SUFFOLK took up a position on the starboard quarter of the enemy within R.D.F. range of the edge of the ice, to ensure that the enemy could not turn back unseen between her and the ice; NORFOLK on the port quarter covered any possible turn to the southward. The Rear-Admiral Commanding, First Cruiser Squadron, reports that a third, smaller, ship was thought to be present; but SUFFOLK never saw this ship and in view of her position it is considered that its presence is not established. It is curious, however, that PRINCE OF WALES also obtained 3 echoes soon after meeting the enemy. It is possible that two separate R.D.F. echoes were being received from the BISMARCK. Aircraft from Iceland were also sent to shadow, and one made a report of enemy's course and speed to NORFOLK.

Battle Cruiser Force.

I6. HOOD and PRINCE OF WALES and their screen were meanwhile closing at high speed. They arrived in the vicinity of the enemy sooner than I had expected. At 0205 the Vice-Admiral Commanding, Battle Cruiser Squadron turned to a course nearly parallel to that of the enemy to wait for the relative positions to become clear and for daylight. The opposing forces were in close proximity at this time, and it is possible that the ship sighted by NORFOLK at 0229 was the PRINCE OF WALES. During the rest of the night PRINCE OF WALES obtained frequent D/F† bearings of NORFOLK and SUFFOLK and passed them in to the Vice-Admiral Commanding,

Battle Cruiser Squadron. At 0340 HOOD and PRINCE OF WALES increased to 28 knots and altered in to make contact.

I7. It was the intention of the Vice-Admiral Commanding, Battle Cruiser Squadron, that HOOD and PRINCE OF WALES should engage the BISMARCK, leaving the PRINZ EUGEN to the cruisers, but the Rear-Admiral Commanding, First Cruiser Squadron, was not aware that the battle-cruiser force was so near; NORFOLK and SUFFOLK, therefore, shadowing from the eastward and northward respectively at a range of about I5 miles, were not in a position to engage the PRINZ EUGEN who was now stationed ahead of the BISMARCK on a course of 240°.

I8. HOOD and PRINCE OF WALES sighted the enemy at 0535 from a direction just before his beam and came into action at 0553 steering to close the range as fast as possible. All three ships opened fire practically simultaneously at a range of about 25,000 yards. The shooting of both the HOOD and the BISMARCK was excellent from the start and both scored hits almost at once. The BISMARCK's second or third salvo started a fire in HOOD in the vicinity of the port after 4-inch mounting. This fire spread rapidly and, at 0600, just after the ships had turned together to open 'A' arcs,‡ HOOD was straddled again: there was a huge explosion between the after funnel and the mainmast and the ship sank in 3 or 4 minutes. She had fired only 5 or 6 salvos. The loss by one unlucky hit of this famous ship with Vice-Admiral Lancelot Ernest Holland, C.B., Captain Ralph Kerr, C.B.E., and her fine company, was a grievous blow.

I9. PRINCE OF WALES had started off well for so new and unpractised a ship and had straddled with her sixth salvo. She had been engaging the BISMARCK, while herself being engaged by the PRINZ EUGEN. After emptying her aircraft in preparation for a night encounter, she had been unable to refuel it in time to fly off before contact was made. It was just about to be catapulted when it was hit by splinters and had to be jettisoned. As soon as HOOD had been disposed of, the BISMARCK shifted her main and secondary armament fire quickly and accurately on to the PRINCE OF WALES. The range was now about I8,000 yards and PRINCE OF WALES' starboard 5.25-inch battery had also come into action. Within a very few minutes she was hit by four I5-inch and three smaller, probably 8-inch shells; her compass platform was damaged and most of the people on it killed or wounded; both forward H.A. Directors and the starboard after one were out of action; one four-gunned turret had jammed and the ship, was holed underwater aft. The Rear-Admiral Commanding, First Cruiser Squadron, reports that PRINCE OF WALES' salvos were now falling short and had a very large spread. The Commanding Officer considered it expedient temporarily to break off the action and, at 06I3, turned away under smoke. The range on ceasing fire was I4,600 yards.

20. SUFFOLK reported that the BISMARCK had suffered three hits, but neither the Rear-Admiral Commanding, First Cruiser Squadron, nor PRINCE OF WALES had been able to observe any hits for certain, though black smoke had been seen at times. Her fire at any rate was still very accurate. (It is now known that she did probably suffer three hits, one of which caused her to leave an oil track and may have had a considerable effect on her endurance.)

2I. The Rear-Admiral Commanding, First Cruiser Squadron, ordered the destroyers in the area to search for survivors of the HOOD and told PRINCE OF WALES to remain in company with him and maintain her best speed. By 0720 she had cleared away most of the debris on the bridge, and resumed conning from the compass platform; two guns of 'Y' turret were again in action and her best speed had been reported as 27 knots.

Admiralty footnotes:-
* *R.D.F. – radar.*
†*D/F – direction finding.*
‡*A' arcs are the arcs on which all guns of a ship's main armament will bear, thus allowing them to fire simultaneously at the enemy.*

Decision to Break Off the Action.

22. The Commanding Officer of the PRINCE OF WALES in this report says:-

"Some explanation remains to be made as to my decision to break off the engagement after the sinking of H.M.S. HOOD – a decision which clearly invites most critical examination. Prior to the disaster to HOOD I felt confident that together we could deal adequately with the BISMARCK and her consort. The sinking of the HOOD obviously changed the immediate situation, and there were three further considerations requiring to be weighed up, of which the first two had been in my mind before action was joined, namely:-

(*a*) The practical certainty that owing to mechanical 'teething troubles' a full output from the main armament was not to be expected.

(*b*) The working tip of the ship after commissioning had only just reached a stage where I had felt able to report to the Commander-in-Chief, Home Fleet, that I considered her reasonably fit to take part in service operations. This was the first occasion on which she had done so. From the gunnery point of view the personnel was immensely keen and well drilled, but inexperienced.

(*c*) The likelihood of a decisive concentration being effected at a later stage.

In all the circumstances I did not consider it sound tactics to continue single-handed the engagement with two German ships, both of whom might be expected to be at the peak of their efficiency. Accordingly I turned away and broke off the action pending a more favourable opportunity."

23. The Rear-Admiral Commanding, First Cruiser Squadron, in his report says:-

"At I545 Admiralty signal I445* had been received. At that time I had no evidence that the enemy's speed was in any way reduced by damage and I did not consider it likely that he would fight or that we could catch him, as his policy was obviously evasion.

The question whether I should re-engage with PRINCE OF WALES had been exercising my mind for some time before the receipt of this signal. The factors to be considered were as follows:-

In the first place, the state of efficiency of PRINCE OF WALES. I had seen her forced out of action after 10 minutes' engagement, at the end of which her salvos were falling short and had a very large spread indeed. As a result of the action she was short of one gun and her bridge was wrecked. She was a brand new ship, with new turrets in which mechanical breakdowns had occurred and were to be expected, apart from damage, and she had had a bare minimum period for working up. I had been unable to observe for certain any hits on the BISMARCK and her shooting had given striking proof of its efficiency. To put it in a nutshell, I did not and do not consider that in her then state of efficiency the PRINCE OF WALES was a match for the BISMARCK.

This, however, was in no way a deciding factor. My object was the destruction of the BISMARCK and I knew that other forces were on the way to intercept her. I had therefore two broad alternatives, one to ensure that she was intercepted by the Commander-in-Chief, the other to attempt her destruction with my own force.

This second alternative involved my being able to bring her to action and this required an excess of speed. I had no evidence that, with PRINCE OF WALES reduced to 27 knots, I possessed it. If, however, the attempt had shown that we could overtake her I would have had to engage with the whole force and press the action to a range at which the 8-inch cruisers' fire would be effective – and could be spotted – namely 20,000 yards or less.

In view of the relative efficiency of the two heavy ships I was of the opinion that such an action would almost certainly result as follows. A gradual reduction of PRINCE OF WALES gunfire due to material failures and damage, in return for which the BISMARCK would receive some damage. That such damage, though it would affect her fighting efficiency, would also have any large effect on her speed I considered improbable, as in a modern well-protected ship the most that could be expected would be some loss of draught due to damaged funnels or fans, or waterline damage forward or aft.

At the range to which the action must be pressed the cruisers might well be left to bear the brunt of the BISMARCK's and PRINZ EUGEN's fire and suffer a reduction of speed due to hits in their large and unprotected machinery spaces or waterline. I should then have a damaged PRINCE OF WALES, and possibly damaged cruisers, with which to try and maintain touch with a BISMARCK damaged but still capable of a high speed.

The alternative was to ensure her interception by the Commander-in-Chief. This I felt I had good reason for thinking I could achieve. At this time I was expecting the Commander-in-Chief to be able to make contact about 0100[†]on the 25th – before dark – and I saw no reason why our success so far in keeping touch should not continue. Even if we had to wait till next day for the Commander-in-Chief, the conditions of darkness were no more difficult than those of low visibility with which we had been able to deal by the use of R.D.F. and it would only be dark from 0200 to 0500."

(†This was due to a miscalculation. The earliest the Commander-in-Chief could arrive, even if he forecast exactly the enemy's movements, was between 0600 and 0700/25th May.)

"The decision was not an easy one. I appreciated that my force was superior in number and the weight of the moral factors involved. I could not feel, however, that PRINCE OF WALES in her then state of efficiency was worth her face value or that my extra cruiser would counterbalance her weakness. But for the probability of a T/B‡ attack from VICTORIOUS and interception by the Commander-in-Chief the situation would have been fundamentally different, and any other course but to re-engage could not have been considered. As it was, however, the alternatives could be summed up as follows:-

(i) To engage with my whole force; this had possibilities varying from the highly problematical result of the destruction of the enemy, through the gamut of a long stern chase at high speed which would make interception by the Commander-in-Chief impossible, to that of being driven off with loss of speed and inability to keep touch.

(ii) Against this was the alternative of continuing to keep touch, with the possibility that we might fail to do so, though with PRINCE OF WALES in support I had no fear of being driven off.

Weighing these alternatives, I chose the latter. This did not preclude the possibility of attacking the enemy, but in so doing my object must be to ensure interception rather than attempt his destruction, and on this policy I acted.

Their Lordships' signal had enquired my "intentions" as regards re-engaging with PRINCE OF WALES. I was careful in my reply to state my "opinions" and not my intentions, and I was grateful that they left the matter to my judgment."

24. After full consideration of the facts, I am of the opinion that this decision was justified and correct. Some of the factors affecting it require emphasis. The PRINCE OF WALES, with many of the contractor's workmen still on board, had joined the Fleet on 25th March. It was not till 27th April that the last of her turrets could be accepted from the contractors and that practice drills with the whole main armament could be started. Captain Leach had been able to report on 17th May, shortly before the Fleet sailed for this operation, that he considered his ship fit to operate; but neither he nor I interpreted that report as implying that she was fully worked up. Her turrets, of a new and untried model, were known to be liable to teething troubles and could already be seen to be suffering them. The effects of all this on her gunnery had been witnessed by the Rear-Admiral Commanding, First Cruiser Squadron, and he knew, in addition, that her bridge was seriously damaged, that she had taken in 400 tons of water aft and could not exceed 27 knots. The BISMARCK and PRINZ EUGEN, on the other hand, after working up for many months under ideal conditions in the Baltic, had given evidence of a very high degree of efficiency: the BISMARCK had been hit, but the Rear-Admiral Commanding, First Cruiser Squadron, could see no sign of damage.

25. In these circumstances, the senior officer on the spot was clearly justified in his conclusion that he was more likely to achieve his object of ensuring the enemy's destruction by keeping touch until the approaching reinforcements should arrive. If these powerful reinforcements had not been in the vicinity, the problem would, of course, have been a different one.

26. At 1445 the Admiralty asked the Rear-Admiral Commanding, First Cruiser

Squadron, to report on the percentage fighting efficiency of the BISMARCK and requested his intentions as regards PRINCE OF WALES re-engaging. The Rear-Admiral Commanding, First Cruiser Squadron, replied that the BISMARCK's efficiency was uncertain but high, and that he considered that PRINCE OF WALES, "should not re-engage until other heavy ships are in contact unless interception fails. Doubtful if she has speed to force action." From his reply I assumed that the Rear-Admiral Commanding, First Cruiser Squadron, would not force action unless the situation changed materially, or instructions were received either from the Admiralty or myself. I had complete confidence in Rear-Admiral Wake-Walker's judgment, nor did I wish, the enemy to be forced away to the westward.

Shadowing during Daylight on 24th May.

27. After the action had been broken off, the three ships continued to shadow. The enemy proceeded on a south-westerly course, with minor alterations, until 1240. They tried hard, by frequent alterations of course and speed, to throw off the shadowers; and the rapid variations of visibility, between two and seventeen miles, were of great assistance to them; but their efforts were without success. SUFFOLK, using, her R.D.F. in a masterly manner to overcome the difficulties of varying visibility, shadowed from the starboard quarter to cover any attempt to break back along the ice; NORFOLK, with PRINCE OF WALES in company, kept out on the port quarter to ensure the detection of any alteration to the southward. About 1240 the enemy seem to have abandoned hope of evasion by daylight, for they turned south, presumably to gain sea-room for another attempt by night, and reduced to 24 knots.

Movements of the Battlefleet.

28. At the time the first report of the sighting of the enemy was received by me, KING GEORGE V, with REPULSE, VICTORIOUS, GALATEA, AURORA, KENYA, HERMIONE and nine destroyers in company, was in approximate position 60° 20' N. 13° W. I had always thought the enemy, when breaking out, might have long distance aircraft reconnoitring ahead of them, to give warning of any of our forces in a position to intercept; if either or both of our capital ship forces were reported, the enemy might turn back through the Denmark Strait or shape course and speed to avoid contact. I therefore altered course to 280° and increased to 27 knots with the idea of reaching a position from which I could intercept the enemy to the eastward of the Denmark Strait, and at the same time be able to reinforce HOOD and PRINCE OF WALES if they were able to bring him to action and reduce his speed, or force him in my direction. As more information was received, it became clear that the enemy intended to continue his attempt to break out; though there was still the chance that he would turn back when he encountered HOOD and PRINCE of WALES or, if

HOOD and PRINCE OF WALES were to the westward of him when contact was made, he might endeavour to break to the south or south-eastward.

29. The sinking of the HOOD and the damage to PRINCE OF WALES made it unlikely that the enemy would be forced to turn back, and the best hope lay for interception by my force, though this would not become possible unless he reduced his speed. Course was altered accordingly to 260°, and later to 240°. Reports suggested that the enemy was keeping a few miles off the edge of the ice, possibly in the hope of finding thick weather. From my point of view the greatest danger lay in his hugging the coast of Greenland, and then making his way to the westward, where I suspected he might have an oiler: for, if he could refuel, he would be able to use higher speeds than KING GEORGE V could maintain and so get away.

30. The enemy's alteration to the southward and his reduction of speed were a great relief, although there seemed a good chance that he was leading our forces into a concentration of U-boats. It suggested that he did not know of my force and it made interception possible.

3I. There was still a grave risk of his getting away by sheer speed, and though I knew the lack of experience of the crews of the aircraft in VICTORIOUS and of VICTORIOUS's own officers and ship's company, I decided I must call upon their aid in an endeavour to reduce the BISMARCK's speed and to ensure my being able to bring her to action with KING GEORGE V and REPULSE – a call they responded to with such splendid gallantry and success.

32. I therefore detached the Rear-Admiral Commanding, Second Cruiser Squadron, at I509 with VICTORIOUS and the four cruisers with instructions to steer the best course to get within I00 miles of the enemy and deliver a T/B attack. Though VICTORIOUS would be of great value in company with me the next morning to locate the enemy if they escaped during the night, a reduction of speed was the more important object and could only be achieved by detaching her at this stage.

33. KING GEORGE V and REPULSE steered an intercepting course with the object of bringing the enemy to action soon after sunrise with the sun low behind us. The situation at this time was as follows:-

(*a*) The enemy appeared to have settled down to a course of I80° at about 22-24 knots. They were, for no apparent reason, zig-zagging. They were shadowed by SUFFOLK from astern and by PRINCE OF WALES and NORFOLK from the port quarter. The BISMARCK had suffered some damage but retained her fighting efficiency, though an aircraft had reported that she was leaving an oil wake. Their reduced speed was probably dictated by the need for economy of fuel and to afford an opportunity of breaking contact by an increase of speed after dark. PRINCE OF WALES had two guns out of action and considerable damage to her bridge.

(*b*) KING GEORGE V and REPULSE were closing from the eastward and would, if the enemy held their course, make contact about 0830, half an hour after sunrise. REPULSE was short of fuel, but had just enough to fight a short action and then reach Newfoundland. By midnight all destroyers had left for Reykjavik to fuel.

(*c*) RODNEY (Captain Frederick H.G. Dalrymple-Hamilton), with three destroyers, was approaching from the south-eastward and would join about 1000.

(*d*) RAMILLIES (Captain Arthur D. Read) was approaching from the south, steering to get to the westward of the enemy, and would make contact about 1100.

Admiralty footnotes:-
*Admiralty signal 1445/24 asked the Rear-Admiral Commanding 1st Cruiser Squadron, to state:-
(i) the remaining percentage of the BISMARCK's fighting efficiency;
(ii) what ammunition she had expended;
(iii) the reasons for her frequent alterations of course;
(iv) his intention as regards the PRINCE OF WALES re-engaging.
‡ T/B – Torpedo/Bomber aircraft.

Attack by Aircraft of VICTORIOUS.

34. The Rear-Admiral Commanding, Second Cruiser Squadron, with his force proceeded at 28 knots on the course which would bring him soonest within 100 miles. He hoped to get near enough to launch the attack by 2100, but a short engagement with PRINCE OF WALES caused the enemy to make ground to the westward; and. it became apparent that VICTORIOUS could not be within 100 miles of them before 2300. The Rear-Admiral Commanding. Second Cruiser Squadron, therefore ordered the striking force to be flown off at 2200, some 120 miles from the objective.

35. VICTORIOUS had only just commissioned. She was about to carry a large consignment of crated Hurricanes to Gibraltar, there to be assembled and flown to Malta, when she was put under my command for this operation. The only operational aircraft she had on board were, nine Swordfish of 825 and six Fulmars of 802 Squadron. She had only had a week to work up and the Fulmar crews were far from fully trained. The Commanding Officer had decided that nothing less than the whole of 825 Squadron could be expected to produce any result in a torpedo attack. He realised that the Fulmars were far from ideal for shadowing, but decided to use them to maintain touch, in the hope of being able to launch another torpedo attack in the morning.

36. The nine Swordfish were flown off at 2210, followed at 2300 by three Fulmars and at 0100 by two more as reliefs. The weather was showery with squalls; wind north-westerly fresh; visibility good except during showers. Sunset was at 0052.

37. 825 Squadron, by very good navigation and with the assistance of the A.S.V. located the BISMARCK at 2330 and altered to the southward with the object of making their attack from ahead. The cloud was increasing and they lost touch, but after circling round for some time located NORFOLK and PRINCE OF WALES and were re-directed by the former. A few minutes later the A.S.V. gear again indicated a ship and the squadron broke cloud to deliver their attack, only to find themselves over a United States coastguard cutter. The BISMARCK was six miles away and, observing this incident, opened H.A. barrage fire, keeping it up throughout the attack. Eight aircraft got in their attacks, the ninth losing touch in a cloud layer and failing to find the target. At least one hit was obtained.

38. This attack, by a squadron so lately embarked in a new carrier in unfavourable weather conditions, was magnificently carried out and reflects the greatest credit on all concerned. There can be little doubt that the hit was largely responsible for the BISMARCK being finally brought to action and sunk.* The value of A.S.V. was once more demonstrated; without it, it is doubtful whether any attack would have been possible.

39. The Fulmars, whose object was to shadow and to distract the enemy, were less successful. Only one of each group made contact and these did not succeed in holding the enemy for long. The crews were inexperienced, some of the observers finding themselves in a two-seater aircraft for the first time, with a wireless set tuned only on deck and no homing beacon. Night shadowing is a task which tries the most experienced of crews and it is not surprising in these difficult conditions that they failed to achieve it. The utmost gallantry was shown by the crews of these aircraft in their attempt. Two of the Fulmars failed to return, but the crew of one was rescued later by a merchant vessel.

40. The Rear-Admiral Commanding, Second Cruiser Squadron, meanwhile, had been steaming towards the position of the BISMARCK, to shorten the return journey of the aircraft. The homing beacon of VICTORIOUS had broken down and the return of the striking force unfortunately coincided with a rain squall round the ship. They missed her in the darkness and it was necessary to home them by D/F on medium frequency and to carry out an all-round sweep with a signal projector. It was with considerable relief that the Rear-Admiral Commanding, Second Cruiser Squadron, sighted them at 0I55, one hour after they were due and uncomfortably close to the end of their endurance. The homing procedure was continued for the benefit of the missing Fulmars until 0250 when the Rear-Admiral Commanding, Second Cruiser Squadron, was regretfully compelled to order VICTORIOUS to stop it. It was by then quite dark and searchlight sweeps in waters close to the enemy, and where attack by submarines had to be expected, were too hazardous. Course was set to close the last reported position of the enemy, in preparation for a search at dawn; this course was also considered to be the best calculated to avoid an encounter before daylight.

First Cruiser Squadron and PRINCE OF WALES.

4I. Throughout the afternoon NORFOLK, SUFFOLK and PRINCE OF WALES continued to shadow. The enemy's alterations of course to the southward and south-eastward and their reduction of speed were all in our favour. The Rear-Admiral Commanding, First Cruiser Squadron, endeavoured further to delay them, and so to assist me to intercept, by engaging the enemy from astern: but the enemy must have made an alteration of course to the south-westward while the shadowing force was temporarily out of touch, for when he did come within gun range at I840, the Rear-Admiral Commanding, First Cruiser Squadron, found himself still on the port quarter instead of astern. A few salvos were exchanged at long range, and the brief action had the undesirable result of forcing the enemy further to the westward, away from my force. The unreliability of PRINCE OF WALES' armament was demonstrated once more, as two guns again went out of action.

42. The Rear-Admiral Commanding, First Cruiser Squadron, considered the possibility of working to the westward of the enemy to force them towards me; but the risk of losing touch altogether was too great and he continued shadowing as before, instructing PRINCE OF WALES not to open fire except in response to enemy fire.

43. Just when the torpedo attack by the aircraft of VICTORIOUS was developing, the shadowing ships were confused by an American coastguard cutter, which appeared on the bearing of the enemy, and touch was again temporarily lost. It was regained at 0II5, but the light was very bad and only two salvos were fired.

44. By 0I40 it was getting dark and SUFFOLK was ordered to act independently and keep touch by R.D.F., the Commanding Officer having previously been instructed to concentrate on the BISMARCK if the enemy should separate. Experience had suggested that the R.D.F. of PRINCE OF WALES was not reliable; the R.D.F. fitted in NORFOLK had the disadvantage of working on limited bow bearings only, so that she would lose touch at once if forced to turn away. The Rear-Admiral Commanding, First Cruiser, Squadron, therefore, with NORFOLK and PRINCE OF WALES, maintained a position in close support of SUFFOLK.

45. The loss of touch, when it came, was caused primarily by over-confidence. The R.D.F. had been giving such consistently good results and had been used so skilfully that it had engendered a false sense of security. The attention of the Rear-Admiral Commanding, First Cruiser Squadron, had been drawn, both by the Admiralty and by me, to the evident danger of U-boat attack, and he had ordered the ships in company to zig-zag. SUFFOLK was shadowing from the extreme range of her instrument, losing touch on those parts of her zig-zag which took her furthest from the enemy. The enemy altered sharply to starboard while SUFFOLK was moving to port, and, by the time she got back, had gone. It is of interest that on both her last two contacts at 0229 and at 0306, SUFFOLK detected two ships; it would appear that the PRINZ EUGEN was still in company with the BISMARCK.[†]

Admiralty footnotes:-

[*] *It is now known that the hit received in the action with the HOOD about 0600 on May 24th and the resulting loss of oil fuel caused Admiral Lutjens to decide at 0800/24 to make for the French coast. The torpedo hit by the VICTORIOUS at 00I5/25 no doubt confirmed him in this decision. The immediate and principal cause however of the BISMARCK being brought to action was the hit at 2I05/26th May by the aircraft of the ARK ROYAL, which demolished her rudder and left her out of control.*

[†] *It is now known that the PRINZ EUGEN parted company from the BISMARCK at about I8I4 on 24th May.*

Search – Morning of 25th May.

46. SUFFOLK searched towards the enemy's last bearing until it became certain that

they had succeeded in evading and then reported the fact (at 040I). The Commanding Officer decided that it was essential first to allow for an increase of speed, coupled with a small alteration to starboard, since failure to do so now could not subsequently be retrieved. He acted accordingly. By 1100 his curve of search had covered enemy courses up to 220°. The Rear-Admiral Commanding, First Cruiser Squadron, informed me that the enemy had probably made a 90° turn to the west, or had turned back and cut away to the eastward under the stern of the shadowers. At 0620 he detached PRINCE OF WALES to join me and himself searched to the westward, north of SUFFOLK.

47. When I heard that the enemy had succeeded in breaking away from the shadowing force, it seemed probable that they would either make for an oiler or they would make for a dockyard. If the former, they would probably steer north-west towards the Davis Strait, which offered an excellent hiding place for an oiler, or southwards towards where an oiler was suspected to be operating in about 25° 30' N. 42° W. If they were making for a dockyard port, they could steer north-east for the North Sea or south-east for Brest, the Straits of Gibraltar or Dakar. In view of the limited capabilities of VICTORIOUS, I had insufficient forces to search all the possible courses of the enemy. I therefore decided to cover the possibility that they were joining a tanker, for these two ships, refuelled, at large in the Atlantic, would constitute a much more serious and immediate menace to our interests than they would, damaged, in a French or German port.

48. The enemy's courses west of south were being covered by SUFFOLK and, to a lesser extent, by NORFOLK and PRINCE OF WALES. KING GEORGE V worked across to the south-westward to cover a southerly course, allowing for an increase of speed by the enemy. Consideration was given to flying off the Walrus from KING GEORGE V to search the perimeter astern of the ship and so cover a south-easterly course of the enemy; but the swell was such that the sacrifice of the aircraft would almost certainly result, and I did not wish to expose KING GEORGE V to U-boat attack whilst picking up the crew. Subsequent analysis shows that such a search might possibly have located the BISMARCK.

49. The Rear-Admiral Commanding, Second Cruiser Squadron, was ordered by signal to organise an air and surface search, with VICTORIOUS and his four cruisers, northwest of the last known position of the enemy. When I issued these instructions, I estimated that the Rear-Admiral Commanding, Second Cruiser Squadron, and VICTORIOUS were well to the northward of this position; but in point of fact he had been steaming south at high speed and was now close to it. It is probable therefore that the air search carried out did not extend as far as the circle on which the enemy now was and would not have found them even if the aircraft had searched to the eastward, as the Rear-Admiral Commanding, Second Cruiser Squadron, and the Commanding Officer of VICTORIOUS had originally intended.

50. This completed the immediate search, leaving a sector between north and south-east unwatched. The search was backed up to a certain extent by the ships which had been detached by the Admiralty from various other duties and which were approaching the scene. RODNEY recovered her screen, which had earlier been forced

by bad weather to drop astern, and took up an extremely well chosen position on the route for the Bay of Biscay. RAMILLIES patrolled to the southward of KING GEORGE V and PRINCE OF WALES. EDINBURGH (flying the flag of Commodore Charles M. Blackman, D.S.O., Commodore Commanding, Eighteenth Cruiser Squadron), who had been patrolling off the Bay of Biscay and had been sent by the Admiralty to act as relief shadower, was near the track for Gibraltar. In addition, some degree of search was provided by REPULSE, whom I had been compelled to detach to Newfoundland for fuel, and by LONDON (Captain Reginald M. Servaes, C.B.E.), who had been instructed by the Admiralty to search for an enemy tanker believed to be in the area round 25° 30' N. 42° W. Force "H" some 1,300 miles to the south-eastward, had been instructed by the Admiralty to steer to intercept the BISMARCK from the southward.

51. The track of the BISMARCK as drawn on the attached strategical plot (see Plan, i) [*not published*] is probably reasonably accurate. It shows how narrowly she avoided contact with the various British forces during her run east. She started by crossing about 100 miles astern of KING GEORGE V at 0800 on 25th May and then passed about 50 miles from RODNEY and 45 miles from EDINBURGH. On the next day she passed 85 miles under the stern of convoy W.S.8B and 25-30 miles ahead of the Captain (D), Fourth Destroyer Flotilla, who had parted company with this convoy. It is understood that the Captain (D), Fourth Destroyer Flotilla, had disposed the convoy escort to the westward of the convoy in the hope that the BISMARCK would be deflected if she appeared steaming towards it.

52. At 1030 on 25th May, a series of D/F bearings was received from the Admiralty which indicated that the enemy was breaking back across the Atlantic. The signals appeared to come from the same ship which had transmitted several signals soon after the T/B attack of the night before; they could therefore reasonably be attributed to the BISMARCK. These bearings, as plotted in KING GEORGE V, showed a position too far to the northward, which gave the misleading impression that the enemy was making for the North Sea. I broadcast this position of the enemy and instructed all Home Fleet forces to search accordingly. PRINCE OF WALES had not yet joined, but the course of KING GEORGE V was altered to 55°, 27 knots, to make for the Iceland-Faeroes gap.

53. A position of the enemy transmitted by the Admiralty made it clear that the enemy was making for a French port and had a lead of about 100 miles. The accuracy of the information which was issued by the Admiralty throughout this stage of the operation and the speed with which it was passed out were beyond praise. The situation could be clearly envisaged by all the forces concerned and I was able to preserve wireless silence.

54. KING GEORGE V, RODNEY, NORFOLK, EDINBURGH and Force "H" all proceeded at their best speed towards the Bay of Biscay; and a sweep was flown in the evening by Coastal Command flying boats as far as longitude 30° W. When this failed to locate the enemy, two cross-over patrols by flying boats were arranged to start at 1000 on 26th May, across his probable track. In addition to these forces, COSSACK (Captain (D) Fourth Destroyer Flotilla), with SIKH (Commander Graham H. Stokes), ZULU (Commander Harry R. Graham, D.S.O.), MAORI (Commander

Harold T. Armstrong, D.S.C.), and the Polish Ship PIORUN (Commander E. Plawski) were detached by the Admiralty from convoy W.S. 8B early on 26th May and instructed to join and screen KING GEORGE V and RODNEY, to be joined by JUPITER (Lieutenant-Commander Norman V.J.T. Thew) from Londonderry; and DORSETSHIRE (Captain Benjamin C.S. Martin), on receipt of the first enemy report, reported that she intended to leave convoy S.L. 74, which she was escorting, and came up from the south-west to intercept and shadow.

Other Dispositions.

55. Meanwhile, those forces which could not reach the most probable track of the enemy were moving to cover alternative possible movements. MANCHESTER and BIRMINGHAM took up the Iceland-Faeroes patrol and ARETHUSA that of the Denmark Strait, with air patrols of all the northern passages to assist. The Rear-Admiral Commanding, Second Cruiser Squadron, in GALATEA, with VICTORIOUS, KENYA, AURORA and HERMIONE in company, proceeded towards the Iceland-Faeroes passage, carrying out air searches on the way. The cruisers had not enough fuel left to escort VICTORIOUS to the Bay and she could not be allowed to proceed unescorted.

56. Two Swordfish aircraft were lost during air searches on 25th and 26th May; but the crew of one of them had a remarkable escape. The aircraft landed alongside a ship's lifeboat, unoccupied but complete with provisions and water, and the crew spent nine days in the boat before being picked up by a merchant vessel. One of the Fulmar crews was also rescued by a merchant vessel.

57. PRINCE OF WALES also proceeded towards Iceland; and destroyers were sent out to screen her and VICTORIOUS. SUFFOLK, after her search, was too short of fuel to steam at the high speed necessary to come up with the BISMARCK; considerable forces were better placed than she was for intercepting an enemy movement to the south-eastward and the Commanding Officer considered he would be better employed covering VICTORIOUS in the northern area, where there was nothing more powerful than a 6-inch cruiser. He therefore set course to the north-eastward until he was instructed, on 26th May, to proceed to an area in the Davis Strait south-west of Cape Farewell and search for enemy supply ships.

58. Two ether precautions were taken by the Admiralty: the Flag Officer Commanding, North Atlantic, was instructed to arrange air and submarine patrols to prevent passage of the Straits of Gibraltar, NELSON being sailed from Freetown to reinforce; and LONDON was recalled from her search for a tanker and instructed to escort convoy S.L. 75, which was approaching the area west of the Bay of Biscay.

59. At II00 on 25th May, when in position 4I° 30' N. I7° I0' W., the Flag Officer Commanding, Force "H" (Vice-Admiral Sir James F. Somerville, K.C.B., D.S.O.) in RENOWN (Captain Rhoderick R. McGrigor), with ARK ROYAL (Captain Loben E.H. Maund) and SHEFFIELD (Captain Charles A.A. Larcom) in company, was instructed by the Admiralty to act on the assumption that the enemy was proceeding to Brest. Course was set for a favourable initial position and a comprehensive scheme

of air search, to cover all enemy speeds between 25 and 15 knots, was prepared for the following day.

60. No information had been received since 23rd May of the two German battlecruisers at Brest, so a security patrol was flown off in the morning to search to the west and northward in case one or both of these ships should be at sea in support of the BISMARCK. Ten Swordfish were flown off at 0835 on 26th May for the first search, whose western edge was next to the flying boat patrols arranged by the Admiralty. It had been hoped to thicken the search with Fulmars, but the weather conditions rendered this impracticable. The wind was from 320°, force 7,* sea rough, sky overcast, visibility 10-12 miles; the round down of ARK ROYAL was rising and falling 56 feet and the handling of aircraft on deck was extremely difficult. While the search was in progress Force "H" proceeded to reach a position to windward, so that the operation of aircraft would not be impeded by subsequent movements of the BISMARCK, if the latter were located.

The BISMARCK Located.

61. At 1030 on 26th May one of the Coastal Command flying boats on cross-over patrol sighted and reported the BISMARCK. The Flag Officer Commanding, Force "H", on receipt of this report, ordered ARK ROYAL to fly off two shadowing aircraft fitted with long range tanks to gain touch, as he feared that the flying boat's position might be inaccurate in view of the weather conditions and the distance from her base. (It was, in fact, about 35 miles in error.) Three quarters of an hour after the first sighting, one of ARK ROYAL's searching aircraft also located the enemy, followed shortly by another. The flying boat reported at this time that her hull had been holed by shrapnel and soon after she lost touch. The reports of the aircraft from ARK ROYAL placed the enemy about 20 miles north of her correct position, but this error was due to the reference position passed out by the Flag Officer Commanding, Force "H" and was corrected later in the day.

62. The BISMARCK was shadowed continuously by aircraft from ARK ROYAL for the rest of the day and excellent reports were made. Particular credit is due to the crews of these aircraft whose part, though unspectacular and often forgotten, is as important and frequently as dangerous as that of the aircraft which attack with torpedoes. The Flag Officer Commanding, Force "H", manoeuvred his force throughout the day to maintain the weather gage for flying operations, to avoid loss of bearing on the BISMARCK and to keep within 50 miles of her to facilitate the launching of T/B attacks. He was instructed by the Admiralty that RENOWN was not to become engaged with the BISMARCK unless the latter was already heavily engaged by either KING GEORGE V or RODNEY.

63. The first report of the BISMARCK placed her about 130 miles south of me, steering a south-easterly course at 22 knots. It was evident that she had too great a lead for KING GEORGE V to come up with her unless her speed could be further reduced or she could be deflected from her course; our only hope lay in torpedo attacks by the aircraft of ARK ROYAL.

Fuel.

64. The shortage of fuel in the Home Fleet battleships was a matter of grave anxiety; KING GEORGE V had only 32 per cent remaining, and RODNEY reported that she would have to part company at 0800 the next morning. When these ships joined company later in the day, they had to share an A/S screen of three destroyers SOMALI (Captain Clifford Caslon), TARTAR (Commander Lionel P. Skipwith) and MASHONA (Commander William H. Selby)) and even these were due to leave that night for lack of fuel. There were known to be several U-boats in the area and it was safe to assume that every available destroyer and U-boat in the ports of Western France would also be ordered to sea. The Admiralty had also warned me to expect heavy air attack. It was therefore essential to allow a sufficient reserve of fuel to enable the battleships to return to United Kingdom ports at a reasonably high speed. The loss of HOOD and the damage to PRINCE OF WALES had left KING GEORGE V as the only effective capital ship remaining in Home Waters. I was not prepared to expose her unscreened at low speed to almost certain attack by U-boats unless there was very good prospect of achieving a result commensurate with the risk. I therefore decided that unless the enemy's speed had been reduced, KING GEORGE V should return at 2400 on 26th May to refuel.

First T/B Attack.

65. The speed of KING GEORGE V was reduced to 22 knots at I705 on 26th May to economise fuel and RODNEY, who had by then been overhauled, was formed astern. I had recommended the Flag Officer Commanding, Force "H", to remain with ARK ROYAL; he was maintaining his position on the beam of the BISMARCK and had detached SHEFFIELD to shadow. The visual signal ordering this latter movement was not repeated to ARK ROYAL, an omission which, as will be seen later, had serious consequences.

66. A striking force of I5 Swordfish, one of which had to return, was flown off at I450; they were armed with Duplex pistols set to 30 feet instead of 34 feet, in consequence of the doubt which then existed in ARK ROYAL whether the enemy ship was the BISMARCK or the PRINZ EUGEN. The weather was particularly bad in the vicinity of the target and reliance was placed on the A.S.V. set carried in one of the aircraft; this aircraft located a ship at I550, about 20 miles from the expected position of the enemy, and an attack through the cloud was ordered. The ship detected was SHEFFIELD, of whose presence near the BISMARCK the striking force was not aware, and eleven torpedoes were dropped at her. Two of the torpedoes exploded on hitting the water, and three more on crossing the wake, the remainder being successfully avoided by SHEFFIELD, who, with great forbearance, did not fire a single round in reply.

67. The flying boat was still shadowing, though her reports now differed widely in position from those of the aircraft of ARK ROYAL. Her signals were made on

H/F† and her position could not therefore be checked by D/F. She reported twice during the afternoon that she was being attacked by enemy aircraft, but these were probably shadowing Swordfish from ARK ROYAL.

Admiralty footnotes:-
* *Wind force 7 – moderate gale, 27-33 m.p.h.*
† *H/F – high frequency.*

Second T/B Attack.

68. A second striking force of I5 aircraft was launched at I9I5. Owing to the limited number of serviceable aircraft, it had been necessary to re-arm and refuel most of those which had taken part in the first attack. In view of the apparent failures with Duplex pistols in the first attack, contact pistols were employed on this occasion. The striking force was ordered to make contact with SHEFFIELD before launching the attack and the latter was instructed to home the striking force by D/F.

69. The aircraft approached SHEFFIELD below the clouds and then climbed to 6,000 feet to make their final approach. The weather in the vicinity of SHEFFIELD appeared to be ideal for a synchonised torpedo attack, but when the aircraft came near the BISMARCK, they found that she was under a cold front. A thick bank of cloud with base about 700 feet and top between 6,000 and I0,000 feet was encountered and the force became split up. The torpedo attacks had therefore to be made by sub-flights or pairs of aircraft over a long period in the face of intense and accurate fire; they were pressed home with a gallantry and determination which cannot be praised too highly. One aircraft, having lost touch with his sub-flight, returned to SHEFFIELD for a fresh range and bearing of the enemy and went in again by himself in the face of very heavy fire to score a hit on the port side of the BISMARCK. At least two hits were scored, one of which so damaged the BISMARCK's rudders that she was unable to keep off the wind, which providentially was from the northwest, for any length of time; a result which ARK ROYAL and her aircraft crews had well earned and which ensured my being able to bring the BISMARCK to action next morning.

70. When I received the first report that the BISMARCK had altered course to 340° I dared not hope that it was more than a temporary alteration to avoid a T/B attack; a further report four minutes later that she was steering 000° suggested, however, that her rudders had been damaged and that she had been forced up into the wind towards KING GEORGE V and RODNEY. I immediately, turned towards our estimated position of the BISMARCK in an endeavour to make contact in time to engage her from the eastward in the failing light. But with frequent rain squalls and gathering darkness the light conditions became too unreliable, and with no certainty of the enemy's position or of that of our own forces, but with confirmation of the damage to the enemy and the knowledge that the Fourth Destroyer Flotilla was shadowing, I decided to haul off to the north-north-eastward and work round to engage from the westward at dawn.

7I. The Flag Officer Commanding, Force "H", had informed me that no further T/B attacks were possible that evening and that he was preparing all remaining Swordfish for a strong attack at dawn. He was instructed to keep not less than 20 miles to the southward of the BISMARCK so as to be clear of my approach.

Night Shadowing and Attack by Destroyers.

72. SHEFFIELD made, her last enemy report at 2I40 on 26th May. At this time the BISMARCK turned and fired six accurate I5-inch salvos at her, at a range of nine miles. SHEFFIELD turned away at full speed and made smoke, but suffered a few casualties from splinters. The turn caused her to lose touch, but shortly afterwards she made contact with the Captain (D), Fourth Destroyer Flotilla (Captain Philip L. Vian, D.S.O.), in COSSACK, who with MAORI, ZULU, SIKH and the Polish destroyer PIORUN, was approaching the BISMARCK. The Captain (D), Fourth Destroyer Flotilla, as I knew he would, had decided to shadow and attack the BISMARCK, instead of screening KING GEORGE V and RODNEY; and was wisely proceeding at high speed, in spite of fuel shortage, to get in touch before dark. Ships were spread 2.5 miles apart at right angles to the estimated bearing of the enemy. The approximate bearing and distance of the enemy was obtained from SHEFFIELD and, in view of the heavy sea running, speed was reduced and the flotilla manoeuvred to avoid a high speed end-on contact.

73. The BISMARCK was sighted by PIORUN, on the port wing, at 2238, just after the last shadowing aircraft left to return to ARK ROYAL: destroyers were ordered to take up stations for shadowing: at 2242 the enemy opened a heavy fire on PIORUN, who made a spirited reply before turning away under smoke. It was evident to the Captain (D), Fourth Destroyer Flotilla, that the enemy's speed had been so seriously reduced by the torpedo bomber attack that interception by the battlefleet was a certainty, provided that the enemy could be held. He therefore decided that his main object was to keep touch and his secondary object to attack with torpedoes if he thought this would not involve the destroyers in serious losses. He ordered the destroyers to attack independently as opportunity offered.

74. Throughout the night and until 0845 on 27th May, when the battlefleet came into action, these destroyers maintained touch in spite of heavy seas, rain squalls and low visibility. They were frequently and accurately engaged by the main and secondary armaments of the BISMARCK, who was apparently firing by R.D.F.; but by skilful handling they avoided serious damage and suffered a very small number of casualties. The four ships of the 7th Division all delivered torpedo attacks during the night, COSSACK and MAORI making two each; hits were scored by COSSACK and by MAORI, the latter's torpedo causing a fire on the forecastle of the BISMARCK; SIKH may also have scored a hit.

75. The Commanding Officer of the PIORUN had not worked with the Fourth Destroyer Flotilla before and he therefore decided to wait until last to deliver his attack as he did not wish to interfere with the flotilla and was not fully conversant

with their methods. He had drawn the BISMARCK's fire for an hour during the period of dusk, hoping that this would assist the other destroyers to get in their attacks, but after dark he retired, to a distance of some 6 to 8 miles to wait for them to finish. He had not succeeded in regaining touch when, at 0500, he was ordered by the Captain (D), Fourth Destroyer Flotilla, to proceed to Plymouth to fuel if not in contact with the enemy. The Captain (D), Fourth Destroyer Flotilla, knew that Commander Plawski would certainly attack the enemy as soon as he could find him: conditions as light came would not be easy and the Captain (D), Fourth Destroyer Flotilla, was concerned lest a valuable ship and a fine crew should be lost without need. PIORUN continued to search until 0600 and left an hour later.

76. The conduct of the night operations by these five destroyers under the Captain (D), Fourth Destroyer Flotilla, was a model of its kind. In heavy weather, frequently under fire, they hung on to their prey with the utmost determination, hit her with torpedoes and delivered her to me the next morning, without suffering damage, other than by splinters, to any of their ships.

77. During the night NORFOLK arrived in the area and made her way round to the north-eastward of the enemy, ready to flank mark for the battleships in the morning: EDINBURGH was compelled to leave for Londonderry owing to lack of fuel (she arrived there with 5½ per cent, remaining): and the DORSETSHIRE was also approaching, to arrive soon after the battlefleet joined action. KING GEORGE V and RODNEY worked round to the westward ready to engage at dawn.

78. The BISMARCK was making frequent alterations of course, possibly involuntary, and it was difficult to gauge her progress from the frequent course reports which were received. As was only to be expected with forces which had been widely separated in weather unsuitable for taking sights, considerable differences in reckoning were now apparent. I instructed destroyers to fire starshell to indicate the position of the enemy, but frequent rain squalls prevented these from being seen in KING GEORGE V, while the Captain (D), Fourth Destroyer Flotilla, reported that the reactions of the BISMARCK to this practice were unpleasant. Destroyers in touch were then instructed to transmit on medium frequency so that bearings might be obtained by D/F, but some had their aerials shot away and ZULU had a smashed deck insulator, which caused enough sparking when transmitting to illuminate, the whole ship. It became evident that the relative positions were not known with sufficient accuracy for a dawn approach to be practicable. The visibility, too, was uncertain; and I decided to wait for full light.

ACTION OF 27TH MAY.
Weather: Wind – north-west, force 8.*
Weather – overcast; rain squalls.
Visibility – 12-13 miles.
Sea and swell – 45.
Sunrise – 0722.

Choice of Tactics.

79. It was clear from the reports of the ships which had come under her fire that, in spite of the damage she had already received from guns and torpedoes, the gun armament and control of the BISMARCK were not seriously affected. Everything suggested, however, that her rudders had been so seriously damaged that she could not steer; in the strong wind prevailing, she could, by working her engines, haul off the wind only for short periods. So it was possible for me to select the direction and time of my approach and to close to whatever range I chose. The experience of the Fourth Destroyer Flotilla made it clear that the BISMARCK had R.D.F which ranged accurately up to 8,000 yards; by day, she could range very accurately up to about 24,000 yards, either by means of the excellent stereoscopic rangefinders the Germans have always had or possibly by R.D.F.

80. I decided to approach with the advantages of wind, sea and light and as nearly end-on as possible, so as to provide a difficult target and to close quickly to a range at which rapid hitting could be ensured. I hoped that the sight of two battleships steering straight for them would shake the nerves of the range-takers and control officers, who had already had four anxious days and nights.

The Approach.

8I. Between 0600 and 0700, D/F bearings of a series of reports by MAORI enabled the relative position of the enemy to be deduced with reasonable accuracy. The BISMARCK had settled down to a course of about 330°, at I0 knots. The horizon to the north-eastward was clear and the light good, but south of east were rain squalls and a poor background. The strong wind and heavy sea made it most undesirable to fight to windward. I decided to approach on a bearing of west-north-west and, if the enemy held his course, to deploy to the southward, engaging him on opposite course at a range of about I5,000 yards and subsequently as events might dictate. At 0737, when the enemy bore I20°, 2I miles, course was altered to 080° to close: RODNEY was stationed on a bearing of 0I0° and instructed not to close within six cables of me and to adjust her own bearing. NORFOLK was shadowing from the north-westward, ready to carry out flank marking for the battleships, and at 0820 she came in sight and provided me with a visual link. It had been necessary to alter course on the way in to avoid rain squalls and to allow for the reported alterations of course of the BISMARCK, but at 0843 she came in sight, bearing II8°, 25,000 yards, steering directly towards us, our course at this time being II0°.

The Action.

82. RODNEY opened fire at 0847, followed one minute later by KING GEORGE V and then by the BISMARCK. The BISMARCK had turned to starboard to open 'A'

arcs, and directed her fire at RODNEY. This turn of the enemy made it look as if it would be better for us to deploy to the north-eastward, and I hoisted the signal to turn to 085°; the BISMARCK, however, almost immediately altered back to port, so the negative was hoisted and I indicated my intention to turn to 170°. RODNEY, who wished to open her 'A' arcs, had anticipated the hauling down of the first signal and started to alter course to port; KING GEORGE V also had altered 20° to starboard to open her distance from RODNEY; so that the ships were well separated, which was entirely in accordance with my wishes. The BISMARCK's fire was accurate at the start, though it soon began to fall off; she made continual alterations of course, but it is doubtful whether these were deliberate.

83. The range was now 20,000 yards and decreasing rapidly, the general trend of the enemy's course being directly towards us. Shortly after our turn to the southward, the BISMARCK shifted her fire to KING GEORGE V. By 0905 both KING GEORGE V and RODNEY had their secondary armaments in action. At this stage the effect of our gunfire was difficult to assess, as hits by armour piercing shell are not easily seen; but after half an hour of action the BISMARCK was on fire in several places and virtually out of control. Only one of her turrets remained in action and the fire of this and of her secondary armament was wild and erratic. But she was still steaming.

84. Some interference from our own funnel and cordite smoke had been experienced, and at 0917 the course of the battlefleet was altered towards the enemy and right round to north, RODNEY again anticipating the signal. When the turn had been completed, the lines of fire of KING GEORGE V and RODNEY were approximately at right angles; a heavy volume of fire could be produced without interference in spotting between the two ships. DORSETSHIRE had been firing intermittently since 0902 from the other side of the enemy, as had NORFOLK from her flank marking position.

85. In order to increase the rate of hitting, the battleships continued to close, the range eventually coming down to 3,300 yards. By 1015 the BISMARCK was a wreck, without a gun firing, on fire fore and aft and wallowing more heavily every moment. Men could be seen jumping overboard, preferring death by drowning in the stormy sea to the appalling effects of our fire. I was confident that the BISMARCK could never get back to harbour and that it was only a matter of hours before she would sink.

86. The shortage of oil fuel in KING GEORGE V and RODNEY had become acute. It was not merely a matter of having sufficient oil to reach one of our harbours: I had to consider the possibility of damage to fuel tanks by a near miss from a bomb or a hit by a torpedo; this might easily result in the ship being stopped in an area where U-boats were known to be concentrating, and where I had been warned to expect heavy air attack. Further gunfire would do little to hasten the BISMARCK's end. I therefore decided to break off the action with KING GEORGE V and RODNEY, and I instructed any ships still with torpedoes to use them on the BISMARCK. DORSETSHIRE anticipated my order and torpedoed the BISMARCK at close range on both sides: she sank at 1037 in position 48° 09' N. 16° 07' W.

Although her sinking had been seen from the after Director Control Tower in KING GEORGE V, the fact did not become known to me until II00 and I informed the Flag Officer Commanding, Force "H", that I could not sink the BISMARCK with gunfire: this signal (I045/27th May), which was perhaps unfortunately phrased, was addressed only to him and was intended to ensure that he should take any steps which might help to hasten her sinking: when intercepted by others, it may have caused some misunderstanding.

87. The BISMARCK had put up a most gallant fight against impossible odds, worthy of the old days of the Imperial German Navy, and she went down with her colours still flying. DORSETSHIRE picked up four officers, including the Third Gunnery Officer, and 75 ratings; MAORI picked up 24 ratings; but at II40 DORSETSHIRE sighted a suspicious object, which might have been a U-boat, and ships were compelled to abandon the work of rescue. Some of the remaining survivors may have been rescued by the Spanish cruiser CANARIAS.

88. From the information available, it appears that the BISMARCK suffered three hits by gunfire on 24th May, one hit by aircraft torpedo on 25th May and two on 26th May, two hits by destroyer torpedoes early on 27th May, one by RODNEY's torpedo, and the subsequent heavy pounding by gunfire. At the end of this she was in a sinking condition, and the final torpedoes from DORSETSHIRE only hastened her end. A few casualties and slight damage from splinters were incurred in SHEFFIELD and the destroyers of the Fourth Destroyer Flotilla during the night of 26th/27th May; there were no casualties or damage to any of our ships during the subsequent day action.

89. In KING GEORGE V W/T transmission on power on certain wavelengths interfered with reception on R.D.F. For this reason I was unable, during the action to keep the Admiralty fully informed of its progress, especially in view of the fact that I had been warned to expect heavy attack by enemy aircraft, and I did not wish to risk being fixed by D/F. The BISMARCK's sinking was reported as soon as it was known and a description of the engagement was deferred until it was practicable to transmit a long signal by wireless. This limitation applies in some degree to all ships and will have to be borne in mind in the future.

Return of the Fleet.

90. KING GEORGE V and RODNEY with COSSACK, SIKH and ZULU, proceeded to the northward, DORSETSHIRE and MAORI rejoined at I230, and the screen was augmented by JUPITER during, the afternoon. Nine further destroyers had joined by I600 the following day. Several signals were received on 28th May, indicating that air attacks on the fleet were impending, but only four enemy aircraft appeared. One of these bombed the screen without effect, while another jettisoned its solitary bomb on being attacked by a Blenheim fighter. MASHONA and TARTAR, I00 miles to the southward, were heavily attacked, MASHONA being sunk at noon, with the loss of one officer and 45 ratings; TARTAR shot down one of the attacking aircraft. PIORUN

underwent six attacks by aircraft on her way back to Plymouth; all were driven off by gunfire.

9I. RODNEY, screened by MAORI, SIKH and COLUMBIA (Lieutenant-Commander Somerville W. Davis), was detached to the Clyde at I700; DORSETSHIRE was detached to the Tyne at 23I6; KING GEORGE V was delayed by fog, but eventually anchored in Loch Ewe at I230 on 29th May. GALATEA (Rear-Admiral Commanding, Second Cruiser Squadron), AURORA and PRINCE OF WALES arrived at Hvalfiord on 27th May; EDINBURGH (Commodore Commanding, Eighteenth Cruiser Squadron) arrived at Londonderry on 28th May and NORFOLK (Rear-Admiral Commanding, First Cruiser Squadron) at the Clyde on 29th May; Force "H" returned to Gibraltar.

Conduct of Officers and Men.

92. Although it was no more than I expected, the co-operation, skill and understanding displayed by all forces during this prolonged chase gave me the utmost satisfaction. Flag and Commanding Officers of detached units invariably took the action I would have wished, before or without receiving instructions from me. The conduct of all officers and men of the Fleet which I have the honour to command was in accordance with the traditions of the Service. Force "H" was handled with conspicuous skill throughout the operation by Vice-Admiral Sir James F. Somerville, K.C.B., D.S.O., and contributed a vital share in its successful conclusion.

Supply of Information and Disposition of Forces.

93. The accuracy of the enemy information supplied by the Admiralty and the speed with which it was passed were remarkable, and the balance struck between information and instructions passed to the forces out of visual touch with me was ideal. The disposition of Force "H", RODNEY and the other forces placed at my disposal, completed my own dispositions and enabled me to avoid breaking W/T silence at a time when this was particularly important.

(Signed) JACK C. TOVEY,
Admiral.
Commander-in-Chief
Home Fleet.

Admiralty footnote:-
* *Wind force 8 – fresh gale, 34-40 m.p.h.*

H.M.S. RENOWN,
4th June, 1941.

To: The Commander-in-Chief, Home Fleet.

The following report of the operations culminating in the destruction of the German battleship BISMARCK is forwarded in accordance with Admiralty message 0032 of 28th May, 1941.

25th May.

2. At 0330 on Sunday, 25th May, Force "H" was in position 39° 35' N. 14° 10' W., steering 310° at 24 knots. At this time instructions were received to steer to intercept BISMARCK from the southward. The enemy had last been located in position 56° 30' N. 36° 00' W. at 0306 when SUFFOLK lost touch. The existing course and speed was therefore maintained.

3. At 0400 instructions were received that destroyers should be sent back to Gibraltar before it became necessary to fuel them, as Force "H" might be required for extended operations. The three screening destroyers were therefore detached at 0900 with instructions to transmit two signals when 150 miles clear, one informing the Admiralty of the position, course and speed of Force "H" at 0730, and the other requesting Commander-in-Chief, Plymouth, to keep me fully informed of the results of Brest reconnaissance.

4. At 1100, when in position 41° 30' N. 17° 10' W., orders were received for Force "H" to act on the assumption that the enemy had turned towards Brest at 0300/25. Course was therefore altered to 360°.

5. At 1215 Force "H" altered course to 345° to reach the initial position for an air search a.m./26 based on the assumption that the enemy's maximum speed of advance was not more than 25 knots. It was my intention to carry out, if necessary, three searches of the area across the Bay of Biscay allowing for the enemy making a substantial detour to the south-ward. The first search was designed to cover enemy, speeds of 25 to 21 knots, the second 21 to 18 knots and the third 18 to 15 knots, Force "H" maintaining an intercepting position to the eastward throughout.

26th May.

6. During the night the north-westerly wind and sea increased, and speed had to be reduced to 23 knots at 2115, to 21 knots at 2340, to 19 knots at 0020 and finally to 17 knots at 0112.

7. In consequence of this reduction of speed, which the BISMARCK with a following sea would not have suffered, course was altered to 000° at 0300/26 to reach the best position for flying off the search.

8. The latest intelligence regarding the German battlecruisers was contained in a reconnaissance report that they were still at Brest at I5I5/23. This lack of information caused me some anxiety as I could not entirely discount the possibility that one or both battlecruisers might have put to sea to support BISMARCK. With this possibility in view a security patrol was flown off at 07I6 to search to the west and northward before assuming A/S duties.

9. It had been intended that the first search should cover the area bounded by 47° 30' N. 2I° 30' W., 49° 00' N. 23° 40' W., 52° 25' N. 20° 00' W., 5I° 40' N. I7° 00' W., but owing to the head seas experienced during the night the area for the search, measuring some 280 miles by I20 miles was transferred 35 miles to the south-east.

I0. Ten Swordfish were flown off at 0835 from position 48° 26' N. I9° I3' W. Two cross-over patrols by Catalinas, arranged by the Admiralty, lay along the western edge of ARK ROYAL's reconnaissance. Weather conditions at this time were wind from 320° force 7, sea rough, sky overcast, visibility I0-I2 miles. It had been hoped to increase the density of the search by the use of Fulmars, but weather conditions rendered this impracticable. ARK ROYAL's round down was rising and falling 56 feet at times, as measured by sextant. The handling of the aircraft on the flight deck was always difficult and several slid bodily across the deck which was wet with spray.

II. At 0930 the A/S patrol was landed on; no relief was flown off in order that every available aircraft should be available for a torpedo striking force. Whilst the search was in progress Force "H" proceeded at I5 knots on a course of 0I5° to reach a position to windward so that the operation of aircraft would not be impeded by subsequent alterations of course of the BISMARCK should the latter be located.

I2. At I030 a Catalina (Duty Z) made a report of "I BS 240° 5 miles steering I50 from position KRGP 33I3". This report, received at I050, placed the enemy 285° II2 miles from RENOWN. An amplifying report five minutes later gave the enemy's speed as 20 knots. I instructed ARK ROYAL to fly off two shadowers fitted with long range tanks to gain touch, as I feared the Catalina's position might be somewhat inaccurate in view of the weather conditions and the distance from her base. As the reconnaissance aircraft had already readied the limit of their search I decided not to recall them by wireless, but informed ARK ROYAL that I would continue the present course and speed until they had returned when a full scale striking force was to be prepared.

I3. At III4 the Catalina reported that her hull had been holed by shrapnel and requested instructions. I asked ARK ROYAL how many aircraft would be required to ensure gaining contact; she replied 6 but proposed to fly off the two aircraft fitted with long range tanks at once to carry out a square search.

I4. At this time (II25) the Catalina lost touch and I instructed ARK ROYAL to send at least 4 aircraft. Before these could be flown off one of ARK ROYAL's aircraft reported in touch (at III4) but also reported the enemy as a cruiser and gave the position of the enemy as 77 miles to the west of Force "H". This was some 25 miles further to the eastward than the Catalina's report but was considered to be a more accurate position in view of the shorter time, interval between departure and sighting. Seven minutes later a second aircraft of the reconnaissance gained touch and reported that the enemy was a battleship. The aircraft on track 305° was the first to sight followed by the aircraft on track 285°. There were five more aircraft to the northward of these two and three more to the southward. These aircraft were on their way back to the ARK ROYAL when touch was first gained. The long range shadowers were flown off at noon and the majority of the reconnaissance landed on. Force "H" was then manoeuvred to the south-east on a course I40° at 24 knots, my intention being to maintain the weather gage for flying operations, to avoid loss of bearing on BISMARCK, and to keep within about 50 miles of the enemy to facilitate the launching of T/B attacks. Should it be desirable for RENOWN to attack unsupported it was my intention to do so from up wind and astern with the object of causing him to turn and thus slow up his retreat, and also to enable full use to be made of smoke.

I5. The two shadowers were relieved as necessary throughout the day. Touch was maintained continuously and excellent reports transmitted until the shadowers were finally recalled at 2230.

I6. Orders were received from Admiralty at II45 that RENOWN was not to become engaged with BISMARCK unless the latter was already heavily engaged by either KING GEORGE V or RODNEY.

I7. The Commander-in-Chief, Home Fleet, reported his position at I050 as 5I° 37' N. 20° 42' W., closing the ship reported by the Catalina, and requested Admiralty confirmation that the report did not refer to RODNEY. This was confirmed by Admiralty.

I8. At I208 the Catalina reported 4 UN* 050° I0 miles steering I40° from position KRG7 473I. It was assumed that these were four of the five destroyers which had just parted from Convoy W.S.8B, and who were now some 50 miles W.N.W. of the BISMARCK.

I9. At I20I the Commander-in-Chief, Home Fleet, reported that his position at II00 was 5I° 33' N. 20° 43' W., course I50°, altering to I30° at II55, speed 26 knots.

20. It was evident at this stage that unless aircraft from ARK ROYAL could reduce the enemy's speed he could not be overhauled by our battleships till well within range of bombing aircraft from the French coast the following day. It was also doubtful whether the Commander-in-Chief, Home Fleet, would have sufficient fuel to enable him to continue the chase until the following day.

2I. At I3I5 I detached SHEFFIELD with orders to close and shadow the enemy, who was then some 40 miles south-west of RENOWN who was in position 49° 39' N. I8° 58' W. at I330. The V/S† signal ordering this movement was not repeated to ARK ROYAL, and as will be seen later this omission had serious consequences.

22. ARK ROYAL informed me that after the interrogation of observers who had sighted the enemy ship, considerable doubt arose, whether the ship was in fact BISMARCK or PRINZ EUGEN. In consequence the torpedoes of the striking force, which was then being ranged, were set to 30 feet instead of 34 as originally intended. The torpedoes were fitted with Duplex pistols: The striking force of I5 Swordfish took off at I450 in position 49° 35' N. I8° 30' W., one aircraft had to return and made a successful emergency landing with the torpedo in place just after the last of the

striking force had left the deck. It had been intended to carry out a synchronised diversion by Fulmars, but this had to be abandoned owing to sea and cloud conditions.

23. Weather and cloud conditions were particularly bad over the target area when the striking force took off. Reliance was therefore placed on the A.S.V. set carried in one of the aircraft of the striking force. This aircraft located a ship 20 miles from the position given to the leader on taking off. This ship was SHEFFIELD, of whose presence near BISMARCK the striking force were not aware. A situation report made to Admiralty at 1345 containing the information that SHEFFIELD had been detached to shadow had been received by ARK ROYAL, but had not been decoded before the striking force left.

24. At 1550 on reaching a position over the supposed target an attack through the cloud was ordered, and eleven torpedoes were dropped at SHEFFIELD. The latter increased to full speed and took successful avoiding action. Of the eleven torpedoes dropped, two were observed by SHEFFIELD to explode on hitting the water and three more exploded when crossing her wake. During this unfortunate incident it is satisfactory to record that not a single round was fired at the attacking aircraft by any gun in SHEFFIELD, where the mistake had been immediately appreciated.

25. At 1525 the Catalina reported having lost touch with the enemy in position 47° 30' N. 19° 00' W. Both this report and the preceding one at 1330 placed the enemy 60 miles south of the position reported by aircraft from ARK ROYAL. It was assumed that the discrepancy was probably caused by navigational errors in the Catalina. The latter made infrequent reports and, as H/F was employed, could not be D/Fd. The need for frequent reports on a D/F-able wave was strongly felt throughout the operation.

26. At 1551, the Commander-in-Chief, Home Fleet, reported his position, course and speed as 50° 18' N. 18° 45' W., 128°, 26 knots, and that RODNEY bore 100° eleven miles from him. This was the first definite information that had been received of RODNEY since her signal timed 0900/25. Course was altered to 140° at 1650 to maintain position on BISMARCK, who had been reported steering that course at 1340.

27. At 1632 the Catalina signalled that she was being attacked by enemy aircraft, type unknown. She had previously made this signal at 1345 but on each occasion the alarm was caused by the ARK ROYAL's shadowing Swordfish.

28. The striking force returned to ARK ROYAL at 1720. Owing to the motion on the ship the three aircraft who had realised that the target was friendly and who had not fired their torpedoes, were ordered to drop them before landing on. Meanwhile the relief shadowers had reported that the enemy ship was definitely BISMARCK.

29. On completion of landing on speed was increased to 29 knots to regain lost ground, and by reducing the distance from the enemy to assist the next striking force in gaining contact.

30. At 1747 SHEFFIELD gained touch with BISMARCK and made her first enemy report. Being in some doubt regarding the Commander-in-Chief's intentions, I requested his position, course and speed and asked whether he wished me to leave the carrier and join him. I added that should no reply be received I would remain with

the carrier. A second striking force of I5 aircraft was prepared with all possible speed. Owing to the limited number of serviceable aircraft to provide this number, it was necessary to refuel and rearm most of the aircraft that had just returned.

3I. At I900 the Polish destroyer PIORUN was sighted 9 miles to the southward and the bearing and distance of the enemy passed to her. The latter portion of the signal, instructing destroyers to shadow and attack as opportunity offered, was not passed owing to visibility closing down. Having sighted PIORUN, it appeared evident that the four destroyers which had been reported by the Catalina at I208 as 4 UN and had also been sighted by first striking force, were Captain (D), 4th Destroyer Flotilla in COSSACK, with ZULU, MAORI and SIKH in company. To assist these destroyers and the striking force in making contact, SHEFFIELD was ordered to make her call sign for D/F-ing purposes.

32. The second striking force took off at I915 in position 48° 35' N. I6° 54' W., when the enemy bore I67°, 38 miles. In view of the failures with Duplex pistols in the preceding attack, contact pistols were employed on this occasion, torpedoes being set to run at 22 feet. The striking force had orders to make contact with SHEFFIELD before launching the attack, both to ensure gaining contact with the enemy and to avoid any possibility of SHEFFIELD being mistaken for the target. SHEFFIELD was instructed to home the striking force by D/F.

33. The aircraft approached SHEFFIELD at I955 below the clouds and then climbed to a height of 6,000 feet. The weather conditions at this time appeared to be ideal for a synchronised torpedo attack cloud 7/I0ths from 2,000 to 5,000 feet. During the climb contact was lost with SHEFFIELD but regained at 2035 when a bearing and distance (II0° I2 miles) of BISMARCK was passed by SHEFFIELD by V/S. The force took departure for the target in sub flights in line astern at 2040. On nearing the enemy a thick bank of cloud with base about 700 feet and top between 6,000 and I0,000 feet was encountered and the force became split up. At 2047, when it was calculated that the enemy would be in a suitable position for an attack down wind from astern, No. I sub flight dived through the cloud, but on reaching the base the enemy was seen four miles down wind to the eastward. Position for an attack on the port beam was gained by approaching just in the clouds, and the final dive to attack was made at 2055. One aircraft from No. 3 sub flight followed closely and also attacked from the port beam. This aircraft observed a hit on BISMARCK about two-thirds of her length from forward. All four aircraft came under intense and accurate fire from the first moment of sighting until out of range.

34. No. 2 sub flight, having climbed to 9,000 feet in cloud, dived down on a bearing obtained by A.S.V. and two aircraft attacked from the starboard beam under intense fire. The third aircraft having lost touch with his sub flight in the clouds returned to SHEFFIELD for a range and bearing on the target. Having obtained this he pressed home a lone and determined attack from the port bow in face of very heavy opposition, and his crew saw the torpedo strike BISMARCK amidships port side.

35. No. 4 sub flight followed No. 3 sub flight into the cloud and became iced up at 6,600 feet. After seven minutes the aircraft dived and found a clear patch at 2,000 feet. BISMARCK was sighted almost at once engaging No. 2 sub flight to starboard.

All four aircraft circled astern of the target and attacked simultaneously from port coming under heavy fire. One aircraft was hit many times and both pilot and air gunner were wounded, the observer being uninjured. I75 holes were counted in this aircraft which had to be written off as one of the longerons had been cut.

36. No. 5 sub flight of two aircraft lost contact with the remainder and with each other in the cloud. Having started to ice up at 7,000 feet they came down and when still in cloud at 3,500 feet one was engaged by A.A. fire. On coming out of the cloud this pilot saw the enemy ahead of him and down wind so retired into the cloud, being engaged continuously while gaining a more favourable position. He eventually came in low on the BISMARCK's starboard bow and dropped just outside I,000 yards. The other aircraft of this sub flight made three attempts to come in but was so heavily engaged on each appearance that he finally jettisoned his torpedo and returned to ARK ROYAL.

37. No. 6 sub flight followed into the cloud and when at 6,300 feet turned 40 degrees to port and climbed clear at 7,450 feet, waited for about I5 minutes and returned to SHEFFIELD for another range and bearing of the enemy. These two aircraft then searched at sea level and attacked on the starboard beam. Intense fire prevented close approach and one dropped at about 4,000 yards while the other returned to the carrier and jettisoned before landing on.

38. The striking force attack took much longer than had been anticipated (2055 to 2I25) owing to bad weather conditions around BISMARCK who appeared to be under a cold front.

39. At 2040 a signal was received from Commander-in-Chief, Home Fleet, giving his position, course and speed at I800 as 49° 48' N. I7° 33' W., I00°, 22 knots, with RODNEY in company. He also stated that unless the enemy's speed was reduced he would have to return in KING GEORGE V at midnight to refuel, leaving RODNEY to continue the chase. He recommended that RENOWN should remain with ARK ROYAL.

40. During and after the torpedo attack on BISMARCK shadowing aircraft reported frequent alterations of course and that she was making smoke. On receipt of these reports RENOWN and ARK ROYAL altered course as requisite to maintain a position some 40 miles distant from the enemy in order that flying operations could not be unexpectedly hampered. It appeared possible that BISMARCK was endeavouring to shake off shadowers before dark; on the other hand she might have suffered damage to shafts or steering gear as a result of the torpedo attacks.

4I. Owing to the time taken to deliver the T/B attack insufficient light remained to carry out another attack before dark. Aircraft could have flown off but in the failing light location of the target would have been difficult, friend might have been mistaken for foe and certainly many of the aircraft would have failed to regain the carrier. It was therefore decided to maintain shadowing aircraft as long as possible and concentrate on preparing all remaining Swordfish for a strong striking force at dawn.

42. Commander-in-Chief, Home Fleet, requested that aircraft might give the destroyers a visual link with the enemy and ARK ROYAL was instructed to comply. The two shadowing aircraft were ordered to remain in touch as long as possible and

establish this link before returning. They left the BISMARCK at 2230 and, after making a detour in heavy rain, located the destroyers. By this time, however, they were not certain of their own position and were unable to assist the destroyers. These two aircraft were D/Fd back to ARK ROYAL, landing on at 2320 when it was practically dark.

43. At 2220 ARK ROYAL reported that one torpedo had definitely hit BISMARCK amidships, and Commander-in-Chief, Home Fleet, was informed accordingly at 2225. Later, information was received from ARK ROYAL that a second hit had most probably been obtained aft, and Commander-in-Chief was again informed at 2240.

44. SHEFFIELD made her last enemy report at 2140. At this time BISMARCK turned and fired six accurate 15-in. salvos at SHEFFIELD at a range of 9 miles. The latter turned away at full speed and made smoke but suffered a few casualties and superficial damage from splinters. These casualties consisted of 1 killed, 2 dangerously wounded who have since died, two seriously and six slightly wounded. All were ratings. After this SHEFFIELD lost touch but at 2142 sighted Captain (D), 4th Destroyer Flotilla, in COSSACK with 3 other destroyers closing the enemy and signalled the last observed bearing and distance of BISMARCK.

45. At 2251 ZULU made a contact and reported the enemy steering 110°. From this time onwards Captain (D), 4th Destroyer Flotilla and his destroyers maintained contact, reporting the enemy's course as 110°, 060°, 340° and finally by midnight 310° into the sea. Rear-Admiral Commanding, 18th Cruiser Squadron in EDINBURGH was sighted to the westward at 2315.

46. Just before midnight a signal was received from Commander-in-Chief, Home Fleet, giving his position, course and speed at 2215 as 49° 10' N. 15° 29' W., 170°, 21 knots, with RODNEY in company. Shortly afterwards Rear-Admiral Commanding, 18th Cruiser Squadron, reported his position, course and speed as 48° 32' N. 15° 22' W., 025°, 13 knots, that he had no fuel left for shadowing and was proceeding to Londonderry.

47. At 2345 I informed Commander-in-Chief, Home Fleet, of my position (48° 42' N. 15° 17' W.), that no further T/B attack was possible that evening and that I intended turning west for a short distance to keep clear of him. Shortly afterwards I received his intentions to engage from the westward at dawn and directions that RENOWN and ARK ROYAL were to keep not less than, 20 miles to the southward of BISMARCK. Course and speed was adjusted during the night to comply.

27th May.

48. At 0036 ARK ROYAL reported that after being torpedoed, BISMARCK made two complete circles and reduced speed. I informed Commander-in-Chief, Home Fleet, accordingly at 0046.

49. It was evident the Commander-in-Chief, Home Fleet, was in some doubt

regarding the position of BISMARCK. I therefore reported to him at 0II2 that the estimated bearing and distance of the enemy from me at 2345 was I65° 4I miles.

50. The situation at this time was as follows. RENOWN and ARK ROYAL some 40 miles to the northward of BISMARCK, working round to the west to reach a position to the southward; Commander-in-Chief, Home Fleet, proceeding southward to engage at dawn; and Rear-Admiral Commanding, Ist Cruiser Squadron, working round to the north-east. DORSETSHIRE who had left S.L. 74 at 0930/26 in position 44° 08' N. 24° 50' W. was closing from the south-west. SHEFFIELD'S position was not known exactly but assumed to be in vicinity of BISMARCK and to the westward of the latter.

5I. At 0II5 a flash was seen bearing I52°, followed four minutes later by heavy gun flashes. Course was altered to 2I0° to keep clear to the westward. During the middle watch the destroyers carried out attacks, and signals were received between 0202 and 02I0 stating that ZULU, MAORI and COSSACK had attacked, the last two claiming one hit each. MAORI added that there was an extensive fire on the forecastle.

52. At 02I0, Rear-Admiral Commanding, Ist Cruiser Squadron, reported his intention to keep to the northward and flank mark for KING GEORGE V and RODNEY. At 030I DORSETSHIRE reported her position, course and speed which indicated she would cross some I0 to I5 miles ahead of RENOWN.

53. The destroyers were instructed by Commander-in-Chief, Home Fleet, that after all attacks were completed they were to fire starshell every half hour to indicate the position of the enemy, whose course and speed was now reported as 3I0°, 8 knots.

54. During the night Commander-in-Chief, Home Fleet, experienced difficulty in making destroyers transmit their call signs on M/F‡ in order that D/F bearings could be obtained. Many D/F bearings obtained proved to be inaccurate and caused considerable doubt as to the exact position of the enemy.

55. At 0335 I informed Commander-in-Chief of my position and reported starshell had been seen bearing I00°, and that an aircraft would be flown off ARK ROYAL at 0500 to spot for KING GEORGE V.

56. At 06I0 I ordered SHEFFIELD who had signalled her position at 0500 to obtain and pass a D/F bearing of MAORI who was in touch with the enemy. The third class bearing of II8° which she gave put BISMARCK further south than her previously estimated position.

57. At dawn visibility was low, and after consultation with ARK ROYAL I decided to delay flying off the striking force as there was a serious risk of mistaking friend for foe and I was in considerable doubt as to the position of KING GEORGE V and RODNEY. Having informed the Commander-in-Chief, Home Fleet, that the striking force would arrive at 07I5, I later informed him that the attack was postponed on account of low visibility, and later still that I had cancelled the attack on account of the difficulty of identifying our own ships in the existing visibility. I was satisfied that until the situation clarified it was undesirable to fly off the striking force.

58. While these signals were being passed the destroyers' reports of the position of the BISMARCK suggested she might be as much as 60 miles to the northward of

RENOWN. Course was therefore altered to the northward, and at 08I0 after ARK ROYAL had struck down her aircraft as it was impossible in existing weather conditions to keep them ranged, MAORI was sighted to the northward. MAORI reported the enemy as being 009° distant II miles from her and thereby only I7 miles from RENOWN. The latest estimate previous to this report placed BISMARCK 40 miles from RENOWN. As contact was now definitely established course was altered to I80° to range the striking force and aircraft were flown off at 0926 in position 47° I6' N. I5° 5I' W.

59. In the meantime the spotting aircraft which had been flown off at 0509 had become lost in rain, failed to establish contact by W/T with KING GEORGE V and eventually had to be D/Fd back.

60. After sighting MAORI I considered detaching ARK ROYAL to the southward to range the striking force, keeping RENOWN in the vicinity of MAORI ready to support KING GEORGE V and RODNEY as required. I decided however that the appearance of RENOWN on the scene before KING GEORGE V established contact was undesirable in view of the low visibility and furthermore it was imperative to afford ARK ROYAL the maximum degree of protection should KING GEORGE V fail to establish contact and thus leave the third striking force as the only means of dealing with BISMARCK.

6I. Heavy gunfire was heard to the northward at 0855 but no report was received indicating what ship or ships were in action.

62. At 0940 SHEFFIELD appeared from the westward, and I ordered her to join ARK ROYAL on a course of 290° while RENOWN turned towards the scene of action to investigate. ARK ROYAL was instructed to fly off a spotting aircraft for RENOWN.

63. At 0952 a signal was intercepted from Commander-in-Chief, Home Fleet, ordering destroyers to close. Five minutes before this I had informed Commander-in-Chief, Home Fleet, that SHEFFIELD and ARK ROYAL had been detached, and that RENOWN was closing him from the southward; I also requested his position, course and speed.

64. The Commander-in-Chief's signal ordering the destroyers to close coupled with NORFOLK'S signal that she had ceased flank marking and Rear-Admiral Commanding, Ist Cruiser Squadron's signal ordering DORSETSHIRE to torpedo BISMARCK at close range, led me to suppose that the action was successfully concluded so in view of the Admiralty signal which had just been received indicating that a heavy scale of air attack was to be expected I decided to rejoin ARK ROYAL to afford A.A. protection. I informed Commander-in-Chief, Home Fleet, accordingly at 0953.

65. At I025 as I still had no definite information I asked Commander-in-Chief if he had disposed of the enemy; he replied that she was still afloat, adding three minutes later that he could not get her to sink by gunfire. Shortly afterwards Commander-in-Chief also informed me that he had been forced to discontinue the action on account of fuel. I was about to order the T/B striking force to finish off the BISMARCK when DORSETSHIRE, who had been ordered by Rear-Admiral Commanding, Ist Cruiser

Squadron to torpedo the enemy at close range, reported at 1034 that the BISMARCK was sinking and at 1039 that she had been sunk.

66. The torpedo striking force from ARK ROYAL located the BISMARCK just in time to see the finish of the action. The enemy was down in the water, on fire and silenced. DORSETSHIRE was seen to be in close proximity to BISMARCK and would have been endangered by a torpedo attack on the latter. The striking force therefore closed KING GEORGE V for instructions but could obtain no answer either by V/S or W/T. The striking force then returned to the vicinity of the BISMARCK and were in time to see DORSETSHIRE sink her with torpedoes from close range.

67. Meanwhile at 0955 an enemy aircraft had been sighted by RENOWN and engaged. About this time COSSACK and NORFOLK both reported that they were being bombed. SHEFFIELD'S R.D.F. was not efficient owing to damage from splinters when she had been engaged by BISMARCK. Enemy aircraft were sighted from time to time and engaged whenever they came out of the clouds. Weather conditions prevented the use of fighters. There appeared to be both Focke-Wolfes and Heinkels present.

68. The striking force returned about 1115 and were ordered to jettison their torpedoes before landing on as the motion of the ship was even greater than the previous day and to land on with torpedoes would have jeopardised the aircraft. Whilst landing on was in progress a Heinkel came out of the clouds and dropped a stick of two large and about five smaller bombs 600 yards astern and to port of ARK ROYAL. This was the last interference experienced by Force "H". Landing on was completed by 1152, and from then on the air appeared clear of enemy aircraft and course was shaped to the southward at 24 knots.

(Signed) J.F. SOMERVILLE,
Vice Admiral.
Flag Officer Commanding.
Force "H".

Admiralty footnotes
* *UN – unknown vessel.*
† *V/S – visual signal.*
‡ *M/F – medium frequency.*

APPENDIX.

COASTAL COMMAND OPERATIONS IN CONNECTION WITH THE BISMARCK AND PRINZ EUGEN 21ST-27TH MAY, 1941.

May 21st.

At I300 hours an aircraft of P.R.U. located and photographed one Bismarck class battleship and one Hipper class cruiser at anchor in small fiords near Bergen.

The weather deteriorated during the afternoon and evening but a strike of 6 Whitleys of No. 6I2 Squadron and I2 Hudsons of Nos. 220 and 269 Squadrons took off between 2I50 and 2330 hours to attack. Owing to bad weather conditions only 2 Hudsons dropped bombs, and poor visibility prevented any results being observed.

May 22nd.

Aircraft patrolled off the Norwegian coast from first light but weather conditions by I000 hours had forced all of them to return. Blenheims of No. 248 Squadron maintained meteorological sorties off the coast all day reporting the weather conditions, which became worse with I0/I0 cloud down to sea level.

Sunderlands of No. 20I Squadron maintained a patrol up the meridian of 5° West between latitudes 6220 N and 6500 N from 0930, but had to return at II00 on account of fog with nil visibility.

At I930 a Fleet Air Arm Maryland succeeded in penetrating to the anchorages and found the billets empty and no sign of the vessels in Bergen roadstead.

May 23rd.

The Norwegian coast patrols could not take off owing to weather conditions. Sunderlands of No. 20I Squadron carried out a patrol between the Faeroes and Iceland from 0650-2000 and Hudsons of No. 220 Squadron patrolled between the Shetlands and Faeroes from 0400-I250, when they had to be recalled as the base was closing down. Catalinas of No. 2I0 Squadron, after a delayed start due to weather, patrolled to the south of Iceland from I300-I650 when they also had to be recalled as the bases in United Kingdom were closing down. Iceland based aircraft should have patrolled the Denmark Strait but here again weather conditions of continuous rain, cloud I0/I0 at 300 feet and visibility of I,000 yards forced the abandonment of all flying. These conditions improved slightly towards the end of the day and, after the sighting of the enemy force by H.M. Ships SUFFOLK and NORFOLK at I922 and 2028 respectively, it was found possible to get aircraft off at 2225 and 2320 to locate and shadow the enemy.

May 24th.

The Sunderland of No. 20I Squadron which had taken off from Reykjavik sent a first sighting report of the enemy at 0620 and followed this up with four subsequent amplifying signals, the last being at 0900. The action between the BISMARCK and

H.M. Ships PRINCE OF WALES and HOOD was witnessed and bearing and distance of enemy signals given to H.M.S. NORFOLK. The Sunderland also signalled the position of survivors of H.M.S. HOOD at 1000 and the fact that BISMARCK was leaving a large trail of oil fuel.

The Hudson of No. 269 Squadron which had taken off at 2320 on the 23rd May did not locate the enemy, but another Hudson of the same Squadron did so and reported at 0554. This aircraft also witnessed the action in which H.M.S. HOOD was sunk, and continued shadowing until 0808. A third Hudson located and shadowed the enemy from 0905 till 1340. A Catalina of No. 240 Squadron from Reykjavik contacted the enemy at 1432, shadowing until 1640. During this time frequent bearings and distances of the enemy were given to the two cruisers and the PRINCE OF WALES. Fire was opened on this aircraft by both enemy ships from time to time. Finally, a Catalina of No. 210 Squadron took off at 1612, but did not sight the enemy in worsening weather visibility although all three H.M. Ships were sighted at 2127 and a formation of F.A.A. aircraft at 0035 on the 25th. During the day 6 aircraft of No. 22 Squadron armed with torpedoes flew from Wick to Kaldadarnes in Iceland as a strike force, together with Catalina and Sunderland reinforcements.

May 25th.

At 0306 hours contact with the enemy force was lost by the two shadowing cruisers and in order to assist re-location a long range sweep by Catalinas was organised. This sweep was designed to cover either a break back to Norway or a course shaped by the enemy for French Biscay ports. The Catalinas took off at 1345 and did not land back until 1030 on 26th May. Some of our own surface forces were sighted but no positive enemy sighting was made, although one Catalina at 0120 on 26th May passed over the wake of a heavy ship which gave no answer to challenge or signals. The aircraft circled for an hour but in the darkness and low cloud at 500 feet it was impossible to establish any identity. The position, course and estimated speed of this unknown ship was signalled to base but fuel supply would not permit shadowing until dawn. As it was, this aircraft did not land back until 1203 on 26th May.

May 26th.

As additional precautions to prevent a break back to Norway, Hudsons of No. 269 Squadron patrolled the Denmark Strait throughout the day in very bad weather conditions, a further sweep was carried out south of Iceland by two Sunderlands, one Catalina and one Hudson, and a continuous patrol was maintained between the Faeroes and Iceland by two Sunderlands. To endeavour to prevent an unseen escape into a French Biscay port two patrols were placed athwart the estimated line of advance from the last sighted position of the enemy towards the Bay of Biscay. On the initiative of the A.O.C.-in-C., Coastal Command, the southern of these two patrols was somewhat to the south of the general appreciation as to the likely course steered by these two ships. A Catalina of No. 240 Squadron flew the northern patrol and a Catalina of No. 209 Squadron the southern patrol. Both were on patrol by 0930 hours.

At 1030 hours aircraft "Z" of No. 209 Squadron sighted the BISMARCK and sent a first-sighting report. An amplifying report was sent five minutes later while the aircraft was taking cover in cloud. At 1039 cloud cover was inadvertently broken almost over the BISMARCK, which immediately opened fire, and before cloud could be regained the aircraft was hit by shrapnel and holed in several places. The other Catalina was diverted to assist in the shadowing and made a sighting report at 1328. Meanwhile "Z" of No. 209 Squadron had lost touch in worsening visibility at 1045. Efforts to re-locate failed, though at 1510 this aircraft sighted and communicated with the other Catalina – "M" of No. 240 Squadron – which by this time had also lost touch. "Z" then left the scene for base, plugging the holes in the hull, and landed safely at Loch Erne. Meanwhile "M" regained contact with an enemy ship at 1600 and continued to report positions and courses until 1800, when contact was lost and the aircraft had to return to base having reached prudent limit of endurance.

A relief Catalina – "O" of No. 210 Squadron – had been flown off at 1215 to continue the shadowing. At 2340 this aircraft sighted and reported an enemy ship and continued to signal positions at intervals until 0240 hours on 27th May.

May 27th.

At 0404 this aircraft reported having lost touch with the enemy ship, though at 0712 it signalled the presence of a Blohm and Voss float plane, after which limit of endurance forced a return to base after a flight of 26 hours 12 minutes.

As the Hipper class cruiser – PRINZ EUGEN – last seen in company with the BISMARCK early on 25th May was unaccounted for, Coastal Command maintained two patrols by Sunderlands of No. 10 Squadron across the mouth of the Bay of Biscay from dawn during the day, and Hudsons of No. 206 Squadron carried out searches in this area from 0900 till 1830, while Wellingtons of No. 221 Squadron completed the patrols across the mouth of the Bay up till 1900 hours.

Over the whole period from the locating of the two enemy ships near Bergen on 21st May until dusk on 27th May, aircraft of Coastal Command flew 69 sorties, totalling 580 hours flying, while searching for or shadowing these two ships

3

THE LOSS OF HMS *PRINCE OF WALES* AND HMS *REPULSE*

10 December 1941

The following Despatch was submitted to the Lords Commissioners of the Admiralty on the I7th December, I94I, by Vice-Admiral Sir Geoffrey Layton, K.C.B., D.S.O., Commander-in-Chief, Eastern Fleet.

> *Office of the British Naval*
> *Commander-in-Chief,*
> *Eastern Fleet,*
> *17th December, 1941.*

Be pleased to lay before the Board the accompanying reports on the operations resulting in the loss of H.M. Ships PRINCE OF WALES and REPULSE on I0th December, I94I.

2. These reports comprise a narrative of the operations drawn up by my direction and the original reports from the Commanding and surviving Officers of H.M. Ships concerned.*

3. The press of time and circumstances have prevented a more thorough analysis of the operations being made so far and I consider it preferable to despatch forthwith the available evidence, as many of the officers concerned are now returning to the United Kingdom.

4. In the circumstances, I feel unable, as I would wish to have done, to bring to the special notice of Their Lordships cases of individual good service, of which there were many. I will submit my further observations at a later stage, but in the meantime I would ask Their Lordships to obtain from Captain W.G. Tennant, R.N., and Lieutenant-Commander A.G. Skipwith, R.N., their recommendations for the recognition of those who were specially deserving.

5. All accounts agree that in coolness, determination, and cheerfulness in adverse circumstances, the ships' companies of these two ships lived up to the best traditions of His Majesty's Service.

(Signed) G. LAYTON,†

Vice-Admiral,

Commander-in-Chief.

Admiralty footnotes:-

* *Only the reports by the Captain of H.M.S. REPULSE and senior surviving officer of H.M.S. PRINCE OF WALES, named in paragraph 4, are here reproduced.*

† *Vice-Admiral Sir Geoffrey Layton, K.C.B., D.S.O., relinquished command of the China Station to Admiral Sir Tom S.V. Phillips, K.C.B., at 0800GH on the 8th December, 1941, it having been decided by the Admiralty to merge the command of the China Station with the Eastern Fleet. Admiral Layton assumed command of the Eastern Fleet at about 1500GH on the 10th December, 1941. He had therefore no responsibility for the operations of Force Z, nor for any other operations during this period.*

NARRATIVE OF OPERATIONS OF FORCE Z.

(All times are Zone GH (-7½ hours) unless otherwise indicated).
Intentions of the Commander-in-Chief.

It was the intention of the Commander-in-Chief to attack Japanese transports and warships which had been reported early on 8th December to be landing troops on the east coast of the Kra Isthmus and at Kota Bharu.

2. It was known by noon on that day that our Air Force and aerodromes in the north were being heavily attacked and that large Japanese forces were landing at Kota Bharu in Malaya and between Singgora and Pattani in Thailand. It appeared likely that our Army and Air Force would both be hard pressed and it seemed to the Commander-in-Chief inacceptable to retain a powerful naval force at Singapore in a state of inaction.

3. The Commander-in-Chief hoped that, with fighter protection if possible, or failing that, by surprise, he might attack the Japanese forces off Singgora and Kota Bharu at dawn on the 10th.

4. The question of fighter protection and reconnaissance was discussed with Royal Air Force Headquarters before the Force sailed. The Air Officer Commanding, Royal Air Force, Far East, stated that he hoped to be able to provide air reconnaissance, but was doubtful about fighter protection off Singgora at daylight on the 10th December. After full investigation, he confirmed later to the Chief of Staff, Eastern Fleet, that such protection could not be provided.*

Admiralty footnote:-

* *Before sailing, the Commander-in-Chief, Eastern Fleet asked the Air Officer Commanding, Royal Air Force, Far East for:*
(a) reconnaissance 100 miles to north of Force daylight 9th December.

(b) reconnaissance 100 miles mid point Singgora 10 miles from coast starting first light 10th December.
(c) fighter protection off Singgora at daylight 10th December.
The Air Officer Commanding subsequently informed the Chief of Staff, Eastern Fleet, who remained ashore, that he could provide (a), hoped to be able to provide (b), but could not provide (c). The Chief of Staff, Eastern Fleet signalled accordingly to the Commander-in- Chief, Eastern Fleet, then at sea (see signals attached as Appendix III).
Chief of Staff was Rear-Admiral A.F.E. Palliser, DSC, who remained ashore in charge of the Commander-in-Chief's office at Singapore.

Composition of Force Z.

5. Force Z consisted of H.M Ships PRINCE OF WALES (Captain J.C. Leach, M.V.O., D.S.O., R.N.) flying the flag of Admiral Sir Tom S.V. Phillips, K.C.B., REPULSE (Captain W.G. Tennant, C.B., M.V.O., R.N), ELECTRA (Commander C.W. May, R.N.), EXPRESS (Lieutenant Commander F.J. Cartwright, R.N.), H.M.A.S. VAMPIRE (Commander W.T.A. Moran, R.A.N.), and H.M.S. TENEDOS (Lieutenant R. Dyer, R.N.).

JUPITER and ENCOUNTER were under repair and STRONGHOLD had to be used for meeting a division of U.S. destroyers expected at Singapore p.m. 9th December.

DURBAN was available but the Commander-in-Chief decided not to take her.

Movements of the Fleet up to the time of Air Attacks.

6. Force Z sailed at 1735 on 8th December and proceeded at 17½ knots to pass to eastward of Anamba Islands thence to the northward. The Commander-in-Chief informed the Force that the enemy Battle cruiser KONGO together with Cruisers and Destroyers were supporting the transports he intended to attack off Singgora and Pattani and that the landing was probably supported by submarines and mining.

7. In signal 2253GH/8 Chief of Staff informed Commander-in-Chief that fighter protection on 10th would not be possible.

8. Weather conditions during most of Tuesday, 9th December were favourable for evasion, with frequent rainstorms and low cloud. There was an unconfirmed report of sighting an enemy aircraft at 0620 on 9th December by VAMPIRE, the machine being seen for one minute by one lookout only. This was disregarded.

Between 1700 and 1830 the weather cleared and three Japanese naval reconnaissance aircraft in swift succession were sighted from the PRINCE OF WALES.

9. TENEDOS was ordered to return to Singapore at 1834 on the 9th December on account of her low endurance.

10. Before these sightings, the Commander-in-Chief had intended to detach the remaining destroyers at 2200 on 9th December and make a high speed descent on

Singgora with the heavy ships only. He considered the destroyers would be very vulnerable to air attack and their low endurance was an anxiety. The Admiral intended to rely on the speed and surprise of the heavy ships' attack to avoid damage to these ships sufficient to slow them down, believing that Japanese aircraft encountered would not be carrying anti-ship bombs or torpedoes and that the Force on retirement would only have to deal with hastily organized long range bombers from bases in Indo-China.

I1. On knowing that the Force had been sighted the Commander-in-Chief decided that the risk of attacking Singgora was no longer justified, as the ships would be expected, their targets might well have been withdrawn and a very large scale of air attack must be faced.

I2. As soon as the reconnaissance aircraft had been shaken off after dusk, Force Z therefore, turned to southward with the intention of returning to Singapore.

I3. The situation was however altered by the receipt of Chief of Staff, Eastern Fleet's message timed I505Z/9 at about midnight, which stated "Enemy reported landing at Kuantan." It seemed improbable that the enemy would expect Force Z, last located steering to the northward in the latitude of Singgora to be as far south as Kuantan by daylight. Kuantan was not far off the return track to Singapore, was 400 miles from Japanese aerodromes in Indo-China and was considered a key military position which every effort must be made to defend. At 0052 on the I0th December, therefore, the Force turned for Kuantan and increased speed to 25 knots.

I4. Between 0630 and 0730 enemy reconnaissance aircraft were sighted. PRINCE OF WALES and REPULSE flew off aircraft for reconnaissance and A/S patrol.*

I5. Force Z arrived off Kuantan at 0800 on I0th December. No enemy forces were sighted and EXPRESS, who was sent to investigate the harbour, reported "complete peace."

I6. One hour before reaching Kuantan, Force Z had passed at extreme range what appeared to be one small ship with a number of barges or junks. On finding Kuantan all quiet, the Commander-in-Chief decided to go back and investigate these barges before returning to Singapore. It was while steaming to the eastward to do this that Force Z was attacked by enemy aircraft.

I7. The only signal from the Commander-in-Chief addressed to his base at Singapore was his I455GH/9 which he directed TENEDOS to transmit at 0800 on I0th December. This stated that 0630 on the IIth December was the earliest time Force Z was likely to pass through position 3° 25' N. I06° 40' E. on return and asked that all available destroyers should be sent out to meet him.

I8. A summary of the aircraft attacks on Force Z follows:-

Admiralty footnote:-
A/S patrol – anti-submarine patrol

(i) Preliminary.

Force Z course 095° speed 20 knots, destroyers in S.D.3* Ships in first degree of A-A readiness.

Aircraft detected by R.D.F.,**sighted 1100, Blue 135°† executed.

Speed increased to 25 knots during first attack.

(ii) *Attack A.* (1118)

9 H.L.‡ Bombers at 10,000 feet in tight line abreast formation attacked REPULSE from ahead, dropping one bomb each simultaneously. One hit on port hangar (entry hole 15m. diameter), bursting on armoured deck below Marines' mess deck, one near miss starboard side abreast B turret, remainder close on port side.

No serious damage.

Admiralty footnotes:-
S.D.3 – an anti-submarine screen formation.
** *R.D.F – radar.*
†*Blue 135° – ships ordered to turn together to course 135°.*
‡ *H.L. – high level.*

(iii) *Attack B.* (1144)

9 T/Bs* attacked PRINCE OF WALES on port side. Ship turned towards but was hit by one torpedo† abreast P.3 and 4 turrets.

Ship listed 13° to port and speed dropped to 15 knots. Both port shafts out of action, steering gear failed and ship was never again under complete control.

Five 5.25 inch turrets out of action temporarily, owing to power failure and/or list.

Two aircraft shot down, falling on disengaged side, one other possibly damaged.

(iv) *Attack C.* (1156)

8 or 9 T/Bs attacked REPULSE on port side. Ship turned towards and was successful in combing the tracks.

(v) *Attack D.* (1158)

H.L.B.‡ attack on REPULSE.

No hits, but near.

REPULSE made emergency report of the attack.

(vi) *Attack E.* (1222)

T/B attack by 9 aircraft, in two groups. 6 came in slightly first on the starboard side and fired at PRINCE OF WALES who was incapable of taking avoiding action and was hit three times on starboard side:-

(*a*) Near stem.

(*b*) Abreast B turret.

(*c*) Aft.

List was reduced to 3° and speed dropped to 8 knots.

One aircraft was shot down.

REPULSE was committed to turning to starboard when three aircraft attacked her from the port side, scoring one hit amidships. The ship stood this hit well, continuing to manoeuvre at 25 knots.

(vii) *Attack F.* (I225)

9 T/Bs attacked REPULSE from various directions First hit abreast gunroom (port side) jammed rudder, putting ship out of control. Three further hits, one port side aft (wardroom bathroom), one abreast port engine room and one starboard side of E boiler room.

Ship listed to port, capsizing and sinking at I235, position 3° 45' N. I04° 24' E.

Two aircraft shot down.

ELECTRA and VAMPIRE picked up survivors.

(viii) *Attack G.* (I246)

9 H.L. Bombers attacked PRINCE OF WALES. One hit near S 3 turret, bursting on Main Deck, and near misses both sides aft. Speed 6 knots. EXPRESS went alongside starboard side at I305 and got clear as PRINCE OF WALES capsized to port and sank at I320 m position 3° 36' N. 104° 28' E.

(ix) *Summary*

PRINCE OF WALES hit by four (possibly five) torpedoes and one bomb.

REPULSE hit by 5 torpedoes and one bomb.

Aircraft shot down – about 8.

I9. When information was received at Singapore at I204 that Force Z was being attacked by aircraft, the fighter squadron which was standing by at Kallang was immediately despatched. Six Buffaloes took off at I2I5 and arrived on the scene of action just as the PRINCE OF WALES was sinking and when all enemy aircraft had taken their departure.

Destroyers, having made a thorough search for survivors, returned to Singapore, arriving between 23I0 and 2400.

Admiralty footnotes:-

* *T/Bs – torpedo bombers.*

† *Subsequent investigation has established the fact that PRINCE OF WALES was struck at this time by two torpedoes simultaneously.*

‡ *H.L.B – high level bombing.*

20. *Japanese aircraft.*

(*a*) *The T/Bs were twin engined monoplanes (Naval type 96) and it is probable that H.L.B.s were the same, viz. shore-based aircraft.*

(b) Four T/B squadrons each of 9 aircraft were used. Three H.L.B. attacks were made, possibly all by the same squadron.

(c) Torpedoes were dropped at ranges between 1,000 and 2,000 yards and at a height noticeably greater than we do. Torpedoes ran very straight and the tracks were readily visible. There is no indication that the pistols were other than contact.

(d) The get-aways appeared clumsy, doubtless partly due to the heavy aircraft. In many cases they continued across the line of advance quite close to their targets. Some opened fire with their machine guns.

(e) No attempt was made to interfere with the rescue of survivors.

INITIAL REPORT BY CAPTAIN W.G. TENNANT, C.B., M.V.O., R.N.

To: – Commander-in-Chief, Eastern Fleet.
From: – Captain W. Tennant (late of H M.S. REPULSE).
Date – IIth December, 1941.

1. In the sinking of H.M.S. REPULSE, I deeply regret to report the loss of 27 officers and 486 men. The survivors number 42 officers and 754 men.

2. I should like to record here the magnificent spirit of my officers and ship's company throughout their ordeal. Cases occurred of men having to be ordered to leave their guns to save themselves as the ship was actually turning over.

3. Should Their Lordships think fit I am ready for a further seagoing command.

4. As I am regrettably the senior surviving officer I am preparing a report of the operation and the loss of the ships PRINCE OF WALES and REPULSE. I would only wish to state here that I was in entire agreement with every action taken by the Commander-in-Chief, Eastern Fleet, with the information that was then, as far as I knew, available to him. REPULSE was attacked constantly between III0 and I233 on the I0th December by H.L.B. and T/B attacks. Altogether she received one bomb hit, several near misses and four or five torpedoes. I was successful in the early attacks in combing the tracks of at least I5 torpedoes but in a later attack when committed to comb one attack another lot came close in on my beam and hit.

5. Shortly after this the ship was torpedoed aft and the rudder jammed; this was followed by attacks coming from all directions, when she suffered two or three further hits. I then knew that she could not survive, and ordered all up from below, and to cast loose Carley floats.

6. The ship remained afloat about six minutes after this and it is fortunate that the number above mentioned were rescued.

7. Lastly I think you should know that the attacks were pressed home by the Japanese with great determination and efficiency – the H.L.B. attacks in close formation at I0,000 feet were remarkably accurate. Large numbers of aircraft, possibly over 50, must have been employed. The torpedoes ran very straight and shallow and showed a distinct track.

8. I understand that Captain L.H. Bell of H.M.S. PRINCE OF WALES has given you a preliminary report of the loss of that ship.

9. The Destroyers ELECTRA, EXPRESS and VAMPIRE were handled most skilfully and I cannot say enough for the rescue work and care of survivors that they showed.

FURTHER REPORT BY CAPTAIN W.G. TENNANT, C.B., M.V.O., R.N.

I. At about I230 Monday, 8th December, I was called to a meeting on board PRINCE OF WALES with the Commander-in-Chief, Eastern Fleet, at which were present the Chief of Staff, the Captain of the Fleet, the Captain of the PRINCE OF WALES and some Staff Officers. The Commander-in-Chief described the intended operation which was broadly to make a raid on the Japanese communications to Kota Bharu, Singgora and Pattani.

2. PRINCE OF WALES, REPULSE, and four Destroyers sailed from Naval Base at I730 and passed the boom at I830. The Commander-in-Chief decided that in view of possible minefields it was necessary to pass to the eastward of Anamba Islands before turning to the northward.

Tuesday, 9th December.

3. Constant low clouds and heavy rain storms continued until about I645 and with the exception of an unconfirmed report of sighting of aircraft by VAMPIRE at about 0630 there was no other reason to suppose that the Force had been sighted. However, at about I645 the sky cleared considerably and the Force was very soon being shadowed by at least three aircraft. One Catalina was seen at about this time. During this period the course of the Force was north so that the enemy had still no knowledge of our intention to turn in towards Kota Bharu. At I900 the course was altered to north-west and speed increased to 26 knots. TENEDOS was ordered to return to base at about this time. At about 2000 I received a signal from the Commander-in-Chief that he had decided to keep the Destroyers in company and to cancel the operation in view of the fact that the whereabouts of the Force was actually known to the enemy; it would therefore be improbable that we should meet any convoy in the morning, and the enemy would have at least twelve hours to concentrate his airforce to attack us. At about 2030 the course was altered to south eastwards, I believe with the intention of shaking off the shadowers, and later to I50° speed being reduced to 20 knots to conserve the destroyers' oil. Later at approximately midnight course was altered to 245° and speed increased to 24 knots; this after signals received reporting an enemy landing at Kuantan. It was understood to be the Commander-in-Chief's intention to be off the coast at daylight in this vicinity. The remainder of the night passed without incident.

4. At about 0630 to 0700 an enemy reconnaissance aircraft appeared. The Force continued steering to the coast and PRINCE OF WALES flew off one aircraft and carried out a reconnaissance of it. Later EXPRESS was also sent in to investigate ashore. The Force passed down inside the seven fathom shoal which lies immediately to the eastward of Kuantan at approximately ten miles from the coast. When EXPRESS rejoined at about 0845 on reaching the northern end of the seven fathom patch, course was altered to the eastward at about 0935. I suggested to the Commander-in-Chief that REPULSE'S aircraft should carry out A/S patrol for two hours and then fly direct to Singapore then only about 140 miles distant. When approaching Kuantan at dawn a small tug with four barges was sighted at 0514. It was thought that they might conceivably be motor landing craft and I signalled to the Commander-in-Chief that we might profitably examine them on our return, with which he agreed. At about 1015 the Commander-in-Chief signalled first degree of H.A. readiness.* REPULSE RDF shortly after picked up enemy aircraft bearing 220 degrees approximately. The aircraft were first sighted at about 1100; the Commander-in-Chief had the Force manoeuvred by blue pennant and the Capital ships were now in quarter line formation.

5. I am now about to describe the various phases of the air attacks which finally caused the destruction of REPULSE. They are divided into five separate attacks with varying periods between them, the interval between numbers four and five being very brief.

6. The first attack developed shortly after 1100 when nine aircraft in close single line abreast formation were seen approaching REPULSE from about Green 50[†] and at a height of about 10,000 feet. Fire was at once opened on them with the Long Range H.A. by PRINCE OF WALES and REPULSE. It was very soon obvious that the attack was about to be entirely concentrated on REPULSE. The formation was very well kept and bombs were dropped with great accuracy, one near miss on the starboard side abreast B turret and one hit on the port hangar burst on the armour below the Marines' messdeck and caused damage. The remainder of the salvo (it was thought seven bombs were dropped altogether), fell very close to the port side and this concluded this attack. There was now a short lull of about twenty minutes during which the damage control parties carried out their duties in a most efficient manner and fires which had been started by this bomb had all been got under control before the next attack; and the bomb having burst on the armour no damage was suffered below in the engine or boiler rooms. It is thought that the bombs dropped were about 250 pounds.

7. The second attack was shared by PRINCE OF WALES and REPULSE and was made by torpedo bomber aircraft. They appeared to be the same type of machine, believed to be Mitsubishi 86 or 88. I am not prepared to say how many machines took part in this attack but on its conclusion I had the impression that we had succeeded in combing the tracks of a large number of torpedoes, possibly as many as twelve. We were steaming at 25 knots at the time I maintained a steady course until the aircraft appeared to be committed to the attack when the wheel was put over

and the attacks providentially combed I would like to record here the valuable work done by all Bridge personnel at this time in calmly pointing out approaching torpedo bombing aircraft which largely contributed to our good fortune in dodging all these torpedoes. PRINCE OF WALES was hit on the port side right aft during this attack and a large column of water appeared to be thrown up, larger than subsequent columns of water which were thrown up when REPULSE was hit later on.

8. The third attack was a high level bombing attack again concentrated on REPULSE. Possibly the enemy were aware, and particularly so if they were using 250 pound bombs, that these bombs would have had little chance of penetrating PRINCE OF WALES'S horizontal armour. I was manoeuvring the ship at high speed at the time and we were actually under helm when the bombs fell. No hits were received. There was one near miss on the starboard side and the remainder fell just clear on the port side. The attack was carried out in the same determined manner as was the first. PRINCE OF WALES had "not under control" balls hoisted at this time and I exchanged some signals with the Commander-in-Chief. I asked PRINCE OF WALES about her damage and she appeared to have a list to port but I got no reply though she still made some signals by Aldis light after this. Although uncertain at this time of the signals PRINCE OF WALES had made, I made an emergency report "Enemy aircraft bombing" followed immediately by an amplifying report which was just about to be transmitted at the time the ship sank. I also made a visual signal to the Commander-in-Chief telling him that we had up to date fortunately avoided all torpedoes fired at REPULSE and that all damage received from the bomb had been got under control. I also asked the Commander-in-Chief whether his wireless was still in action in case he wished me to make any reports. I closed PRINCE OF WALES at this time and reduced to 20 knots, the better to ascertain her damage, and to see if I could be of any assistance. Very shortly after this the fourth attack started to develop.

9. In the fourth attack about eight aircraft were seen low on the horizon on the starboard bow. Being low down it signified another torpedo bombing attack was impending. When about three miles away they split into two formations and I estimated that those on the right hand would launch their torpedoes first and I started to swing the ship to starboard. The torpedoes were dropped at a distance of 2500 yards and it seemed obvious that we should be once more successful in combing their tracks. The left hand formation appeared to be making straight for PRINCE OF WALES who was at this time abaft my port beam. When these aircraft were a little before the port beam at a distance of approximately 2000 yards they turned straight at me and fired their torpedoes. It now became obvious that, if these torpedoes were aimed straight, REPULSE would be most certainly hit as any other alteration of course would have caused me to be hit by the tracks of those torpedoes I was in the process of combing. One torpedo fired from my port side was obviously going to hit the ship and it was possible to watch its track for about a minute and a half before this actually took place. The ship was hit amidships port side. The ship stood this torpedo well and continued to manoeuvre and steamed at about 25 knots. There was now only a very short respite before the final and last attack.

10. I think it is interesting to report here the remarkable height from which the

torpedoes were dropped, estimated to be between three and four hundred feet and all torpedoes appeared to run perfectly straight from the point of dropping.

II. The second Walrus aircraft which had been damaged by the first bombing attack was successfully got over the side to avoid a petrol fire.

I2. From what I saw myself and from evidence I received at this period it became evident that the whole ship's company were carrying out their duties as if they were at ordinary peace exercises. The damage control parties working under Commander R.J.R. Dendy had replaced damaged lighting, had put out fires, and successfully coped with every situation as it arose.

I3. The torpedo bombers had carried out some machine-gunning on the port deck and the gunnery control positions aloft but this was not experienced on the Bridge.

I4. The Navigating Officer, Lieutenant Commander Gill, who controlled the ship under my orders carried out his duties in a most calm and exemplary manner, on one or two occasions when the whole H.A. armament was firing he had considerable difficulty in passing helm orders to the Quartermaster in the Upper Conning Tower but I do not think that this in any way caused the ship to be hit. The delay in giving helm orders in one or two cases was perhaps half a minute

I5. In the attacks up to date and in the last one which I am about to describe, it is estimated that four or five enemy aircraft were shot down but the Air Defence Officer informs me that he did not until the very end engage those torpedo bombers which had dropped their torpedoes but kept his fire for further aircraft approaching. I had previously told the Gunnery Officer that there was not to be any wasteful expenditure of H.A. ammunition.

I6. The enemy attacks were without doubt magnificently carried out and pressed well home. The high level bombers kept tight formation and appeared not to jink. I only observed one torpedo bomber who apparently had cold feet and fired his torpedoes at a distance of at least two miles from the ship. The torpedoes ran very straight and the tracks were exceptionally easy to see in the calm water and the torpedoes appeared to be running shallow although one of the last hits was observed to be under the starboard bilge keel between 87 and I02 stations, when the ship finally rolled over. I think the ship had a list to port at the time of this hit.

I7. I had intended to recover the Walrus aircraft at I2I5. Under the circumstances this became impossible. She subsequently made a forced landing on the sea and was towed into harbour by STRONGHOLD.

Fifth and Last Attack.

I8. The respite from the previous attack was brief. Torpedo bomber aircraft seemed to appear from several directions and the second torpedo hit the ship in the vicinity of the Gunroom and apparently jammed the rudder, and although the ship was still steaming at well over twenty knots she was not under control. Shortly after this at least three torpedoes hit the ship, two being on the port side and one on the starboard side. I knew now that she could not survive and at once gave the order for everyone to come on deck and to cast loose Carley floats. It has been learnt that the broadcasting apparatus was still working throughout the ship with the exception of the compartments down below aft but word was quickly passed down from Y turret and the after control. The decision for a Commanding Officer to make to cease all work in the ship below is an exceedingly difficult one, but I felt very sure that she would not survive four torpedoes and this was borne out for she only remained afloat about six or seven minutes after I gave the order for everyone to come on deck. I attribute the fact that so many men were fortunately able to be saved to these six or seven minutes, combined with the fact that the broadcast apparatus was still in action.

19. When these final two or three torpedoes detonated the ship rapidly commenced to take up a heavy list to port. Men were now pouring up on deck. They had all been warned, 24 hours before, to carry or wear their lifesaving apparatus. When the ship had a 30 degrees list to port I looked over the starboard side of the Bridge and saw the Commander and two or three hundred men collecting on the starboard side I never saw the slightest sign of panic or ill discipline. I told them from the Bridge how well they had fought the ship and wished them good luck. The ship hung for at least a minute and a half to two minutes with a list of about 60 degrees or 70 degrees to port and then rolled over at 1233.

20. With the exception of those officers I have mentioned who were immediately under my notice I find it very difficult specially to recommend any particular officer or man for decoration because every officer and man in the ship carried out his duties to the utmost, and it is possible that if comparison could be made, many of those who were lost are of all the most deserving.

21. Destroyers VAMPIRE and ELECTRA immediately closed and picked up survivors. They did their work in a most efficient manner and I cannot say enough of their work of rescue and care of the ship's company on the way back to harbour. ELECTRA subsequently went off to assist in searching the water round PRINCE OF WALES for survivors while we did the same on the Bridge of VAMPIRE on whose Bridge I was, and I am very certain that no one surviving was left.

22. From what I saw myself and reports I have received the work of the medical officers was tireless and beyond all praise.

(Signed) WILLIAM TENNANT.
Captain, R.N.
14th December, 1941.

REPORT BY LIEUTENANT COMMANDER
A.G. SKIPWITH, R.N.

Singapore.
12th December, 1941.

I have the honour to submit, in accordance with Commander-in-Chief, Eastern Fleet signal 0946GH/IIth December, the following brief narrative of events leading to the loss of H.M.S. PRINCE OF WALES.

2. At the time of the first air attack the squadron was returning to Singapore under the orders of Commander-in-Chief, Eastern Fleet.

3. At III3 on I0th December fire was opened on eight twin-engined high level bombers which attacked REPULSE in close formation.

4. At II4I½ fire was opened on nine torpedo bombers which attacked H.M.S. PRINCE OF WALES from the port side. The ship was hit by a torpedo at II44 in a position approximately abreast P.3 and P.4 turrets. The damage caused by this hit was as follows and the result apparent before the next attack developed:

(*a*) The ship assumed a list of II½° to port and increased her trim by the stern, the port side of the quarterdeck being awash by I220.

(*b*) "B" Engine Room, "Y" Boiler Room, the port Diesel Room and "Y" Action Machinery Room flooded.

(*c*) Both propeller shafts stopped.

(*d*) Steering gear was affected and the ship was never again under complete control, N.U.C. Balls‡ being hoisted at I2I0.

(*e*) The warning telephone system failed.

(*f*) Power failed at both after groups of 5.25 inch guns and P.I turret jammed in training: power failed at P.2.

5. A further torpedo bomber attack developed on the starboard side at I220. Three minutes later the ship was hit by two torpedoes, one at the stem and the other in the after part of the ship, starboard side. At I224½ the ship was hit by a torpedo abreast B turret on the starboard side. Amongst other results "A" propeller shaft became jammed, the list was gradually reduced, and the ship settled appreciably..

6. At I24I fire was opened with remaining 5.25 inch guns, namely S.I., S.2 and P.I, and pom-poms, at a high level bombing formation of eight aircraft. Three minutes later the ship was straddled and a hit sustained on the catapult deck. The armoured deck was not pierced. Near misses may have caused further damage.

7. Soon after this attack H.M.S. EXPRESS closed and came alongside the starboard side of the quarterdeck. Orders were given by the Captain to disembark wounded and those not required to fight the ship. Finally, the order to abandon ship was passed.

8. As much detailed evidence as possible is being taken.

9. I wish to record that H.M.S. EXPRESS was magnificently handled, remaining alongside until the last possible moment.

I0. The officers and ratings whom I saw displayed great courage and steadiness.

II. H.M.S. PRINCE OF WALES heeled over quickly to port and sank at about 1320.

(Signed) A.G. SKIPWITH,
Lieutenant Commander, R.N.

Admiralty footnotes.
* *H.A. readiness – readiness of High Angle anti-aircraft guns.*
† *Green 50 – 50° on the starboard bow.*
‡ *N.U.C. Balls – "not under control" signal.*

APPENDIX I.

Air Headquarters Far East,
Singapore.
12th December, 1941.

Sir,
    I have the honour to forward herewith a report made by Flt./Lt. Vigors, temporarily commanding 453 Squadron, who took his squadron over to provide fighter cover to H.M. Ships PRINCE OF WALES and REPULSE. The tributes paid by Flt./Lt. Vigors to the magnificent conduct of the officers and men of the PRINCE OF WALES and REPULSE are tributes which the whole of the personnel under my command would like to join in.

I have the honour to be, Sir,
Your obedient Servant,
(Signed) C. PULFORD.
Air Vice-Marshal, Commanding,
Royal Air Force, Far East.

The Commander-in-Chief Eastern Fleet,
H.M. Naval Base,
Singapore.
R.A.A.F Station,
Sembawang.
11.12.41.

To: – Commander-in-Chief, Far Eastern Fleet.

Sir,
    I had the privilege to be the first aircraft to reach the crews of the PRINCE OF WALES and the REPULSE after they had been sunk. I say the privilege, for during the next hour while I flew around low over them, I witnessed a show of that

indomitable spirit for which the Royal Navy is so famous. I have seen a show of spirit in this war over Dunkirk, during the "Battle of Britain," and in the London night raids, but never before have I seen anything comparable with what I saw yesterday. I passed over thousands who had been through an ordeal the greatness of which they alone can understand, for it is impossible to pass on one's feelings in disaster to others.

Even to an eye so inexperienced as mine it was obvious that the three destroyers were going to take hours to pick up those hundreds of men clinging to bits of wreckage, and swimming around in the filthy oily water. Above all this, the threat of another bombing and machine-gun attack was imminent. Every one of those men must have realised that. Yet as I flew around, every man waved and put his thumb up as I flew over him.

After an hour, lack of petrol forced me to leave, but during that hour I had seen many men in dire danger waving, cheering and joking as if they were holiday-makers at Brighton waving at a low flying aircraft. It shook me for here was something above human nature. I take off my hat to them, for in them I saw the spirit which wins wars.

I apologise for taking up your valuable time, but I thought you should know of the incredible conduct of your men.

I have the honour to be, Sir,
Your obedient Servant,
(Signed) T.A. VIGORS,
Flt./Lt., O.C. 453 *Squadron.*

APPENDIX II.

Operational Signals made by Commander-in-Chief, Eastern Fleet,
on 9th December, 1941.

TO: Force Z
FROM C.-in-C., E.F.

Besides a minor landing at Kota Bharu which was not followed, landings have been made between Pattani and Singgora and a major landing 90 miles north of Singgora.

2. Little is known of enemy naval forces in the vicinity. It is believed that KONGO is the only capital ship likely to be met. Three Atago type, one Kako type, and two Zintu type cruisers have been reported. A number of destroyers possibly of fleet type are likely to be met.

3. My object is to surprise and sink transports and enemy warships before air attack can develop. Objective chosen will depend on air reconnaissance. Intend to arrive objective after sunrise tomorrow 10th. If an opportunity to bring KONGO to action occurs this is to take precedence over all other action.

4. Subject to Commanding Officer's freedom of manoeuvre in an emergency Force Z will remain in close order and will be manoeuvred as a unit until action is joined. When the signal "Act independently" is made or at discretion of Commanding

Officer, REPULSE will assume freedom of manoeuvre remaining in tactical support but engaging from a wide enough angle to facilitate fall of shot.

5. Intend to operate at 25 knots unless a chase develops and subsequently to retire at maximum speed endurance will allow.

6. Capital ships should attempt to close below 20,000 yards until fire is effective but should avoid offering an end on target. Ships must be prepared to change from delay to non-delay fuzes according to target.

7. PRINCE OF WALES and REPULSE are each to have one aircraft fuelled and ready to fly off if required. If flown off aircraft must return to land base. Kota Bharu aerodrome is understood to be out of action.

8. TENEDOS will be detached before dark to return independently to Singapore.

9. Remaining destroyers may be detached during the night 9th/10th should enemy information require a high speed of advance. In such case these destroyers are to retire towards Anamba Island at 10 knots until a rendezvous is ordered by W/T.

TO: PRINCE OF WALES, REPULSE
FROM: C.-in-C., E.F.

Inform Ships' Companies as follows: Begins – "The enemy has made several landings on the north coast of Malaya and has made local progress. Our Army is not large and is hard pressed in places. Our Air Force has had to destroy and abandon one or more aerodromes. Meanwhile fast transports lie off the coast.

This is our opportunity before the enemy can establish himself. We have made a wide circuit to avoid air reconnaissance and hope to surprise the enemy shortly after sunrise tomorrow Wednesday. We may have the luck to try our metal against the old Japanese battle-cruiser KONGO or against some Japanese cruisers and destroyers which are reported in the Gulf of Siam. We are sure to get some useful practice with the H.A. armament.

Whatever we meet I want to finish quickly and so get well clear to the eastward before the Japanese can mass too formidable a scale of an attack against us. So shoot to sink." – Ends.

APPENDIX III.

*Signals made by Chief of Staff, Eastern Fleet,
to Commander-in-Chief, Eastern Fleet.*

TO: C.-in-C., Eastern Fleet.
FROM: Chief of Staff, Eastern Fleet.

IMMEDIATE.

R.A.F. reconnaissance to depth of 100 miles to the north-westward of you will be provided by I Catalina from 0800 onwards tomorrow 9th.

(ii) It is hoped that a dawn reconnaissance of coast near Singgora can be carried out on Wednesday, I0th.

(iii) Fighter protection on Wednesday, I0th will not, repeat not, be possible.

(iv) Japanese have large bomber forces based Southern Indo-China and possibly also in Thailand. C.-in-C., Far East, has requested General MacArthur to carry out attack with his long range bombers on Indo-China aerodromes as soon as possible.

(v) Kota Bharu aerodrome has been evacuated and we seem to be losing grip on other northern aerodromes due to enemy action.

(vi) Military position near Kota Bharu does not seem good, but details are not available.

T.O.O. 2253GH/8.

TO C-in-C., Eastern Fleet.
FROM. Chief of Staff, Eastern Fleet.

MOST IMMEDIATE.

One battleship, "M" class cruiser, II destroyers and a number of transports reported close to coast between Kota Bharu and Perhentian Island by air reconnaissance this afternoon.

T.O.O. II25Z/9.

Correct my II25/9. Force was sighted at 0900Z/9 (I630GH/9).

T.O.O. II55Z/9

TO: C.-in-C., Eastern Fleet.
FROM: Chief of Staff, Eastern Fleet.

IMMEDIATE.

Only significant enemy report is contained in my II25Z/9th. Enemy apparently continuing landing in Kota Bharu area which should be fruitful as well as Singgora.

2. On the other hand enemy bombers on South Indo-China aerodromes are in force and undisturbed. They could attack you five hours after sighting and much depends on whether you have been seen today.

Two carriers may be in Saigon area.

3. Military situation at Kota Bharu appears difficult. Aerodrome is in enemy hands.

4. All our northern aerodromes are becoming untenable due to enemy air action. C.-in-C., Far East, hints he is considering concentrating all air efforts on defence of Singapore area.

5. Extremely difficult to give you clearer picture because air reconnaissance communications are so slow due partly to damage to aerodromes.

T.O.O. I4I5Z/9 (2I45GH/9).

TO: C.-in-C., Eastern Fleet.
FROM: Chief of Staff, Eastern Fleet.

IMMEDIATE.

Enemy reported landing Kuantan, latitude 03° 50' North.
    T.O.O. I505Z/9.

4

THE X-CRAFT ATTACK ON *TIRPITZ*

20-22 SEPTEMBER 1943

The following Despatch was submitted to the Lords Commissioners of the Admiralty on the 8th November, 1943, by Rear Admiral C.B. Barry, D.S.O., Admiral (Submarines).

8th November, 1943.

REPORT ON OPERATION "SOURCE".

Be pleased to lay before the Lords Commissioners of the Admiralty the following report on operations by X-craft in 1943 against the German main units in their protected anchorages on the Norwegian coast (Operation "Source").

Preliminary.

2. The X type of small submarine was evolved as a result of a study of the problem of how enemy main units could be attacked in their heavily defended and inaccessible anchorages.

3. On completion of the successful trials of the prototype X-craft (X.3), a contract was placed with Messrs. Vickers Armstrong, Limited, on 12th May, 1942, for the construction of six X-craft of a new and improved design, built for the purpose of attacking capital ships in harbour and surrounded by net defences.

4. At the same time, volunteers were called for, for special and hazardous service and training commenced, using the prototype X-craft (X.3) and the second prototype (X.4).

5. The six operational X-craft (X.5-X.10) were delivered from Messrs. Vickers

Armstrong between the 31st December, 1942, and 16th January, 1943, and preliminary plans were put in hand and advanced training commenced with a view to attacking the German main units on the Norwegian coast in the Spring of 1943, before the hours of darkness became too short. The latest date for such an attack was considered to be the 9th March, 1943.

6. Unfortunately the time in hand proved insufficient to allow of the crews and craft being worked up to the high standard required for such an operation, and this was aggravated by a number of teething troubles in the craft themselves – troubles which were to be expected in a new design of weapon but which it had optimistically been hoped would not occur. Nor had the vital problem been solved of how to transport the X-craft to within striking distance of their target. Various methods had been tried before it was proved that the only profitable way was to tow them there by operational submarines. I was thus reluctantly compelled to inform the Vice Chief of Naval Staff on the 11th February, 1943, that the operation must be postponed until the Autumn.

7. The time gained proved invaluable, and that the decision to postpone the operation was the correct one, was proved beyond doubt by subsequent events: it ensured that, when the time came, both the crews and the craft were trained and perfected to that concert pitch so vital to such an operation.

8. On the 17th April, 1943, the 12th Submarine Flotilla was formed under the command of Captain W.E. Banks, D.S.C., R.N., to coordinate, under Admiral (Submarines), the training and material of the special weapons, including X-craft, and Acting Captain P.Q. Roberts, R.N., assumed command of H.M.S. BONAVENTURE, the depot ship for X-craft, under Captain (S), 12th Submarine Flotilla. The officer in charge of training was Commander D.C. Ingram, D.S.C., R.N.

9. On completion of preliminary trials and training, X.5–X.10 joined H.M.S. BONAVENTURE for advanced training and working up at Port HHZ (Loch Cairnbawn, close north of Loch Ewe), where from the 4th July until the commencement of the operation full scale exercises and attacks against capital ships were carried out. This period was also devoted to perfecting the towing of X-craft by submarines. I should like to place on record the great assistance given by the Commander-in-Chief, Home Fleet, in providing capital ships of his Fleet to act as target ships at Port HHZ during this period, and also to mention the part played by the Boom Defence organisation in surrounding these ships with nets and providing net defences and equipment for the necessary trials.

Planning.

10. In the meantime detailed plans for carrying out the operation were prepared by my Staff and operation orders were drawn up. The officer mainly responsible for this work was Commander G.P.S. Davies, R.N., of my Staff.

11. It was decided that the attack should take place at the earliest date the hours of darkness allowed, so as to complete the operation before the weather conditions

deteriorated. It was also desirable to have a certain amount of moon, to assist the X-craft in their passage by night up the fiords. The period 20th-25th September, 1943, with the moon in the last quarter, was therefore selected, and Day D, the day on which the X-craft were if possible to be slipped from their towing submarines to proceed for the attack, was provisionally fixed for the 20th September, 1943.

I2. To allow for the attack to be carried out at any of the protected anchorages used by German main units on the Norwegian coast it was necessary to provide operation orders for attacks on Alten Fiord, the Narvik area and on Trondheim, and Operation "Source" was divided into three operations, as follows:

	Operation
Operations north of 70° N	"Funnel"
Operations between 67° and 69° N	"Empire"
Operations between 63° and 65° N	"Forced"

It was thus possible to direct operations against the enemy in whichever of these three areas he might be detected.

Photographic Reconnaissance.

I3. Preliminary photographic reconnaissance of the anchorages, with special reference to net defences, was considered most necessary for the success of the operation, and last minute reconnaissances, to give the disposition of targets, essential.

I4. This presented difficulties for the Alten area, which was outside the range of home-based P.R. aircraft. In May, 1943, I discussed this question with the Commander-in-Chief, Home Fleet, who was fully in agreement with me on the importance of establishing reliable P.R. cover for the area. On I2th May, 1943, he addressed a signal to Admiralty and repeated to Admiral (Submarines) and Headquarters, Coastal Command, in which he proposed that the necessary British air crews and photographic personnel should be sent to North Russia for this most important duty.

I5. Agreement was reached with the Air Ministry by 30th July, and Admiral Fisher (in Moscow) was asked for his views after consultation with the Russian authorities.

I6. As a result, and after agreement with the Russians, it was agreed to send a British photographic unit to Murmansk by destroyer, to run a shuttle service between the United Kingdom and North Russia by Mosquito aircraft for the preliminary reconnaissances, and to base Spitfires at Vaenga for the last-minute sorties. In addition, Catalina aircraft would be available to run a shuttle service to and from North Russia with photographs.

I7. All preliminary arrangements for putting this into operation had been made by the I8th August and negotiations concluded with the Russians on the question of visas. On the 27th August, H.M. Ships MUSKETEER and MAHRATTA sailed from Faroes with R.A.F. photographic personnel and stores and arrived in Kola Inlet on the 3Ist August.

18. The weather was still to be reckoned with, however, and although the Mosquito aircraft for the preliminary reconnaissances had been ready to leave the United Kingdom from the 21st August, weather conditions were never satisfactory for this aircraft to carry out her part of the plan.

19. The three Spitfires, however, arrived at Vaenga on the 3rd September, exactly eight days before Operation "Source" was due to sail from Port HHZ, and the first sortie was flown on the 7th September.

20. The subsequent reconnaissances flown by this unit were invaluable to the operation. Full details of the dispositions of the enemy units and net defences were signalled from Russia and given to all the personnel taking part before they left harbour. No actual photographs of the preliminary reconnaissances were available for the final briefing as, in spite of every effort to obtain them in time, the first photographs taken by this unit did not arrive until a few hours after the X-craft had sailed, but this did not in fact matter as the relevant information was complete, in the signalled report.

Preliminary Movements.

21. For security reasons it was decided that the operation should sail from Port HHZ (Loch Cairnbawn), where the X-craft taking part had been working up from H.M.S. BONAVENTURE since the 4th July, 1943.

22. H.M.S. TITANIA was sailed for and arrived at Port HHZ on the 30th August to act as depot ship to the submarines taking part, and H.M. Submarines THRASHER, TRUCULENT, STUBBORN, SYRTIS, SCEPTRE and SEANYMPH arrived between the 31st August and 1st September. These submarines had all been fitted with special towing equipment.

23. In addition, H.M. Submarines SATYR and SEADOG, also specially fitted for towing, were held at 24 hours' notice at Scapa as reserves.

24. Towing trials, and trials of changing over passage and operational crews between X-craft and submarines at sea, were carried out between the 1st and 5th September; then, after final swinging for compasses, all X-craft were hoisted inboard of H.M.S. BONAVENTURE for the fitting of side charges, storing, final preparations and the full briefing of crews and the Commanding Officers of the submarines.

This briefing was carried out by the officer of my Staff (Commander Davies) who had been responsible for the planning.

Security.

25. Special security measures at Port HHZ were increased as from the 1st September. No leave was allowed, none but specially selected officers and ratings were permitted to leave the area, and all ships present were retained in the port until the completion of the operation. It is considered that the security of the operation was well maintained.

Departure for the Operation.

26. Soviet reconnaissance on the 3rd September had shown that TIRPITZ, SCHARNHORST and LUTZOW were present in the Alten area, and it appeared likely therefore that the operation would be carried out in that area (Operation "Funnel"). On the 7th September, however, the first Spitfire sortie showed only LUTZOW present, and the TIRPITZ and SCHARNHORST were later reported off Ice Fiord, Spitzbergen.

27. In order for Day D to be the 20th September in the case of Operation "Funnel," it was necessary for the X-craft to be sailed from Port HHZ on IIth-I2th September. Furthermore it was not desirable to postpone Day D by more than two or three days owing to the waning moon. It was therefore vital to obtain the re-disposition of the main units as soon as possible.

28. However, visual reconnaissance at I000A on the I0th September confirmed the return of the TIRPITZ and SCHARNHORST to Alten Fiord, and the S.B.N.O., North Russia that evening signalled the exact positions of both ships in their berth in Kaafiord. LUTZOW was not seen.

29. I arrived at Port HHZ on the morning of the I0th September, to see the crews before they sailed and to witness the start of this great enterprise.

30. On the following morning I signalled to Admiralty, Commander-in-Chief, Home Fleet, and Admiral Commanding Orkney and Shetlands, my intention to carry out Operations "Source" and "Funnel", Day D being 20th September.

3I. Submarines, each with an X-craft in tow, sailed from Port HHZ as follows:-

    I600Z, IIth September – TRUCULENT and X.6.
                                SYRTIS and X.9.
    I800Z, IIth September – THRASHER and X.5.
    2000Z, IIth September – SEANYMPH and X.8.
    2I30Z, IIth September – STUBBORN and X.7.
    I300Z, I2th September – SCEPTRE and X.I0.

The operational crews of the X-craft were embarked in the towing submarines and the X-craft were manned for the passage by passage crews.[*]

Admiralty footnote:-

[*] *The Commanding Officers of the towing submarines, and of the operational and passage crews of the X-craft were:-*

TRUCULENT	*Lieut. R.L. Alexander, D.S.O., R.N.*
X.6	*Lieut. D. Cameron, R.N.R.*
	(Passage) Lieut. A. Wilson, R.N.V.R.
SYRTIS	*Lieut. M.H. Jupp, D.S.C., R.N.*
X.9	*Lieut. T. L. Martin, R.N.*
	(Passage) Sub-Lieut. E. Kearon, R.N.V.R.
THRASHER	*Lieut. A.R. Hezlet, D.S.C., RN.*
X.5	*Lieut. H. Henty-Creer, R.N.V.R.*
	(Passage) Lieut. J.V. Terry-Lloyd, S.A.N.F.

SEANYMPH	Lieut. J.P.H. Oakley, D.S.C, R.N.
X.8	Lieut. B.M. McFarlane, R.A.N.
	(Passage) Lieut. J. Smart, R.N.V.R.
STUBBORN	Lieut. A.A. Duff, R.N.
X.7	Lieut. B.C.G. Place, D.S.C., R.N,
	(Passage) Lieut. P.H. Philip, S.A.N.F.
SCEPTRE	Lieut. I.S. McIntosh, M.B.E, D.S.C., R.N.
X.10	Lieut. K.R. Hudspeth, R.A.N.V.R.
	(Passage) Sub-Lieut. E.V. Page, R.N.V.R.

The Passage.

32. The passage was uneventful from the IIth to I4th September. Good weather was experienced and all submarines made good speed with their X-craft dived in tow. X-craft surfaced to ventilate three or four times every 24 hours for approximately I5 minutes during which time speed was reduced. The average speed made good over this period was approximately:

| "T" class submarines | I0 knots. |
| "S" class submarines | 8½ knots. |

33. With the arrival of photographs, flown to this country from Russia by Catalina, of the preliminary Spitfire sorties, a detailed interpretation of the net defences was carried out and on I5th September the results were signalled to the submarines taking part in the operation. The presence of LUTZOW in Langfiord was confirmed by P.R. on the I4th September which also showed TIRPITZ and SCHARNHORST in Kaafiord, and the geographical positions of these ships were signalled to the submarines and Target Plan No. 4 ordered.

Target Plan No. 4 allocated X.5, X.6 and X.7 to attack TIRPITZ, X.9 and X.I0 to attack SCHARNHORST, and X.8 LUTZOW.

I5th September.

34. At 0400Z on the I5th September, when X.8 was being towed by SEANYMPH at 8 knots, the tow parted. X.8, who was dived at the time, surfaced five minutes later, but, although the visibility was estimated at 5 miles, there was no sign of the SEANYMPH. X.8's estimated position at that time was latitude 69° 04' N. 08° I4' E. At 0430Z, X. 8 set course 029°, speed 3 knots, on main engines.

35. The fact of the tow parting was not immediately apparent to the SEANYMPH, and it was not until 0600Z, when X.8 was due to surface to ventilate, that it became apparent.

SEANYMPH thereupon turned back on her track and set course 209° to search. The weather at I200Z, I5th September, was reported as: Wind S. to S.E. 4, sky 0, sea 4-5, visibility 7.*

A watercolour by Edward Tufnell, RN (Retd), depicting the cruisers HMS *Exeter* (foreground) and HMNZS *Achilles* (right centre background) in action with the *Admiral Graf Spee* (right background) on 13 December 1939. (US Naval Historical Center)

A photograph of the port bow of *Admiral Graf Spee* which was taken whilst the warship was anchored in Montevideo Harbour following the Battle of the River Plate. (US Naval Historical Center).

A 15cm gun recovered from the wreck of *Admiral Graf Spee*. On display at the Uruguayan Naval Museum, the gun is trained towards the River Plate, site of the battleship's last action in December 1939. (With the kind permission of Vince Alongi)

The German pocket battleship *Admiral Graf Spee* after being scuttled off Montevideo, Uruguay, in the estuary of the River Plate, 17 December 1939. (HMP)

On 10 February 2006, the 6.6ft tall eagle figurehead from *Admiral Graf Spee*'s stern was recovered from the waters of the River Plate. It still bears the impact of a heavy calibre round through its chest, almost certainly caused during the Battle of the River Plate. (With the kind permission of Vince Alongi)

After *Admiral Graf Spee* was scuttled in the shallow water just outside Montevideo Harbou much of the ship's superstructure remained above water. Over the years the wreck has subsided into the muddy seabed and today only the tip of the mast remains above the surfa – as can be seen here. (With the kind permission of Anthony Papini)

The German battleship *Bismarck* photographed from the heavy cruiser *Prinz Eugen* on 24 May 1941, following the Battle of the Denmark Strait and shortly before the two German ships separated. This is the last photograph of *Bismarck* taken by the Germans. (US Naval Historical Center)

Taken from a Japanese aircraft, this poor quality image shows HMS *Prince of Wales* at far left and HMS *Repulse* beyond her. A destroyer, either HMS *Express* or HMS *Electra*, is in the foreground. (US Navy Photograph)

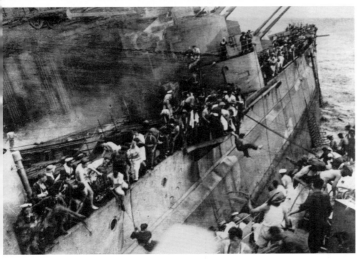

As the disaster unfolds, some of the crew of the sinking HMS *Prince of Wales* abandon ship, transferring, where they can, to the destroyer HMS *Express*. Moments later, the list on *Prince of Wales* suddenly increased and *Express* had to withdraw. (HMP)

Also taken from a Japanese aircraft, this picture captures the early stages of the attack, the initial high-level bombing, on HMS *Prince of Wales* (top) and HMS *Repulse*. (US Naval History and Heritage Command Photograph).

A remarkable image of the German battleship *Tirpitz* which was taken by Flight Lieutenant Albert Fane, of the RAF's No.1 Photographic Reconnaissance Unit, during a sortie over Norway. The original caption states that the "arrows indicate gun crews at action stations". (HMP)

The crews of the X-craft involved in Operation *Source*, including the passage crews, pose for a group photograph on HMS *Bonaventure* in September 1943. Soon after this image was taken, the midget submarines departed on their mission to attack *Tirptiz*, the "Beast", as Winston Churchill so famously referred to her. (HMP)

Four of the X-craft involved in the attack on *Tirpitz* during Operation *Source* are pictured in a floating dock at Port Bannatyne. (HMP)

One of the Operation *Source* X-craft, X-6, pictured being floated alongside HMS *Bonaventure* at Port HHZ in August 1943, prior to the attack. (HMP)

A remarkable shot taken the moment that gun crews on *Tirpitz* open fire on an X-craft sighted in Kåfjord during Operation *Source*. Both X-6 and X-7 managed to drop their charges underneath *Tirpitz*, but were unable to make good their escape as they were observed and attacked. Both craft were abandoned and six crew members survived to be captured. (Courtesy of Chris Goss)

In 1974 divers located the missing bow and battery section of X-7, at a depth of forty-nine metres. They were successfully raised and donated to the Imperial War Museum at Duxford. (Courtesy of Dr Scott Arthur, Edinburgh)

A vertica[l]
photographi[c]
reconnaissance imag[e]
taken from 8,500 fee[t]
showing *Tirpit[z]*
surrounded by repa[ir]
vessels, whils[t]
anchored behin[d]
double torpedo boom[s]
in Kaa Fjord on 1[2?]
July 1944. (HMP[)]

The man who wrote the last
two despatches in this
volume: Admiral Sir Bruce
A. Fraser. (HMP)

36. At 1213Z STUBBORN, towing X.7, and on the adjacent route to SEANYMPH and X.8, sighted what was at that time believed to be a U-boat in an estimated position 68° 51' N. 8° 34' E. and dived, surfacing at 1323Z.

37. At 1550Z, while proceeding at 7 knots, X.7, in tow of STUBBORN, broke from her tow. X.7 surfaced immediately and the auxiliary tow was passed. At 1700Z, STUBBORN again proceeded with X.7 in tow.

38. At 1630Z, X.8 sighted and closed STUBBORN who was at that time getting X.7 in tow again, and at 1718Z STUBBORN, with X.7 in tow and X.8 in company, proceeded to look for SEANYMPH. No contact was made, however, and at dusk (1900Z) STUBBORN proceeded northwards with X.7 and X.8. STUBBORN reported the situation by W/T to Admiral (Submarines) at 1954, who passed the information to SEANYMPH.

39. Meanwhile, SEANYMPH, having searched the area unsuccessfully, passed a signal to Admiral (Submarines) at 2045Z informing him of the loss of X.8. At 2151 she received Admiral (Submarines) signal referred to in paragraph 38 and proceeded to intercept.

40. X.8 proceeded in company with STUBBORN and X.7 until 2359, when contact was lost.

Admiralty footnote:-
* *Wind force 4 – moderate breeze (11-15 m.p.h.)*
   Sky 0 – overcast.
   Sea 4-5 – rough to very rough.
   Visibility 7-7 miles.

16th September.

The reason was explained at 0400Z, when it was found that since 0001Z, X.8 had been steering 146° instead of 046° (the result of a phonetic error in passing orders for the course).

41. At 0300Z, dawn showed to STUBBORN that there was no X.8; but at 0315Z a submarine was sighted and identified as SEANYMPH, in position 69° 35' N. 10° 16' E. All relative information was passed to SEANYMPH who proceeded to look for her errant charge, STUBBORN and X.7 proceeding to the northward.

42. Between 1200 and 1350Z, SEANYMPH sighted and spoke SCEPTRE, and at 1700Z she made contact with X.8. By 2005 she had her once more in tow and, as the weather was favourable, transferred to her the operational crew.

43. In the meantime there had been another case of tow-parting which was not to have such a happy ending. Until 0145Z on the 16th, in estimated position 70° 49' N. 11° 40' E., SYRTIS and X.9 had had an uneventful passage. At 0102Z, X.9 dived after her period on the surface for ventilating and charging. Speed was then gradually increased to 8½ knots. SYRTIS reports the weather at 0001Z/16 as: Wind S.S.E. 3, sea and swell 2-3.* SYRTIS decided not to bring X.9 to the surface at 0300 after so short a spell dived but continued until 0855Z, when speed was reduced to 5 knots.

At 0907Z, three signals-underwater-exploding were fired to surface X.9. X.9 did not surface and at 0920Z the tow was hauled in and found to have parted. SYRTIS turned to the reciprocal course at 0955Z, to return as soon as possible to the vicinity of where it was thought X.9 might have broken adrift. From the log readings and fuel consumption this was estimated to have been between 0I45 and 0300Z. However, no contact was made with X.9; but at I545Z SYRTIS sighted a well defined oil track which it was considered might have come from an X-craft, running in a direction 088°-090°, which was the direct course for the slipping position, 200 miles distant.

44. Subsequent search revealed no sign of X.9 and no further news has been received of her. It can only be hoped that the Passage Commanding Officer (Sub-Lieutenant E. Kearon, R.N.V.R.) made the Norwegian coast, scuttled his craft, and made his way ashore with his crew. It is not considered that X.9 took any part in the attack. The passage crew were not trained for it, neither did they have sufficient information to carry it out.

Admiralty footnote:-
* *Wind force 3 – gentle breeze (7-I0 m.p.h)*
  Sea 2-3 – slight to moderate.

I7th September.

45. The regrettable loss of X.9 was not known to Admiral (Submarines) until some days later, as at the time the loss was discovered, SYRTIS was in an area where, by the orders, it was forbidden to break W/T silence. At 0I43Z therefore, having abandoned the search, SYRTIS proceeded north to pass a signal by W/T from north of 73° North.

46. Meanwhile the remaining five submarines were proceeding with their X-craft in tow, and TRUCULENT and THRASHER, neither of which had had any difficulties, both made their landfalls from the vicinity of their ordered landfall positions during the day. At approximately 0600Z STUBBORN and SEANYMPH sighted each other in the vicinity of position 7I° 04' N. I5° 56' E., and later, between I447 and I508Z, STUBBORN and SEANYMPH were again in contact and spoke to each other by S.S.T.* It was comforting to STUBBORN to learn that X.8 had been met.

47. At 0725Z X.8 experienced some difficulty in maintaining trim. Trim became worse as the day went on, air could be heard escaping from the starboard side charge and the craft took up a list to starboard. It was apparent that the buoyancy chambers of the starboard charge were leaking. At I630Z, with the compensating tank dry and No. 2 main ballast fully blown, and trim still difficult to hold, the Commanding Officer of X.8 (Lieutenant B.M. McFarlane, R.A.N.) decided to jettison the starboard charge, and this was set to "safe" and released at I635Z in about I80 fathoms. In spite of the "safe" setting, however, the charge exploded at I650Z, about I,000 yards astern of X.8, in tow of SEANYMPH. Both vessels were dived at the time. The explosion was loud but caused no damage.

48. Although this charge had been released, X.8 still had difficulty in maintaining trim and now had a list to port, indicating that the port charge also had flooded buoyancy chambers; and the Commanding Officer decided he must jettison it too. Before doing so X.8 surfaced and, distrusting the "safe" setting, set the charge to fire 2 hours after release. It was released at 1655Z, as was verified by the Commanding Officer. At 1840Z – 1¾ hours after release – by which time, from log readings and revolutions taken by SEANYMPH, X.8 was distant 3½ miles from the position of release, the charge detonated astern with tremendous force. This caused such damage to X.8 as to flood the "wet and dry" compartment, distorting the doors to this compartment, fracturing pipes, and generally causing such damage to the craft that she was no longer capable of diving. The explosion also caused a number of lights to be broken in SEANYMPH.

49. It is not clear why the second explosion caused such damage at an apparent range of 3½ miles while the first explosion, only 1,000 yards away, did none. Both charges had been dropped in approximately the same depth of water (180 fathoms). It may be that only partial detonation occurred in the first charge, which had been set to "safe". Whatever the reason the force of the second explosion would appear to have illustrated the efficiency of the charges. I find it hard to believe that the explosion was in fact 3½ miles away; but whatever the horizontal range was, there is no doubt about the depth of water, so that in any event the result of the explosion was indeed remarkable.

50. The 17th September was the first day (D-3) on which the transfer of crews was to take place if the weather permitted; but the weather had deteriorated and by the evening the wind was from the south-west, force 4, with a sea and swell of 4-5, and it was too rough to make the change-over.

51. The P.R. on the 15th September had shown no change in the disposition of the targets, and submarines were so informed by signal on 17th September, which also confirmed the Target Plan as No. 4. Further information on the nets round LUTZOW and the A/S† net across Langfiord was also passed by signal this day.

Admiralty footnote:-
* S.S.T. – submarine sound signalling apparatus.
† A/S – anti-submarine.

18th September.

52. X.8 informed SEANYMPH at daylight of the full particulars of her damage; and as she could now serve no useful purpose in the operation and, if sighted on the surface, might compromise it, the Commanding Officer, H.M.S. SEANYMPH, decided to embark her crew and scuttle her. In anticipation of the possibility of just such a situation, Admiral (Submarines) had transmitted a signal on 16th September, informing the Commanding Officer, H.M.S. SEANYMPH, that if he considered it necessary in the interests of the general security of the operation as a whole to scuttle X.8, such action would have his full approval.

53. By 0345Z the crew had been embarked from X.8 and the craft sunk in position 7I° 4I.5' N. I8° II' E.

54. I consider that the Commanding Officer of X.8 acted correctly in releasing the side charges when it became apparent that they were flooded, and that the Commanding Officer, H.M.S. SEANYMPH's decision to sink X.8, to avoid compromising the operation, was the correct one.

55. After sinking X.8, SEANYMPH proceeded to the north of 73° North to report by W/T.

56. At 0555 SYRTIS, having transmitted the signal reporting the loss of X.9, set course for her patrol area. SYRTIS's signal was never received, and it was not until the 3rd October, when Admiral (Submarines) received SYRTIS's signal timed 200IA/2nd, that is was known that X.9 had broken adrift from her tow and had not been seen since I6th September, and therefore had not taken part in the attack.

57. Weather conditions had improved slightly by dusk on the I8th, and at 20I5Z STUBBORN, in position 70° 57' N. 20° 35' E., decided to transfer the operational crew to X.7. The change-over was successfully completed by 2I24Z. The remaining submarines with X-craft in tow – TRUCULENT with X.6, THRASHER with X.5 and SCEPTRE with X.I0 – decided that the weather was still too bad to effect the transfer.

58. At 2I28Z STUBBORN, on going ahead after changing over the crews, parted her tow. The main tow had already parted, on the I5th September, and with the auxiliary tow also parted, it was necessary to use a 2½-inch wire spring. Some difficulty was experienced in passing this, but at 2345Z STUBBORN went ahead, only to find that the pin of the screw shackle of X.7's end of the tow had come adrift and the tow had to be passed afresh. It was not until 0I25Z on I9th September that STUBBORN was able to go ahead with X 7 in tow.

I9th September.

59. At 0855 on I9th September, Admiral (Submarines) received SEANYMPH's signal reporting the scuttling of X.8 and that she was herself returning to Lerwick. Although SEANYMPH now had no X-craft to recover, I decided she could still assist in the recovery of other craft or might be required to proceed on patrol to intercept enemy forces should they be "flushed" by the X-craft attack and try to escape to the southward. SEANYMPH was therefore ordered to patrol in the vicinity of position 7I° 25' N. I7° I6' E., until the 2Ist September, when she was to proceed to her patrol sector to assist in the recovery of X-craft. I decided not to inform the other submarines taking part that X.8 had been scuttled, as to do so might have had a slightly dampening effect, nor to alter the Target Plan though it meant that LUTZOW (who was the target for X.8) would not be attacked.

60. SCEPTRE and SYRTIS made their landfalls from the vicinity of their ordered landfall positions during the day and THRASHER, TRUCULENT and SCEPTRE (the weather having moderated since the previous evening) all successfully transferred their crews after dark.

6I. At I843Z SYRTIS from position 7I° 03' 40" N. 22° I3' E. sighted a submarine bearing 308°, 2 to 3 miles, which dived five minutes later. From an analysis of track charts and other patrol reports, this was probably a U-boat.

20th September: Day D.

62. The position now was that the operational crews of the four X-craft still remaining had all been transferred successfully. TRUCULENT, THRASHER, SCEPTRE and SYRTIS – the latter with no X-craft – had all made successful landfalls and were in their patrol sectors. STUBBORN, who had been delayed by parting tows but with X.7 still in tow with her operational crew on board, was closing the land to make her landfall. SEANYMPH, having sunk X.8, was on patrol some 60 miles to the westward of Alten Fiord.

63. At 0300Z, SYRTIS sighted a submarine on the surface bearing 030° and five minutes later this was identified as a U-boat: position 7I° 00' N. 22° I0' E., course 235°, proceeding at about 9 knots at a range from SYRTIS of about 3,500 yards. In order not to compromise the operation in any way submarines had been forbidden to attack anything below capital ships while on passage out to or in their patrol areas off Alten, and the Commanding Officer of H.M.S. SYRTIS had no option but to let this tempting target pass by, at I,500 yards range and a sitting shot. The U-boat, which had originally appeared to be making for the entrance to Soroy Sound, altered to I05° at 03I5Z and disappeared in the direction of Tarhalsen Point, presumably entering the Leads round the eastern end of Soroy Island and possibly being bound for Hammerfest.

This may have been the same U-boat previously sighted by SYRTIS on the evening of the previous day. It reflects credit on the lookout kept by our submarines that, with six of them in the vicinity and four of them with X-craft in tow, none were sighted. A single sighting might have compromised the operation, or at least led to A/S activity in the area.

64. At 0I05Z STUBBORN was in position 70° 45' N. 2I° 03' E. when she sighted a floating mine. The mine itself passed clear of STUBBORN but the mooring wire caught in the tow astern and slid down the tow until it became impaled on the bows of X.7. This brought the Commanding Officer of X.7 (Lieutenant B.C.G. Place, D S.C., R.N.) on to the casing, where by deft foot-work he was able to clear this unpleasant obstruction, remarking as he did so that this was the first time he had kicked a mine away by its horns.

After this interlude STUBBORN proceeded to make her landfall off Soroy and set course for her slipping position.

65. The weather had by now improved considerably, the wind had dropped to a south-easterly breeze, the sea had gone right down and visibility was good, enabling all submarines to fix their positions accurately. All was now staged to slip for the attack, and between I830 and 2000Z the four X-craft – X.5, X.6, X.7 and X.10 – were slipped from THRASHER, TRUCULENT, STUBBORN and SCEPTRE respectively

from their slipping positions and proceeded independently into Soroy Sound. The submarines then withdrew to seaward within their patrol sectors.

66. That four out of the six X-craft which set forth from Port HHZ should have made these passages, varying between I,000 and I,500 miles, in tow of submarines, without major incident, to be slipped from their exact positions at the time ordered ten days later, was more than I had ever anticipated.

67. The Commanding Officer, H.M.S. STUBBORN (Lieutenant A.A. Duff, R.N.), deserves special mention for his determination in the way he battled against the difficulties of parted tows and brought his X-craft to the right position at the right time in spite of everything.

68. The passage crews of the X-craft deserve great credit for the way they stuck the long and weary passage and for the efficient state of the craft when they were turned over to the operational crews. The passage crews played a big part in the subsequent success of the operation.

69. I consider this passage a fine example of seamanship and determination by all concerned.

The Attack.

70. The crews of all four X-craft were reported to be in great spirits and full of confidence when they parted company with their towing submarines. The Commanding Officers all reported that their craft were in an efficient state when they took over from their passage crews except that X.I0 had a defect in her periscope hoist motor and in the motor of her "wet and dry" pump, and a slight gland leak; however, these defects were accepted by the operational crew, who were confident that they could remedy them.

7I. As X.5, X.6 and X.7 have not returned from the operation, it is impossible to trace their movements in their approach to and subsequent attacks. The target was TIRPITZ in each case. The intentions of the Commanding Officers were, after passing across the declared mined area to the westward of Soroy on the surface during the night 20th/2Ist September, to proceed dived up Stjernsund during daylight on the 2Ist September in order to reach Alten Fiord by dusk: then to proceed southward to charge batteries in the vicinity of the Brattholm group of islands, about four miles from the entrance to Kaafiord. All three had intended to be at the entrance to Kaafiord shortly after daylight on 22nd September. To give all X-craft ample time to reach their objective, and to guard against loss of surprise through one X-craft attacking before the remainder, X-craft were forbidden by their orders to attack before 0I00Z, 22nd September, but were free to do so at any time after that, setting their charges in accordance with the firing rules table given in the operation orders. As all X-craft Commanding Officers had agreed between themselves not to set their charges to fire in the 0400-0500 firing period, it was expected that they would carry out their attacks somewhere between 0500 and 0800Z, laying their charges set to fire about 0830Z on

22nd September, by which time it was hoped that they would have been able to withdraw from the area.

72. That these three very gallant Commanding Officers succeeded in carrying out their intentions and pressing home their attacks to the full, I have no doubt; but what difficulties and hazards they were called on to negotiate in the execution of the attack are not known; nor is it known how some of them (if the German wireless broadcast is to be believed) came to be taken prisoner. It is certain that outstanding devotion to duty and courage of the highest order were displayed, the full story of this gallant attack must remain untold for the time being.*

Admiralty footnote:-
* For further information on the attacks by X.5, X.6 and X.7 see Admiral (Submarines) supplementary despatch dated 2nd February, 1944, compiled from information received from German prisoners subsequently taken and other sources.

Narrative of X.10.

73. X.10 (Lieutenant K.R. Hudspeth, R.A.N.V.R.) was slipped from H.M.S. SCEPTRE from the slipping position – 70° 40' N. 21° 07' E. – at 2000Z on 20th September, and after a trim dive proceeded on the surface at full speed across the declared mined area in the direction of Stjernsund. The entrance to Stjernsund was identified at 2300Z from a distance of 20 miles, and at daylight (0205Z) on 21st September; X.10 was in a position 5 miles from the west point of Stjernoy Island, when she dived.

74. Difficulty was experienced in trimming, and the defect to the periscope motor which was present on taking over from the passage crew had become worse. Further electrical defects also developed and the gyro compass failed. Lieutenant Hudspeth therefore decided to proceed into Smalfiord on the north coast of Stjernoy to remedy these defects. The choice of Smalfiord was made as it was considered there was less risk of detection there than in one of the small fiords in Stjernsund in which it had been the original intention to bottom during daylight on 21st September.

75. X.10 arrived in Smalfiord at 0700Z on 21st September, bottomed at the head of the fiord on a sandy bottom and spent the day making good defects. By 1750Z the defects had been sufficiently overcome to warrant proceeding – though they were by no means cured – and X.10 proceeded out of Smalfiord and at 2035Z entered and proceeded up Stjernsund, keeping close to the north shore. The only sign of activity was a small ship of fishing craft type which was sighted with navigation lights burning at 2135Z. She appeared to enter Storelokker Fiord.

76. Alten Fiord was reached by 2320Z on 21st September, and intending to press on so as to be close to the entrance of Kaafiord by daylight on 22nd September, course was shaped to the southward, keeping to the eastern side of the fiord.

77. At 0110Z on 22nd September it was realised that the gyro compass was wandering. At 0135Z, the steaming lights of a vessel were sighted ahead, approaching X.10; and at 0104Z, X.10 dived to avoid being sighted. On diving it was found that

the damping bottles of the gyro compass were not working, and on raising the magnetic compass the light refused to function. As this light can only be replaced by taking off the top cover from outside, the result of these two defects was to leave X.10 with no compass whatsoever. At 0150Z X.10 came to periscope depth; but on attempting to raise the periscope a brisk fire developed from the periscope hoisting motor, filling the craft with smoke, and Lieutenant Hudspeth was forced to come to the surface to ventilate and clear the craft of fumes. Dawn was then breaking and X.10 was almost within sight of the entrance to Kaafiord.

78. Lieutenant Hudspeth then decided that, with the craft in its then condition, with no compass, and no means of raising or lowering the periscope, he was in no state to carry out his attack. He therefore decided to bottom before daylight set in, in the only possible position within reach at the time. At 0215Z on 22nd September he bottomed in 195 feet half a cable S.E. of Tommerholm Island, 4½ miles from the entrance to Kaafiord, and took immediate steps to make good defects.

79. At 0830Z – the exact time at which an explosion of charges might have been expected from the other craft attacking – two very heavy explosions were heard at a few seconds interval. Five minutes later – at 0835Z – nine further heavy explosions were heard at short and irregular intervals. These were followed between 0900 and 1000Z by a burst of about twelve lighter explosions, which were repeated, but this time louder and closer, at about 1100Z.

80. The two heavy explosions at 0830Z would appear undoubtedly to have been one or more of the X-craft charges detonating, while the lighter explosions between 0900 and 1000 and at 1100 would seem probably to have been depth charges. It is difficult to understand the nine heavy explosions at 0835Z. They might have been some form of controlled mine, either in the nets or in the entrance, or depth charges: though it does not seem probable that craft carrying depth charges could have been got under way in so short a time. The possibility of their having been other X-craft charges should not be discounted, echoes and a possible miscounting of the number of explosions heard being responsible for the figures given.

81. After spending the whole of daylight on 22nd September on the bottom, the defects in X.10 had still not been overcome; and Lieutenant Hudspeth reluctantly decided to abandon any idea of attacking and to withdraw. His decision was influenced by the explosions he had heard during the day, which convinced him that other craft had carried out their attack. At this time he still thought that all five of the other X-craft had been able to attack: he had no knowledge of the sinking of X.8 or the loss of X.9.

82. I consider Lieutenant Hudspeth's decision to abandon the attack was in every way correct. To have made the attempt without a compass, and with a periscope which could not be operated and must remain in the fully raised position, would have made any chance of success remote indeed. With the attack already compromised it would have been doomed to failure from the outset and would merely have been an unnecessary loss of valuable lives.*

83. X.10 surfaced at 1800Z on 22nd September and made for deep water. At 1825Z both charges were jettisoned in 135 fathoms, set to "safe". X.10 then proceeded on

main engines out of Alten Fiord. A darkened vessel was sighted at about 2100Z off the entrance to Langfiord but was lost to sight in a snow squall. The western end of Stjernsund was reached by 2350Z. As it was impossible to cross the declared mined area before daylight, X.10 proceeded into Smalfiord, where she arrived at 0215Z on 23rd September. As the fiord was completely deserted and snow squalls frequent, X.10 secured alongside the shore with her grapnel, considering the risk of detection negligible with shore and craft covered with snow. The opportunity was taken to get some rest and try to make good some of the defects.

84. At 1100Z on 23rd September after the light in the projector compass had been replaced and with the periscope lashed in the "up" position, X.10 proceeded out of Smalfiord and dived towards the southern end of the minefield. Surfacing at 1800Z, she crossed the declared area at full speed on the engines towards the recovery position, where it was hoped a submarine would be encountered.

85. Recovery position F.B. was reached about 2300Z on 23rd September and a search was carried out. X.10 patrolled in the vicinity of the recovery position all day 24th September, spending some time on the surface in the hope of being sighted; and that night she carried out a further search. At 0430Z on 25th September, when no contact had been made, X.10 set course for Sandoy Fiord, on the northern coast of Soroy Island. This was reached at 1200Z and by 1525Z X.10 was secured alongside the beach in Ytre Reppafiord, on the northwest of Sandoy Fiord. This bay was completely deserted and here the crew got some much needed rest.

86. X.10 remained in Ytre Reppafiord until the morning of 27th September, when Lieutenant Hudspeth decided to move to O Fiord, which it was expected a submarine would close that night. O Fiord was reached at 1550Z on 27th September and a search was carried out across the entrance after dark.

87. At 0100 on 28th September contact was made with STUBBORN, and at 0150 X.10 was in tow. It was by this time too late for her crew to be taken on board STUBBORN and the weather was none too good for the transfer, and it was not until 2200Z on the following day that the crew were taken off and the passage crew from X.7 took over X.10. By this time the crew of X.10 had been on board their craft for almost exactly ten days. They had been subjected to much hardship and disappointment, but were none the worse for their experience.

88. Apart from the sighting of the three vessels mentioned, two of which (since they were burning navigation lights) may have been fishing vessels or small coasting craft, no patrol activity was encountered either on the inward passage up the fiords or, after the attack, on the way out; nor, apparently, was there any A/S activity or counter-measures in Alten Fiord directly subsequent to the attack.

89. X.10 also reports that all shore navigation lights were burning normally and showing normal characteristics, and that the weather on the 22nd September was ideal for X-craft attack, with the sky dull and overcast and a fresh breeze raising white horses to assist an unseen approach.

90. From these facts there appears to be no reason to doubt that other X-craft, free from defects, should have experienced no difficulty in making the passage to the entrance to Kaafiord.

9I. X.I0 also reports that before diving in the vicinity of Tommerholm Island at 02I5Z on the 22nd September, and again on surfacing that evening at I800Z, lights were observed in the entrance to Kaafiord which appeared to be of the nature of low powered flood lights, possibly for illuminating the net across the entrance to the fiord.

92. The Commanding Officer expresses the highest opinion of all his crew throughout the whole time they were on board. They worked long and arduously in the face of ever-growing disappointment, and at no time did their zeal or enthusiasm fail. I consider that the Commanding Officer himself showed determination and high qualities of leadership in a gallant attempt to reach his objective. He was frustrated by defects for which he was in no way responsible and which he made every endeavour to overcome. He showed good judgment in coming to his decision to abandon the attack, thereby enabling the craft to be recovered and bringing back valuable information.

Admiralty footnote:-
* It is now known that on the morning of 22nd September, SCHARNHORST was returning to her anchorage in Kaafiord, after carrying out gunnery exercises in Alten Fiord, when she received a signal stating that TIRPITZ had been torpedoed. She thereupon put about and proceeded to Langfiord, so it is clear that in any case X.I0 would not have found her quarry.

Movements of Submarines after Slipping X-craft.

20th September.

93. After slipping X-craft to proceed to the attack, THRASHER, TRUCULENT, STUBBORN and SCEPTRE withdrew within their patrol sectors and assumed patrol. SYRTIS remained on patrol within her sector, and SEANYMPH was patrolling in the vicinity of 70° 25' N. I7° I6' E.

2Ist September.

94. I had decided to order SEANYMPH to patrol off Andoy in order to intercept any main units endeavouring to escape to the southward, and in my signal at I205 – which could be read by all submarines taking part – I ordered SEANYMPH to patrol in the vicinity of position 69° II' N. I5° 27' E., proceeding so as to arrive after dark on 22nd September, her object being to attack main units proceeding from Alten to Narvik. I also informed all submarines taking part that X.8 had had to be sunk.

SEANYMPH proceeded towards her patrol area at I856Z, 22nd September.

22nd September.

95. As no reports had been received, other than SEANYMPH's, to indicate that any X-craft apart from X.8 were out of the running, it was assumed that the remaining five had proceeded according to plan. It was therefore confidently hoped that some would be attacking in the early hours of the 22nd September and that the "bang" would occur about 0830Z.

96. Senior British Naval Officer, North Russia, had been asked to fly a P.R. over the area p.m. on 22nd September if possible. LUTZOW at least was not likely to have become a casualty: with the loss of X.8 she was not liable to attack: and it was possible that this reconnaissance might show signs of a move of main units southwards, having been "flushed" by the attack. In anticipation of such a movement I ordered SCEPTRE to leave her patrol sector and proceed to patrol in position 69° 44' N. 17° 43' E. to arrive as soon as possible after daylight on 23rd September.

97. I also decided that should sufficient information of a major movement be received in time I would send one of the "T" class submarines into Soroy Sound, accepting the risk of crossing the declared mined area. I therefore ordered THRASHER to close to the south-east of her area, and to charge her batteries full out after dark. For the same reason I ordered TRUCULENT to proceed from Sector FFF into Sector FDD – which was left vacant by SEANYMPH – so that she should be closer at hand if required.

98. SCEPTRE received my signal referred to in paragraph 96 at 1203 22nd September, and at once set course for the patrol as ordered. At the time of receipt SCEPTRE found herself to have been set some 15 miles to the eastward of her patrol area, and this delayed her arrival in her new patrol position just sufficiently to make her miss sighting LUTZOW on her passage south.

99. STUBBORN had also experienced a set. At 0813Z on 22nd September she found herself inside the declared mined area, having been set 13 miles, 117°, in 24 hours. The S.T.U.* was operated but no contacts were gained, and STUBBORN regained safer waters

100. The P.R. of the Alten area on the 22nd September failed.

Admiralty footnote:-
* S T U – a form of asdic.

23rd September onwards.

101. Four submarines were now left to patrol off Alten Fiord for the recovery of X-craft, and I signalled ordering THRASHER to cover the two westernmost recovery sectors (FAA and FBB), TRUCULENT to cover Sector FDD and Sector FEE west of 22° East, and SYRTIS Sector FEE east of 22° East and Sector FFF. STUBBORN continued in Sector FCC.

102. These four submarines patrolled without incident on the 23rd, 24th, 25th and 26th September, encountering no A/S or air activity. This would appear to be a clear

indication that the enemy were unaware how the X-craft had been transported or how they had made the passage.

103. Senior British Naval Officer, North Russia has stated in a monthly report of proceedings that there was an enemy air raid on Polyarnoe on the 24th September, apparently directed against the submarine base. This may have been in connection with Operation "Source", and it is considered not unlikely that the enemy thought the X-craft were operated from Kola Inlet.

Recovery of X-craft.

104. X-craft who were able to withdraw after the attack were to endeavour to contact a submarine patrolling in one of the sectors off Alten Fiord. If unable to make contact, they were to make for one of the bays off the north coast of Soroy, which, circumstances permitting, would be closed and examined by certain of the patrolling submarines on the nights of the 27th/28th and 28th/29th September.

105. Submarines were ordered by signal on 25th September that if no contact had been made with X-craft by daylight on the 27th September, they were to assume patrol as follows: SYRTIS in Sector FFF, TRUCULENT in Sector FEE and STUBBORN in Sector FDD. These submarines were then to act in accordance with the orders for recovery.

106. SYRTIS closed the coast off Soroy during daylight on the 27th September and at 1835Z surfaced between Bondoy Island and Store Kamoy. At 2149Z she sighted and spoke TRUCULENT, who was also searching for X-craft in the vicinity of Bondoy, and then proceeded into Finn Fiord. Sighting nothing, SYRTIS withdrew and patrolled to seaward during the day of the 28th September. That night she again searched Finn Fiord and the islands of Bondoy and Store Kamoy. When by 0215Z on the 29th September nothing had been sighted, SYRTIS withdrew to seaward and set course to return to base.

107. Similarly TRUCULENT closed Staalet Point and Presten Leads at 1822Z on the 27th September. Nothing was sighted, and she passed through the Bondoy-Kamoy passage, speaking SYRTIS at 2151Z. The following night TRUCULENT again closed Staalet Point to within 2½ miles, but the weather was so bad that it was considered that it would have been impossible to have recovered any X-craft or her crew. At 2030Z on the 28th September TRUCULENT withdrew to return to base.

108. However, the recovery plans were fruitful in the case of STUBBORN. She had set course to close O Fiord at 2200Z on the 27th September, and by 0055Z on the 28th had closed to within half a mile of the entrance to the Fiord. Here she sighted "X"s – the prearranged identification signal for X-craft – being made on a blue lamp. A few minutes later X.10 closed and, STUBBORN being short of towing gear after her outward passage, an extemporised tow was passed. By 0150Z on the 28th September X.10 was in tow and both withdrew to seaward.

109. STUBBORN had still not covered Sandfiord which was on her beat, and during the day she attempted to communicate with TRUCULENT, to request her to

cover Sandfiord that night: but she failed to get in touch. However, the weather, wind force 6 from the west and sea and swell 5-6,* decided STUBBORN against attempting to close the land once more: it might have meant losing X.I0 and at 0600Z on the 29th September STUBBORN with X.I0 in tow proceeded by the route ordered to return to base at slow speed.

II0. It seems unlikely that any other X-craft were able to withdraw after the attack, and the recovery of the sole survivor must be regarded as a fine piece of seamanship on the part of the Commanding Officer, H.M.S. STUBBORN. The Commanding Officers of TRUCULENT and SYRTIS also made close approaches to an unknown coast in darkness and in bad weather to try to locate any missing X-craft. They withdrew their submarines safely to seaward in accordance with their orders when they had satisfied themselves that a proper search had been carried out.

III. As a further alternative should they not be recovered from the vicinity of Soroy, Commanding Officers of X-craft had the opportunity to proceed to Kola Inlet. Here the Senior British Naval Officer, North Russia, maintained a minesweeper on patrol off the entrance from the 25th September until the 3rd October to intercept any X-craft who had decided on this course. However, no X-craft arrived.

The Return Passage.

II2. THRASHER, TRUCULENT, SYRTIS and STUBBORN – the latter with X.I0 in tow – proceeded a.m. on the 29th September to return to base by the reverse of their outward routes. SCEPTRE and SEANYMPH remained on patrol off Andoy.

II3. THRASHER, TRUCULENT and SYRTIS arrived without incident at Lerwick on 3rd and 5th October.

II4. At about I700A on the 3rd October a weather forecast was received from the Admiralty that weather was expected to deteriorate and liable to reach gale force 8† from the south-west in the vicinity of STUBBORN's position. Realising that darkness was approaching and that should STUBBORN, with X.I0 in tow, meet this gale during the night it might be impossible to take off the crew, and that there would be little chance of regaining contact with X.I0 if the tow parted, I decided that the passage crew should be embarked in STUBBORN while there was still time. I informed STUBBORN to this effect, instructing him to scuttle X.I0 at his discretion, since the chances of being able to tow her the 400 miles to base without a crew on board were slight and should she break adrift she might drift into the enemy's hands.

II5. STUBBORN was in fact already having trouble with her tow, for at I230Z on the 3rd October the tow had parted in a heavy astern swell and considerable difficulty had been experienced in getting X.I0 in tow again. The last wire on board was already in use and this had had to be recovered and passed again, using the still serviceable portions; and it was not until I700Z that STUBBORN had been able to proceed, at dead slow speed as the swell showed no signs of going down. The operational Commanding Officer and First Lieutenant of X.I0 had been transferred back to their craft to relieve the seaman and stoker passage crew while this operation was taking place.

II6. On receipt of my signal (see paragraph II4), STUBBORN decided to sink X.I0 after the crew had been recovered. The crew were embarked by 2040Z and at 2045Z X.I0 sank in position 66° I3' N. 04° 02' E. STUBBORN then proceeded and arrived at Lerwick at I330Z on the 5th October.

II7. Whether X.I0 could have been brought into port is doubtful. The expected gale did not materialise until the 6th October. Even so, at the slow speed at which X.I0 had to be towed, STUBBORN could not have arrived at Lerwick by that time. The loss of X.I0, after all she had done and all the efforts to bring her safely home, is very much regretted however.

Admiralty footnote:-

The portion of this despatch in which consideration is given to the extent of success achieved on the information then available has been omitted in view of the Admiral (Submarines) later despatch, dated 2nd February, 1944, which is appended.

I20. The success of this operation is the culmination of many months spent in developing and perfecting the new weapon, in the intensive training of the crews for the hazardous enterprise, and in detailed and careful planning for the actual operation.

I2I. The officers and men under my command who have been responsible for the technical development in its early stages and for the preparation of the craft immediately prior to the operation have shown skill and perseverance in overcoming the many difficulties which have arisen. That so many of the craft were able to reach their destination in such good condition after so long a passage is a credit to all those concerned with their material and equipment. In this they have received every assistance from the Admiralty Departments concerned.

I22. The operation involved the strictest and most intensive training. By his leadership and ability, Commander D.C. Ingram, D.S.C., R.N., as officer in charge of training inspired all officers and ratings alike and achieved that high standard of training and fitness which was so essential. He was responsible that the crews were at the peak of their efficiency at the time the operation began.

I23. The skill and seamanship shown by the Commanding Officers of the towing submarines played a most important part in the operation, and the safe and timely arrival at the slipping positions of four X-craft of the six which set out is in no small measure due to the skill with which these officers handled the submarines under their command. I would like to pay special tribute to the Commanding Officer of H.M.S. STUBBORN, Lieutenant A.A. Duff, R.N., for the determination and fine seamanship he displayed both on the outward passage with X.7 and in the recovery of X.I0 and his later efforts to bring her safely to port.

I24. The part played by the passage crews of the X-craft contributed to a large extent to the final success of the operation. During the long and arduous passage these crews kept their craft in a high state of efficiency by constant care and attention, so that with one exception when the time came for the operational crews to take over, the craft were in an efficient state for the final stages of the operation. They showed fine seamanship, determination and endurance. The one exception was X.I0, and her passage crew were in no way responsible for the defects which developed on passage.

I25. Finally, I cannot fully express my admiration for the three Commanding Officers, Lieutenants H. Henty-Creer, R.N.V.R., D. Cameron, R.N.R. and B.C.G. Place, D.S.C., R.N., and the crews of X.5, X.6 and X.7, who pressed home their attack and who failed to return. In the full knowledge of the hazards they were to encounter, these gallant crews penetrated into a heavily defended fleet anchorage. There, with cool courage and determination and in spite of all the modern devices that ingenuity could devise for their detection and destruction, they pressed home their attack to the full and some must have penetrated to inside the A/T‡ net defences surrounding the TIRPITZ. It is clear that courage and enterprise of the very highest order in the close presence of the enemy were shown by these very gallant gentlemen, whose daring attack will surely go down to history as one of the most courageous acts of all time.

(Signed) C.B. BARRY.
Rear Admiral.
Admiral (Submarines).

Admiralty footnotes:-
* *Wind force 6 – strong breeze (2I-26 m.p.h.).*
  Sea and swell 5-6 – very rough to high sea.
† *Wind force 8 – fresh gale (34-40 m.p.h.).*

‡ A/T – anti-torpedo.

The following Despatch was submitted to the Lords Commissioners of the Admiralty on the 2nd February, I944 by Rear Admiral C.B. Barry, D.S.0., Admiral (Submarines).

2nd February, I944.

With reference to my submission of 8th November, I943, be pleased to lay before the Lords Commissioners of the Admiralty the following further report on operations by X-craft against the German main units (Operation "Source").

2. It is now possible to reconstruct the attacks carried out by His Majesty's midget submarines on the battleship TIRPITZ on 22nd September, I943, and to make some assessment of the damage sustained by this ship as the result of the attacks.

3. Three X-craft, X.5 (Lieutenant H. Henty-Creer, R.N.V.R.), X.6 (Lieutenant D. Cameron, R.N.R.), and X.7 (Lieutenant B.C.G. Place, D.S.C., R.N.), failed to return as a result of the operation, and, while it was known that one or more of these craft succeeded in carrying out a successful attack on TIRPITZ, at the time of my previous report no information was available as to which of the craft had succeeded in this daring attack, nor were there details of how it was accomplished.

4. It was the intention of each of the three Commanding Officers, all of whom had TIRPITZ as their target, to close the entrance to Kaafiord at first light on the morning

of the 22nd September, having fully charged up their batteries during the night. Having negotiated the A/S* net at the entrance to Kaafiord they would then attack TIRPITZ by passing under the A/T † nets surrounding her, drop their charges set to detonate at approximately 0830 G.M.T., and then retire to seaward, hoping to be well clear of the fiord by the time of the explosion.

5. P.R.U. photographs had shown that the close A/T nets around TIRPITZ consisted of three lines of nets. The flotation indicated that the nets were for anti-torpedo protection, and it was considered unlikely that they would reach the bottom in the depth of water, twenty fathoms. In fact it was estimated they would only extend downwards about fifty feet.

6. The following is a reconstruction of the movements of these three X-craft in their attacks, as far as is known at present.

X. 6 (Lieutenant D. Cameron, R.N.R.)

7. At some time unknown the periscope of X.6 became flooded. The Commanding Officer was therefore completely "blind" with no means of conning his craft when dived.

Having negotiated the A/S net at the entrance to Kaafiord and entered the fleet anchorage, Lieutenant Cameron, with a complete disregard for danger, proceeded on the surface in broad daylight astern of a small coaster through the boat gate entrance in the nets, situated only two hundred yards away from TIRPITZ.

After passing safely through the entrance on the surface, X.6 dived, and steering straight for TIRPITZ, proceeded to attack.

8. X.6 had, however, been sighted from TIRPITZ off the port bow, as Lieutenant Cameron must have realised that he would be. The time of sighting is reported as 0800 G.M.T. The alarm was raised, and hand grenades thrown at him from the deck of TIRPITZ, and a pinnace started to drop depth charges.

9. Lieutenant Cameron continued to carry out his attack, and on passing under the bridge of TIRPITZ, he probably released one charge. Having passed under the ship, X.6 failed to turn to starboard in time and ran into the nets on the starboard side of TIRPITZ before he could carry out the second run of the attack.

Finding himself foul of the nets Cameron was obliged to go astern to clear himself, and in so doing went astern into TIRPITZ.

10. Lieutenant Cameron, realising that he had been sighted, released his second charge, and surfaced his ship almost alongside the TIRPITZ. Cameron then saw all his crew safely out of the craft before scuttling her.

Lieutenant Cameron and the crew of X.6 (Sub-Lieutenant J.T. Lorimer, R.N.V.R., Sub-Lieutenant R.H. Kendall, R.N.V.R., E.R.A.4 E. Goddard, C/MX 89069) were picked up and taken on board, the time being then approximately 0805.

X.7 (Lieutenant B.C.G. Place, D.S.C., R.N.)

II. In the meantime X.7 had also attacked.

Proceeding according to plan, X.7 penetrated safely past the A/S nets at the entrance to the fiord, and Lieutenant Place decided to attack by passing under the close A/T nets.

Here he met unexpected difficulties, for instead of the expected gap under the nets he found that they extended to I20 feet, which, with a depth of water of only twenty fathoms, meant that the nets were almost, if not quite, down to the bottom.

Lieutenant Place was not to be deterred, and at the third attempt he managed to worm X.7 along the bottom under the nets to carry out a successful attack, dropping one charge under the funnel and one under the after turret.

I2. In negotiating the A/T nets he was able to ascertain its details which were fine wire 4" mesh – a most formidable type of A/T net.

I3. Having completed the attack undetected, Place was then faced with the difficulty of getting through under the nets again to make his escape. To add to his difficulties the tide was by then ebbing, which meant that the nets would be even nearer to the bottom than before. Once again X.7 found herself foul of the nets; and as they were only I70 feet from TIRPITZ and from the line on which the charges had been laid, and with the time for the explosion drawing nearer every minute, the feelings of those on board while they were struggling to extricate themselves may well be imagined.

As it was, X.7 cleared the nets with only a few minutes to spare, as at 0830, when the explosion took place, X.7 was only some 400 yards to seaward of the nets.

Even at this distance the force of the explosion so damaged X.7 that she was put out of action, and Lieutenant Place decided to remain on the bottom for the next hour and await events.

Around about 0930, when depth charges were being dropped indiscriminately about the fiord, although they did no damage to the craft, Lieutenant Place realised, that owing to damage sustained nothing further could be done and that the operation was by now compromised. He therefore decided to surface the craft to give his crew the chance of escaping.

X.7 was brought to the surface, but was immediately hotly engaged by gunfire and sunk. Place was left swimming when she sank, and Lieutenant Aitken, the 3rd Officer, escaped by using D.S.E.A.‡

Of the other two members of the crew nothing is known, nor, apparently, have their bodies been discovered.

X.5 (Lieutenant H. Henty-Creer, R.N.V R.)

I4. The information so far available is insufficient to show what part X.5 took in the attack.

Wreckage, presumably from this craft, was discovered by divers either on the day of or the day after the attack, about one mile to seaward of TIRPITZ berth, about halfway between TIRPITZ and the entrance to Kaafiord. Some of the wreckage from this craft was also flung to the surface.

No bodies or personal gear have been found, and there is no knowledge of any survivors from X.5.

I5. X.5 may therefore already have attacked and laid her charges and have been on the way out when depth-charged and destroyed, or she may have been waiting to attack at the next attacking period after 0900.

The Explosion

I6. At 0830 a huge explosion took place, and TIRPITZ was heaved five or six feet out of the water before settling down again. The explosion extended from amidships to aft, and a large column of water was flung into the air on the port side. The explosion appeared to be caused by two or more simultaneous detonations.

Members of the ship's company on deck aft were hurled into the air, and several casualties resulted. The ship took on an immediate list to port of about five degrees; this was later adjusted by trimming. All the ship's lights failed temporarily, but lighting was soon restored. Oil fuel started to leak out from amidships.

I7. Panic seems to have reigned for a short time immediately following the explosion.

More than I00 casualties were caused by panic firing, and destroyers and small craft went into action up and down the fiord.

I8. Meanwhile, the survivors from X.6 were being questioned by officers from the Admiral's staff.

Prior to the explosion it is reported that the crew of X.6 were seen looking anxiously at their watches.

They were joined about an hour after the explosion by Lieutenant's Place and Aitken from X.7.

All of them were well treated and given hot coffee and schnapps. Everyone on board TIRPITZ expressed great admiration of their bravery.

Salvage of Craft

I9. X.7 was salvaged eight days after the attack, being recovered from a position some 400 yards off the starboard bow of TIRPITZ, outside the nets. She was taken in tow and beached in Kaafiord. The whole of her bow was missing, probably caused either by the gunfire or depth charges.

Although divers made a thorough search, no signs of X.6 could be found inside the A/T nets, and it is presumed that she was totally destroyed by the explosion, which must have taken place very close to where she was scuttled.

The wreckage of, presumably, X.5 was found, as previously stated, about a mile to seaward from TIRPITZ, but there was insufficient of the craft left to make salvage worth while.

Damage to TIRPITZ

20. The explosive charges (of which at least two detonated, the others possibly being destroyed by their close proximity to each other) badly buckled and possibly holed the hull in two places, causing flooding and loss of oil fuel.

The harbour boiler and turbo generator rooms were affected, with consequent effect on the lighting system and forward turret machinery.

Damage aft was also caused, and one report states that all four turrets were damaged, the guns put out of alignment, and that the shaft tunnel was stove in in parts.

A further report assesses the damage as follows:-

"The upper bridge is awry and the guns aft rendered useless. On the after deck, especially, there are large dents and bulges. The engine room area was particularly badly damaged."

The fact that a large proportion of the 50-60 victims among the crew, who were later buried on Norwegian soil, were engineers, stokers, etc., seems to confirm this last statement.

2I. Several hundreds of workmen have been transported to Alten Fiord to effect temporary repairs with the aid of repair ships which have been seen alongside, and there is a repair hut on deck, and welding is in progress. On I0th January, I944, a I00 ft. raft with superstructure had been towed alongside, apparently for divers.

22. It would appear conclusive that TIRPITZ has sustained considerable damage to the hull, machinery and armament as a result of the attack. Temporary repairs are still being carried out in Kaafiord which it is estimated will not be completed for a further one or two months, and the ship cannot be made effective for prolonged operations without docking at a German port.

23. With the full story of this very gallant attack now unfolded, my admiration for Lieutenant D. Cameron and Lieutenant Place and their crews is beyond words. I take special note of the complete disregard for danger in the immediate vicinity of the enemy shown by Lieutenant Cameron in taking X.6 through the net defences in broad daylight on the surface with the full knowledge that he must be sighted, and the cool and calculated way in which he carried out his attack and then ensured the safety of his crew.

Lieutenant Place, undaunted by encountering unexpected obstacles, carried on with cool determination to worm X.7 under the nets under the very eyes of those on board TIRPITZ to carry out his successful attack. Then, when again caught in the nets and with the time drawing close for the explosion to take place, rather than bring his craft to the surface and so compromise the operation and thereby jeopardise the chances of other craft who might be attacking, he proceeded coolly to extricate his craft and remained submerged after the explosion, although fully aware of the danger, for sufficient time to ensure that other craft who might be attacking were clear of the area.

The acts of these two officers speak for themselves. They can seldom have been surpassed in the history of the Royal Navy. The proceedings of the two Commanding Officers would have been of no avail had they not been supported by the undaunted spirit of their crews.

24. It is very much regretted that insufficient evidence is available to assess the part played by Lieutenant Henty-Creer and the crew of X.5, but, from the position in which their craft was found, it is clear that they, too, showed courage of the highest order in penetrating the fleet anchorage, and that they lived up to the highest traditions of the Service.

(Signed) C.B. BARRY,
Rear Admiral.
Admiral (Submarines).

Admiralty footnotes:-
* *A/S – anti-submarine.*
† *A/T – anti-torpedo.*
‡ *D.S.E.A. – Davis Submarine Escape Apparatus, a form of diving equipment.*

The following Despatch was submitted to the Lords Commissioners of the Admiralty on the 26th July, 1945 by Rear Admiral G.E. Creasy, C.B., C.B.E., D.S.O., M.V.O.,

Admiral (Submarines).
26th July, 1945.

FINAL REPORT ON OPERATION "SOURCE".

Be pleased to lay before Their Lordships the following final report on operations by X-craft against the German main units (Operation "Source").

2. The return from Germany of the Commanding Officers of X.6 (Lieutenant D. Cameron, V.C., R N.R.) and X.7 (Lieutenant B.C.G. Place, V.C., D.S.C., R.N.), and the receipt of their patrol reports, together with the release of certain information from captured German documents (notably the deck log of TIRPITZ and portions of the German High Command War Diary), have brought to light new facts which, as is to be expected, are in some cases different from those that had been inferred in my predecessor's submission of 2nd February, 1944.

The opinions expressed by my predecessor in paragraphs 23 and 24 of that report, however, remain with added force.

3. Whilst further knowledge of the total damage inflicted on TIRPITZ by X.6 and X.7 may yet become available from German official documents, it is considered fit

to forward this report in continuation of my predecessor's submission of 2nd February, 1944.

4. The following is the sequence of events from the time of slipping the X-craft from their parent submarines to the conclusion of the attack. No reference has been made to X.I0, as her movements were fully covered in my predecessor's report of 8th November, 1943, and have no bearing on the approach and attack of the other three X-craft.

20th September, 1943 (All times are G.M.T.)

All three X-craft slipped from their towing submarines between I845 and 2000, all being in good heart and trim. X.6's starboard charge had flooded since IIth September, but experiments with stores and spare gear had put the ship into a working trim, provided that the inland waters of the fiords were sufficiently saline.

The minefields reported off Soroy were negotiated on the surface successfully, although X.6 sighted a patrol vessel at 2200.

At 23I5 X.7 sighted another X-craft and exchanged shouts of good luck and good hunting. Although not definitely identified, the other X-craft was certainly X.5. X.5 now, unfortunately, passes out of the picture until her sighting and destruction on 22nd September.

2Ist September

X.6 and X.7 both dived between 0I45 and 02I5, each finding trimming difficult.

During the passage through Stjernsund, X.7 had to dodge several vessels and X.6 started a defect on her periscope which was to prove a major handicap throughout, but a triumph of mind over matter to her crew.

The advance through the fiords toward the agreed waiting and charging positions in Alten Fiord went according to plan, neither X-craft experiencing any difficulty in the calm weather prevailing, and at I245 X.7, taking advantage of a freshening breeze, was able to ventilate the boat through the induction trunk.

An occasional A/S patrol vessel, and a solitary aircraft had to be dodged, but at I630 X.7 sighted a large vessel in the lee of Aaroy Island. This vessel is noted in X.7's report as "believed to be SCHARNHORST" and was thereafter disregarded. All thoughts were centred on TIRPITZ, which, under Plan No. 4, was the target for X.5, X.6 and X.7.

X.6 was first into her waiting billet, arriving at I845 I mile north of Brattholm where she spent a rather disturbed night, charging, making good defects (particularly to her periscope) and dodging traffic. This traffic became so trying that the Commanding Officer surfaced to continue his charge at 2I45, endeavouring to make contact with other X-craft during the night.

On inspecting the clock settings of his fuzes at 2300, it was discovered that the port (unflooded charge) clock was defective. To guard against any hold up, both I0 point plugs were released and the charges set to fire at one hour from release.

X.7 had also reached her waiting position and spent the night charging and making good defects. Among this "making good defects" was the fitting of the spare exhaust pipe, the discovery that it did not fit, and its eventual "make do and mend" with the aid of tape, canvas and chewing gum. X.7 also suffered some inconveniences due to small boats and minor war vessels.

22nd September

Phase I

X.7 left the lee of the Brattholm group of islands at 0045 to commence the penetration of the known and unknown defences of Kaafiord, followed an hour later by X.6; neither boat having made friendly contact during the night. Operationally such contact was not necessary and it had not been allowed for in the plan.

At 0340, X.7, first in the field, straightened up for the entrance through the A/S boom defence gap at the entrance to Kaafiord and by 0400 was through, only to be put deep by an M.L. outward bound. As a result of this temporary blindness X.7 got caught in the unoccupied square of A/T nets, once used to house LUTZOW but now empty. X.6 following later, and having increasing trouble with her periscope, dodged a small ferry boat and an A/S patrol vessel and at 0505 also passed through the A/S boom gap.

Meanwhile, life in Kaafiord in general and TIRPITZ in particular pursued its normal course. Hands were called, normal A/A defence and anti-sabotage watch ashore and afloat were set, the boat-gate in the A/T nets was opened for boat and tug traffic, and the hydrophone listening office ceased work, all at 0500.

Phase II

X.6, suffering from a flooded periscope, went to 60 feet to strip and clean it, while proceeding by D.R.* towards the western end of the fiord. On coming to periscope depth again she found she was so close to NORDMARK that she had to alter course to avoid the mooring buoy. To add to her difficulties, the periscope again clouded over and the periscope hoisting motor brake burnt out resulting in manual control of the brake being necessary when raising or lowering the periscope.

By 0705 X.6 had closed the A/T shore net defence of TIRPITZ and was through the boat entrance, and within striking distance of the target.

X.7 having got caught in the unoccupied A/T defences in the middle of the fiord spent a busy, if cautious, hour in getting clear at the expense of breaking surface, unseen, and putting the trim pump out of action. The violent action required to break free of the nets also put the gyro compass off the board. By 0600, having had another incident with a wire across the periscope standard, X.7 was clear, though precariously trimmed at periscope depth, and headed for the target.

At 0710, having decided in favour of passing under the TIRPITZ A/T net defences, X.7 endeavoured to do so at 75 feet and got caught.

Up to this point no suspicions had been aroused in TIRPITZ and normal harbour routine was in progress.

Phase III

After passing through the gate X.6 ran aground on the north shore of the enclosure and broke surface. This was observed in TIRPITZ but, although reported as a "long black submarine-like object" there was a five minute delay passing the information on to higher authority as it was thought that the object sighted might be a porpoise.

Five minutes later, X.6 in backing and filling to get clear of the ground and to get pointed in the right direction to close TIRPITZ, again broke surface about 80 yards abeam of TIRPITZ and was sighted and correctly identified.

X.6 by this time had no gyro compass, as this had been put out of action by the grounding and subsequent violent angles on the boat, and the periscope was almost completely flooded. She was therefore taken blindly in what was imagined to be the target's direction, hoping to fix her position by the shadow of the battleship.

After five minutes X.6 got caught in an obstruction which she took to be the A/T net on the far (starboard) side of TIRPITZ but which was probably something hanging down either from TIRPITZ or one of the craft alongside. Lieutenant Cameron straightened his craft up, manoeuvred clear of the obstruction, and surfaced close on the port bow of TIRPITZ when a brisk fire from small arms and hand grenades was opened on the submarine. The submarine was too close to the ship for any of the heavy A/A or main armament to bear.

Realising that escape was hopeless, Cameron destroyed the most secret equipment, backed his craft down until the stern was scraping TIRPITZ hull abreast "B" turret, released his charges and scuttled the craft. X.6 started to sink as a power boat from TIRPITZ came alongside, picked off the crew of four and vainly attempted to take X.6 in tow, but X.6 followed her explosives to the bottom.

On board TIRPITZ and in Kaafiord the alarm had now been properly raised, and it is clear from the entries in the battleship's log that complete surprise had been achieved by our forces. Although the first sighting had been made at about 0707 (a note in the log states that times between 0705 and 0730 are inaccurate) it was not until 0720 that the order was given to close watertight doors, and the A/A guns' crews closed up. A power boat "manned by one officer and equipped with hand grenades" left the ship at about 0715, and was the one which took off the crew of X.6, having used her hand grenades, happily to no effect.

"Action stations" was sounded, steam raised and the ship was prepared for sea, in order to get her outside the nets. This order was apparently not given until 0736, when watertight doors were reported closed. Divers were ordered to go down to examine the hull for limpet mines† but it appears that some form of charge dropped under the ship was also expected, as the extract from the log recording the preparations for sea, reads "in order to leave the net enclosure if possible before the time-fuzed mines detonate".

Destroyers in the fiord had also raised steam, and were requesting depth charges.

While TIRPITZ was making up her mind how to deal with the situation, X.7, so far unseen but stuck in the nets ahead of TIRPITZ, was trying to extricate herself. The following is taken from Lieutenant Place's report:-

September 22nd

". . . 07I0. Set both charges to one hour and released ten pin plugs. Went to 75 feet and stuck in the net. Although we had still heard nothing it was thought essential to get out as soon as possible and blowing to full buoyancy and going full astern were immediately tried. X.7 came out but turned beam on to the net and broke surface close on to the buoys, going astern to the northward.

We went down again immediately but had to go ahead towards the net to avoid catching our stern and the boat stuck again by the bow at 95 feet. Here more difficulty in getting out was experienced, but after about 5 minutes of wriggling and blowing X.7 started to rise. The compass had, of course, gone wild on the previous surface and I was uncertain how close to the shore we were; so the motor was stopped and X.7 was allowed to come right up to the surface with very little way on. By some extraordinary lucky chance we must have either passed under the nets or worked our way through the boat passage, for on breaking surface the TIRPITZ with no intervening nets, was sighted right ahead not more than 30 yards away. 40 ft. was ordered and X.7 at full speed, struck the TIRPITZ at 20 ft on the port side approximately below 'B' turret and slid gently under the keel where the starboard charge was released in the full shadow of the ship. Here, at 60 ft., a quick stop trim was caught – at the collision X.7 had swung to port so we were now heading approximately down the keel of TIRPITZ. Going slowly astern the port charge was released about I50 to 200 ft. further aft – as I estimated, about under 'X' turret. I am uncertain as to the exact time of release, but the first depth charges were heard just after the collision, which, from Lieutenant Cameron's report would fix the time at 0722.

After releasing the port charge, I00 ft. was ordered and an alteration of course guessed to try and make the position where we had come in. At 60 ft. we were in the net again. Without a compass I had no exact idea of where we were; the difficulties we had experienced and the air trimming had used two air bottles and only I200 lbs. were left in the third. X.7's charges were due to explode in an hour – not to mention others which might go up any time after 0800.

A new technique in getting out of nets had by this time been developed. The procedure was to go full ahead blowing economically and then go full astern, the idea being to get as much way on the boat as the slack of the nets would allow and thus have a certain impetus as well as the thrust of the screws when actually disengaging from the net. In about the next three quarters of an hour X.7 was in and out of several nets, the air in the last bottle was soon exhausted and the compressor had to be run. When at about 40 ft., at 0740, X.7 came out while still going ahead and slid over the top of the net between the buoys on the surface. I did not look at the TIRPITZ at this time as this method of overcoming net defences was new and absorbing, but I believe we were at the time on her starboard bow – we had certainly passed underneath her since the attack. We were too close, of course, for heavy fire but a large number of machine gun bullets were heard hitting the casing. Immediately after passing over the nets all main ballast tanks were vented and X.7 went to the bottom in 120 ft. The compressor was run again and we tried to come to the surface or periscope depth for a look so that the direction indicator could be started and as much distance as possible put between ourselves and the coming explosion. It was extremely annoying to run into another net at 60 ft. Shortly after this there was a tremendous explosion (0812). This evidently shook us out of the net and on surfacing it was tiresome to see the TIRPITZ still afloat – this made me uncertain as to whether the explosion we had just heard was our own charges or depth charges, so X.7 was taken to the bottom . . ."

This last excursion into the nets was apparently well on TIRPITZ's starboard bow and from outside. After getting clear X.7 sat on the bottom to survey the damage. Compasses and diving gauges were out of action but there appeared to be little structural damage. The boat was impossible to control, however, and broke surface on several occasions. On each occasion fire was opened on her from TIRPITZ causing damage to the hull, and finally it was decided to abandon the boat. X.7 was brought to the surface rather than use D.S.E.A., owing to the depth charging that was being experienced. The boat surfaced close to a target allowing Lieutenant Place to step on to it, but before the remainder of the crew could escape, X.7 sank at 0835. Sub-Lieutenant Aitken was able to get out by the use of D.S.E.A. at 1115, but no trace was discovered of the remaining two members of the crew. Both Lieutenant Place and Sub-Lieutenant Aitken were brought on board TIRPITZ and well treated, as had been the crew of X.6.

The first knowledge on board TIRPITZ that more than one midget submarine was attacking came at 0740, when X.7 was seen just outside the A/T nets, having made her escape after dropping her charges. Hand grenades were thrown, fire opened from the 2 cm. and 3.7 cm. armament, and aircraft made ready to take off and carry out a search.

As other craft were outside the nets in unknown numbers, it was decided not to take TIRPITZ out of the enclosure, so the gate was shut, and the ship moved as far away from the position in which X.6 had sunk by heaving in on the starboard cable and veering port. This brought the bows away from both of X.6's charges and the first of X.7's, but left X.7's second charge still under the engine room; those on board TIRPITZ being unaware that a second attack had been carried out.

TIRPITZ's log records at 0812 "two heavy consecutive detonations to port at 1/10 sec. interval. Ship vibrates strongly in vertical direction and sways slightly between the anchors." The first explosion abreast Section VII ("X" turret) about 6 to 8 yards away from the ship, the other 56-60 yards off the bow in the position where X.6 sank.

The weight of the charge was estimated at 900 lbs. whereas, in fact, each of the four charges weighed 2 tons. It is not clear from this how many of the three charges laid off the port bow actually went off, although subsequent examination of the sea-bed failed to discover any of the charges, or even fragments.

It seems likely, therefore, that all four charges detonated completely and that only the action to move the bows of the ship bodily to starboard on her cables saved her from far worse damage and even, perhaps, from destruction.

Before dealing with the damage resulting from the attack it remains to be recorded that at 0843 a third X-craft was sighted some 500 yards outside the nets. TIRPITZ opened fire and claims to have hit and sunk this X-craft. Depth charges were also dropped in the position in which the craft disappeared. This was X.5 (Lieutenant H. Henty-Creer, R.N.V.R.) which had last been seen off Soroy on 2Ist September by X.7.

Nothing is known of her movements, nor was any member of her crew saved.

X.7 was salved, minus her bows, by Ist October, I943, but there is nothing to substantiate a statement, made to Lieutenant Place by German interrogators, that the bodies of the two missing members of his crew had been recovered and buried with full military honours.

Damage to TIRPITZ

According to the first Damage Report:-

Port propulsion installation out of action, one generator room flooding and damage to the lower platform deck in Section VIII (Engine Room) and T.S.

In the whole ship nearly all the lighting and electrical equipment as well as the W/T rooms and hydrophone station were put out of action, as well as two aircraft outside the hangar.

By 0833 there were 300 tons of water in the ship, which had increased to 500 tons by 0942.

At 0900, 50 minutes after explosion, pumping out of the middle and port turbine rooms was being successfully accomplished, and the hydrophone office was again in order, but there were oil fuel leaks and No. 2 Generator Room and Dynamo Control Room were still flooded with oil and water.

At I045 the following report was made on the condition of the TIRPITZ:-

"(I) *Schiffssicherung* (Ship's safety measures)

Approx. 800 cubic m. water in ship. Probable hits on port side in Section VIII. Flooding under control. Ship out of danger.

(2) *Propulsion installation*

So far, all three main engines out of action. Damage to condenser in port power installation. One boiler lit.

(3) *Electrical installation*

Generator room 2 flooded and dynamo control installation 2.50 cm. water, electricity out of action.

Forward turbo-generators are brought into operation.

(4) *Gunnery*

Turret A and C raised by blast, so far out of action.

A/A control positions out of action. Considerable breakdown of range-finding gear including revolving hoods (Drehhauben), aft position and foretop.

(5) *Communications Section*

Communication with W/T room C established. Breakdown of several transmitters, receivers, radar sets and echo-ranging equipment.

(6) *Steering*

Rudder compartment 2 flooded. Port rudder installation out of action, cannot be examined yet.

In all sections breakdown (probably only temporary) of apparatus and electrical equipment through lack of current, as well as damage to casings and bedplate propellers.

I killed, about 40 wounded, among them the First Lieutenant, slightly injured (concussion)."

Final effect of the attack

According to an entry in the War Diary of the German Naval Staff for September, 1943, it was decided that the repair of TIRPITZ should be carried out in a northern port, and this decision was sanctioned by Hitler and the Commander-in-Chief, German Navy. It was, however, considered that the ship might never regain complete operational efficiency.

Repair ships, equipment and a large staff of dockyard workmen were transferred to Alten Fiord, and the services of a 100 ton crane were requested. The crane never arrived, however, being damaged by weather on passage, and only reaching the Namsos area.

Much time, personnel and work were expended on improving the defences of Kaafiord, and LUTZOW was moved south to Germany. As this ship was overdue for refit in any case, it cannot be claimed that this weakening of the Northern Fleet was altogether due to the X-craft attack.

On 22nd November, 2 months after the attack, again according to the War Diary, MARINE-GRUPPENKOMMANDO NORD reported to the German Naval War Staff that "as a result of the successful midget submarine attack on heavy units of the Battle Group, the battle cruiser TIRPITZ had been put out of action for months", and the truth of this is borne out by the fact that not until April, 1944, did the ship move out from her anchorage, only to be further damaged and finally destroyed, by air attack, from which she had been virtually immune in Kaafiord.

(Signed) G.E. CREASY.

Rear Admiral.
Admiral (Submarines).

Admiralty footnotes:-
* *D R – dead reckoning of navigational position.*
† *Limpet mines – explosives attached to the ship's side or bottom.*

5

THE BATTLE OF NORTH CAPE AND THE SINKING OF *SCHARNHORST*

26 DECEMBER 1943

The accompanying Despatch was submitted on the 28th January, 1944, to the Lords Commissioners of the Admiralty by Admiral Sir BRUCE A. FRASER, K.C.B., K.B.E., Commander-in-Chief, Home Fleet.

Be pleased to lay before The Lords Commissioners of the Admiralty my despatch of the battle of 26th December, 1943, off the North Cape which culminated in the destruction of the German battlecruiser SCHARNHORST. All times are Zone minus one.

PRELIMINARY DISPOSITIONS.

2. After proceeding to Kola Inlet and providing battlefleet cover for J.W.55A* I returned with Force 2 (See paragraph I7) to Akureyri† to refuel preparatory to covering convoy J.W.55B.

3. With the safe arrival of J.W.55A I felt very strongly that the SCHARNHORST would come out and endeavour to attack J.W.55B.

4. Fortunately my small force had now been in company for nearly a fortnight, we knew each other and had practised night encounter tactics together.

5. Before sailing on 23rd December, I had a final meeting with Commanding Officers at which I stated my intentions and stressed on this occasion that every officer and man must be doubly sure that he knew his night action duty. Such a reminder would hardly seem necessary except that within Home Fleet there are frequent changes of officers and men and, with constant escort requirements, adequate training is not easy to achieve.

6. Should the SCHARNHORST be encountered I had decided:–

(*a*) To close the enemy, opening fire with starshell at a range of about I2,000 yards.

(*b*) To form the four destroyers of my screen into sub-divisions and release them in time to take up positions for torpedo attack.

(*c*) To keep the JAMAICA in close support of DUKE OF YORK but with freedom of action to take drastic avoiding action and open the distance if engaged.

7. The endurance of my destroyers did not permit continuous cover to be given for the whole passage of the convoy and my intention was to reach the covering position at a speed of advance of 15 knots when the convoy was just east of Bear Island. This would allow me to spend some thirty hours in the area.

8. Force 2 sailed at 2300 on 23rd December, and in the early morning next day carried out a last practice attack using JAMAICA as target.

9. Meanwhile J.W.55B had been located by enemy air the previous day and during the morning of 24th December, was being continuously shadowed.

10. Although German surface forces had never before made a sortie to the westward, the convoy which had reached the position 70° 40' N. 3° 10' E. at 1200 was entirely unsupported and I was uneasy lest a surface attack should be made.

11. At 1400 on 24th December, I therefore broke W/T silence and reversed the course of the convoy for three hours increasing the speed of Force 2 to 19 knots. If the enemy surface forces had searched to the westward this step would have had little effect in bringing the convoy closer, but it would have prevented the convoy being located by them, before dark.

12. There was no further development that day and the original intentions for the covering force were resumed.

13. The J.W. convoy was not, however, making its scheduled speed and it appeared that the R.A. convoy was passing Bear Island without being contacted by the enemy. Shadowing of the J.W. convoy together with this fact implied that U-boats if present, might be concentrating on the J.W.

14. I therefore requested Rear Admiral, Destroyers, Home Fleet to take the following action if he thought it desirable:–

(*a*) To divert the R.A. convoy to the northward clear of the area.

(*b*) To detach four Fleet destroyers from R.A.55A to J.W.55B. This was successfully carried out.

15. I now felt confident that if the SCHARNHORST attacked the convoy, Force 1 and the escort destroyers would either drive her off or inflict damage which would give me time to close.

16. During the night of 25/26th December, the Battlefleet steamed to the eastward at 17 knots. There was an unpleasant sea and conditions in DUKE OF YORK were most uncomfortable, few people obtaining any sleep.

17. At 0339 Admiralty message timed 0319 was received in which Admiralty appreciated that SCHARNHORST was at sea. The stage was well set except that if SCHARNHORST attacked at daylight and immediately retired, I was not yet sufficiently close to cut her off. At 0400 the dispositions of Forces in the Bear Island area were as follows:

(*a*) *J.W.55B and Through Escorts.*

In position 73° 31' N. I8° 54' E. steering 070 at 8 knots. I9 merchant ships escorted by ONSLOW (Captain J.A. McCoy, D.S.O., R.N.), ONSLAUGHT (Commander W.H. Selby, D.S.C., R.N.), HAIDA (Commander H.G. de Wolf, R.C.N.), IROQUOIS (Commander J.C. Hibberd, D.S.C., R.C.N.), ORWELL (Lieutenant-Commander J.A. Hodges, D.S.O., R.N.), HURON (Lieutenant-Commander H.S. Rayner, D.S.C., R.C.N.), SCOURGE (Lieutenant-Commander G.L.M. Balfour, R.N.), IMPULSIVE (Lieutenant-Commander P. Bekenn, R.N.), and GLEANOR (Lieutenant-Commander F.J.S. Hewitt, D.S.C., R.N.), and the following ships belonging to the Western Approaches Command – WHITEHALL, WRESTLER, HONEYSUCKLE and OXLIP. This escort had also been recently reinforced by the following four destroyers detached from R.A.55A – MUSKETEER (Commander R.L. Fisher, D.S.O., O.B.E., R.N.), OPPORTUNE (Commander J. Barber, D.S.O., R.N.), VIRAGO Lieutenant- Commander A.J.R. White, R.N.), and MATCHLESS (Lieutenant W.D. Shaw, R.N.).

(b) R.A.55.A and Through Escorts.

In approximate position 74° 42' N. 5° 27' E. steering 267 at 8 knots. 22 merchant ships escorted by MILNE (Captain I.M.R. Campbell, D.S.O., R.N.), METEOR (Lieutenant-Commander D.J.P. Jewitt, R.N.), ASHANTI (Lieutenant-Commander J.R. Barnes, R.N.), ATHABASKAN (Lieutenant-Commander J.H. Stubbs, D.S.O. R.C.N.), and SEAGULL (Lieutenant-Commander R.W. Ellis, D.S.C., R.N.R.), and the following ships from the Western Approaches Command – BEAGLE, WESTCOTT, DIANELLA, POPPY and ACANTHUS.

(c) Force I.

In approximate position 73° 52' N. 27° I2' E. steering 235 at I8 knots. BELFAST (Captain F.R. Parham, R.N. wearing the flag of Vice Admiral R.L. Burnett, C.B., D.S.O., O.B.E., Commanding Tenth Cruiser Squadron), NORFOLK (Captain D.K. Bain, R.N.), and SHEFFIELD (Captain C.T. Addis, R.N.).

(d) Force 2.

In position 7I° 7' N. I0° 48' E. steering 080 at 24 knots. DUKE OF YORK (Captain the Honourable G.H.E. Russell, C.B.E., R.N., wearing the flag of the Commander-in-Chief, Home Fleet), JAMAICA (Captain J. Hughes-Hallett, D.S.O., R.N.), SAVAGE (Commander M.D.G. Meyrick, R.N.), SCORPION (Lieutenant-Commander W.S. Clouston, R.N.), SAUMAREZ

(Lieutenant-Commander E.W. Walmsley, D.S.C., R.N.), and STORD
(Lieutenant-Commander S. Storeheill, R.Nor.N.).

18. As J.W.55B had been consistently shadowed and reported by U-boats and aircraft throughout its passage, and R.A.55A was apparently undetected, I appreciated that SCHARNHORST would make for the former convoy.

19. While breaking W/T silence would give away the fact that covering forces were in the vicinity I decided that the safety of the convoy must be the primary object.

20. The following action was therefore taken:-

(*a*) The convoy was diverted to the north in the hope that the change of course would make it more difficult for the SCHARNHORST to find it.

(*b*) C.S. I0‡ was ordered to report his position and D.17§ that of the convoy.

(*c*) My position, course and speed was indicated.

21. On the course and speed of Force 2 and in the following sea my destroyers had much difficulty in avoiding broaching to and the DUKE OF YORK'S bows were constantly under water.

22. At 0628 I altered the course of the convoy to 045 and, having received C.S.I0's signal timed 0540 giving his course as 235, I ordered Force I to close the convoy for mutual support, as I wished C.S.I0 to have destroyers with him. C.S.I0 altered course to 270 at 07I2, in order to approach the convoy from the southward and avoid, in the event of action, steaming into the strong south westerly wind and heavy seas. At 08I5 after receiving the position, course and speed of the convoy from D.I7, the course of Force I was adjusted to 305 and speed increased to 24 knots.

Admiralty footnotes:-
* *J.W. Convoys were those bound for Russia, R.A. Convoys those returning from Russia.*
† *Akurcyri – on N. Coast of Iceland.*
‡ *C.S. I0 – Vice Admiral Commanding, I0th Cruiser Squadron.*
§ *D.I7 – Captain (D), I7th Destroyer Flotilla.*

FIRST CONTACT WITH THE ENEMY BY FORCE I.

23. At 0840 BELFAST'S radar picked up the enemy at 35,000 yards, bearing 295, when in an estimated position 73° 35' N. 23° 2I' E.; at this time C.S.I0 expected the convoy to bear 287, 48 miles. At the same time D.I7 estimated that the enemy's position was about 36 miles bearing I25 from the convoy.

24. In BELFAST the range of the main echo shortened rapidly and at 0900 a second echo was obtained bearing 299 at 24,500 yards. This second echo remained on a steady bearing and was held until 0930 when, from its estimated speed of 8-I0 knots, C.S.I0 considered that it was probably a merchant ship from the convoy and disregarded it. It may well, however, have been one of the enemy destroyers, detached to shadow the convoy, which are mentioned in paragraph 30 below.

25. At 09I5, by which time Force I was formed on a line of bearing I80 the main echo bore 250 at I3,000 yards, speed approximately I8 knots. Force I altered to a line

of bearing I60 and at 092I SHEFFIELD reported enemy in sight bearing 222, range I3,000 yards.

26. At 0924 BELFAST opened fire with starshell and five minutes later Force I was ordered to engage with main armament. At 0930 Force I altered to 265 and NORFOLK opened fire at a range of 9,800 yards but had to drop back to clear BELFAST'S range. At 0938 Force I altered to I05 and at 0946 to I70 by which time the range had opened to 24,000 yards and the enemy had altered course, to I50 steaming at about 30 knots.

27. NORFOLK alone of Force I continued firing until about 0940. She claimed one hit with her second or third salvo and this has since been confirmed by prisoners as a hit either in the crow's nest or the bridge port director which caused several casualties. Other observers consider that she scored a further hit on the forecastle without doing very much damage but prisoners have not yet confirmed this. The 6-inch cruisers did not open fire during this phase of the action and the enemy may at this time have been deceived as to the number of cruisers in Force I and thus made a second attempt to attack the convoy. From prisoners' statements, however, it seems that SCHARNHORST had been expecting to engage two or three cruisers.

28. After NORFOLK ceased firing Force I pursued the enemy to the southward but the range continued to open with the enemy's speed at 30 knots. At 0955 the enemy altered course to the north east and C.S.I0 at once appreciated that he was trying to work round to the northward of the convoy and attack again. Possibly this was the result of an exhortation from Admiral Doenitz which appears to have been received and read to the ship's company at about this time. In the prevailing weather conditions, with wind force 7-8 from the south west, Force I's maximum speed was 24 knots and as that of the enemy was estimated at 28 to 30 knots C.S.I0 decided that Force I must get between SCHARNHORST and the convoy. Force I therefore altered course to 305 at I000 and to 325 at I0I4. Six minutes later contact with the enemy was lost when he was bearing 078 at 36,000 yards and steering to the north east at about 28 knots.

29. During this engagement the convoy was turned to the northward by D.I7 on my instructions at 0930; it remained on that course until I030 when, realising that C.S.I0 had lost touch with the enemy and was closing the convoy, I ordered D.I7 to turn it back to 045. C.S.I0 had previously asked for six destroyers to be detached to Force I but D.I7 received my signal timed 0937 (ordering only four to join Force I) before they were detached and so MUSKETEER, MATCHLESS, OPPORTUNE and VIRAGO (36th Division) left the convoy to join C.S.I0 at 095I.

30.* Throughout this first engagement I had appreciated that enemy destroyers might be in company with SCHARNHORST. In fact no visual contact with them was reported by any of our forces throughout the whole operation, though many unidentified destroyer radar echoes persisted during the day. From prisoners' reports, however, there seems little doubt that SCHARNHORST had three destroyers in company with her and that before Force I first made contact these destroyers had been sent ahead to shadow, report and if possible attack J.W.55B. Prisoners also state that the destroyers did make contact with the convoy and signalled that they had done so by Very lights before Force I engaged. If this is so neither the destroyers nor the Very lights were seen by the convoy escorts who reported nothing unusual until they sighted BELFAST'S starshell at 0925. It may well be that when SCHARNHORST was engaged, these destroyers withdrew from the convoy either to assist her or to make good their escape.

Admiralty footnote:-
* It is known that the three destroyers at sea with SCHARNHORST were detached early on the day of the action to seek and attack the J.W. Convoy and that thereafter they did not rejoin her.

SECOND ENGAGEMENT WITH THE ENEMY BY FORCE I.

3I. Force I closed the convoy and was joined at I024 by the 36th Division. At I045 Force I passed through position 73° 49' N. 2I° 58' E. and five minutes later made radar contact with the convoy bearing 324 at 28,000 yards. The cruisers commenced zig-zagging I0 miles ahead of it with the 36th Division disposed ahead of Force I as a screen.

32. At this time I appreciated that Force 2 would have little chance of finding the enemy unless some unit regained touch with him and shadowed. I informed C.S.I0 of this at I058 but as weather conditions gave the enemy an advantage of 4-6 knots in speed he rightly considered it undesirable to split his force by detaching one or more ships to search, feeling confident that the enemy would return to the convoy from the north or north east.

33. At about noon I found myself in a difficult position on account of the destroyers' fuel situation. I had either to turn back or go on to Kola Inlet*, and if the enemy had turned for home by this time there was obviously no chance of my catching him.

34. The convoy remained on a course of 045 but at II22 I ordered D.I7 to use his discretion regarding its course and at II55 he altered round to I25 to keep Force I between the convoy and the enemy.

35. Force I was still zig-zagging ahead of the convoy. NORFOLK had reported a radar contact at 27,000 yards at II37 but had lost it a few minutes later and by I200, when the convoy was turning to I25, Force I was in 74° II' N. 22° I8' E. steering 045 at I8 knots. Then, at I205 with the convoy about 9 miles on the port quarter of Force I, BELFAST made contact with the enemy by radar at 30,500 yards, bearing 075 and I knew now that there was every chance of catching the enemy.

36. C.S.I0 concentrated the 36th Division on his starboard bow and at I2I9 altered course to I00; the enemy course and speed was estimated at 240, 20 knots. A minute later the SCHARNHORST appeared to alter slightly to the westward, at I22I SHEFFIELD reported enemy in sight and Force I was ordered to open fire at a range of II,000 yards.

37. At the same time the 36th Division was ordered to attack with torpedoes. Unfortunately weather conditions, which reduced the destroyers' speed, and also the enemy's hurried retreat, prevented them from getting within range. MUSKETEER

opened fire on the enemy at a range of 7,000 yards at I222 and continued firing until I236. During this time the range was never less than 4,I00 yards and SCHARNHORST retiring at high speed was not considered to be a possible torpedo target.

38. This second action, fought by the cruisers at ranges from 4½ to 8 miles, lasted about 20 minutes and for the second time SCHARNHORST was most effectively driven off the convoy by Force I's determined attack. The enemy quickly withdrew; his course altered round from west to south-east and the range began to open as his speed increased from I8 to 28 knots. Several hits were claimed by the cruisers during the opening salvos. Only one, which struck the port side aft and did not apparently explode, has been confirmed by prisoners but MUSKETEER from a distance of 4,500 yards considers there were others. Prisoners were agreed that the cruisers' fire was unpleasantly accurate and filled the air with fragments.

39. At I233 NORFOLK received one hit through the barbette of "X" turret, which put the turret out of action and the magazine was flooded as a precaution; a second shell hit amidships. All radar became unserviceable except Type 284 and one officer and six ratings were killed and five ratings seriously wounded. At the same time an eleven inch salvo straddled SHEFFIELD and several pieces of shell described by C.S.I0 as "up to football size" came inboard; fragments also penetrated the ship at various points.

40. By I24I the enemy was on a course of II0 at 28 knots and the range had opened to I2,400 yards. C.S.I0 decided to check fire and shadow with the whole of Force I until SCHARNHORST could be engaged by Force 2. Force I therefore increased speed to 28 knots and at I250 the enemy range and bearing were steady at I3,400 yards, I38°.

The 36th Division to the westward of the cruisers continued to pursue the enemy in line ahead, their range opening to 20,000 yards and then remaining steady.

Admiralty footnote:-
* *Kola Inlet = the entrance to Murmansk.*

SHADOWING OF THE ENEMY BY FORCE I.

4I. For the next three hours SCHARNHORST'S course was to the south-east and southward. Prisoners state that by this time she had given up all idea of attacking the convoy. Force I shadowed and reported SCHARNHORST from a range of 7½ miles and slightly to the eastward of the enemy. As he was retiring on such an advantageous course for interception by Force 2 the cruisers remained in close company and did not attempt to engage, shadowing instead by radar from just outside visibility range.

42. The 36th Division to the westward of SCHARNHORST and rather further astern closed the range slightly but owing to the heavy sea were unable to close to attack and were later stationed to the westward (in accordance with my signal time I559) to guard against SCHARNHORST turning in that direction and breaking back

to the convoy or to Altenfjord. Had this happened neither DUKE OF YORK nor my destroyers could have kept up against the head sea.

43. Despite her damage NORFOLK kept up with Force I. At I603 she was obliged to reduce speed to fight a fire in a wing compartment but she rejoined the Force at I700.

44. At I6I0 SHEFFIELD dropped back and reported that her port inner shaft was out of action and her speed reduced to I0 knots for half an hour, but by I62I she was catching up again at 23 knots. However, the delay, and her reduction in speed, prevented her from rejoining Force I until 2I00 and for the rest of the action she remained some I0 miles astern conforming to the general movement of the battle.

45. At I640 Force I made radar contact with Force 2 at 40,000 yards on a bearing of I76 and C.S.I0 received my order to open fire on the enemy with starshell at the same time. The range of SCHARNHORST from BELFAST was then I9,300 yards. BELFAST opened fire at I647 with starshell and four minutes later Force I observed Force 2 engaging the enemy.

MOVEMENTS OF FORCE 2.

46. Acting on the enemy reports of Force I, Force 2 had been steering throughout the day to intercept.

47. The exemplary fashion in which C.S.I0 with Force I shadowed the enemy until Force 2 made contact had given me all the information I required. At one time I feared that our respective positions might be in error but D/F bearings indicated that the approach was being made on a steady bearing.

48. Soon after I000 three enemy aircraft shadowing from the starboard quarter at about 8½ miles had been picked up by radar and D/F. One was heard making enemy reports and was in radar contact for nearly three hours after which it was heard intermittently by D/F until about I400; it then either lost touch or returned to base.

49. During the first two engagements by the cruisers the composition of the enemy force was not clear as the earlier radar reports from Force I had indicated that SCHARNHORST might be accompanied by destroyers. When C.S.I0 had confirmed that only one heavy unit was present I decided to engage on similar courses with JAMAICA in support, opening fire at about I3,000 yards, detaching the destroyers of the screen to make a torpedo attack.

50. At I400 I appreciated that if the enemy maintained his course and speed Force 2 would engage him about I7I5. In the event he altered round to the south soon afterwards and was first picked up by DUKE OF YORK'S radar at 45,500 yards at I6I7, bearing 020. A radar report was made including my position (my signal timed I6I7).

At I637 destroyers were ordered to take up the most advantageous position for torpedo attack, Force 2's screen having been formed into sub-divisions on either bow shortly after DUKE OF YORK first obtained radar contact.

5I. The range closed rapidly and BELFAST was soon picked up astern of the target.

DUKE OF YORK'S Fire Control Radar found the target at 1632 at 29,700 yards when the enemy appeared to be zigzagging on a mean course of 160. At 1642 the enemy seemed to alter slightly to port. Two minutes later Force 2 altered to 080 to open A arcs* and at 1647 BELFAST opened fire with starshell, followed at 1648 by DUKE OF YORK. At 1650 DUKE OF YORK'S starshell illuminated the enemy, Force 2 opened fire with main armament and my first enemy report was made timed 1650.

Admiralty footnote:-
*7 A arcs are the arcs on which all guns of the main armament will bear, thus allowing them to fire simultaneously at the enemy.

FIRST ENGAGEMENT WITH THE ENEMY BY FORCE 2.

52. When DUKE OF YORK and JAMAICA opened fire at 12,000 yards there was every indication that SCHARNHORST was completely unaware of their presence. Although I assumed that reports of the aircraft which had shadowed Force 2 earlier in the afternoon would have been passed to her, SCHARNHORST was closed on a steady bearing and prisoners confirm that she made no radar contact. When first sighted her turrets were reported trained fore and aft, she did not immediately engage Force 2 and her opening salvos were erratic. Prisoners state they had been told they would not have to engage anything larger than a cruiser and were badly shaken when informed that a capital ship to the southward was engaging them.

53. The enemy altered round at once to the northward and DUKE OF YORK to 060 to follow and to avoid torpedoes which the enemy, had he been on the alert, might have fired.

As SCHARNHORST turned to the northward BELFAST prepared to fire torpedoes and then with NORFOLK engaged her with main armament as she altered round on to an easterly course, probably to avoid Force I and to open her A arcs. By 1708 SCHARNHORST was steady on an easterly course and engaging DUKE OF YORK and JAMAICA with her main armament. Her tactics were to turn to the southward, fire a broadside and then turn end on away to the east until ready to fire the next, making DUKE OF YORK'S gunnery a difficult problem.

54. The situation as the chase to the eastward began showed DUKE OF YORK and JAMAICA to the southward of SCHARNHORST pursuing her and adopting similar tactics. Astern of SCHARNHORST, Force 2's screen, SAVAGE and SAUMAREZ on her port quarter, and SCORPION and STORD on her starboard quarter, crept slowly ahead to deliver their torpedo attacks, taking individual avoiding action from time to time when engaged by the enemy though this, for reasons given later, was not often, until they had closed in to 10,000 yards.

55. To the northward BELFAST and NORFOLK engaged the enemy turning away to the east until 1712, while she remained within range; SCHARNHORST replied to the cruisers' fire with two salvos. These two cruisers then followed the enemy to the eastward keeping to the northward of him. SHEFFIELD was still astern of Force I and dropping slowly back owing to her reduced speed.

56. The 36th Division to the north westward of the enemy altered round at 1700 to follow SCHARNHORST to the east and crept forward to the northward of her to deliver their torpedo attacks. MUSKETEER hoped to synchronise these attacks with those of Force 2's screen but owing to a technical failure in MUSKETEER'S W/T equipment she was never in W/T touch with SAVAGE and Force 2's screen delivered their attack nearly 40 minutes before the 36th Division reached the target area.

57. DUKE OF YORK probably obtained hits with her first and third salvos which prisoners state were low down forward (a hit which may have put "A" turret out of action as it did not fire again) and on the quarterdeck close to "C" turret. Little is known of other hits on the enemy during this first engagement but it seems certain that DUKE OF YORK obtained at least three, the last of which caused underwater damage and eventually reduced the enemy's speed. SCHARNHORST'S own gunfire was erratic to begin with but improved in speed and accuracy as the range increased until, between 17,000 yards and 20,000 yards, DUKE OF YORK was frequently straddled and there were many near misses.

58. JAMAICA, keeping six cables astern of and slightly to one or the other quarter of DUKE OF YORK, conformed to the flagship's movements. She opened fire at 1652 at a range of 13,000 yards and continued firing as opportunity offered until 1742 when the range had opened to 18,000 yards. At this range she considered her blind fire of doubtful value and liable to confuse DUKE OF YORK'S radar spotting. JAMAICA claimed one hit during this engagement.

59. By the time JAMAICA ceased firing all cruisers were out of range and the destroyers had not yet been seriously engaged by the enemy. The gun duel between DUKE OF YORK and SCHARNHORST continued until 1820 when SCHARNHORST ceased firing at 20,000 yards probably due to a hit by DUKE OF YORK which reduced her speed, although this was not apparent at the time. DUKE OF YORK checked fire at 1844 when the range had opened to 21,400 yards.

FIRST DESTROYER TORPEDO ATTACK
BY SCREEN OF FORCE 2.

60. At this time it seemed quite probable that SCHARNHORST would escape and much depended upon the four "S" class destroyers. At 1713 they had been ordered to attack with torpedoes and I could now see them on my radar very slowly gaining bearing on SCHARNHORST waiting for her to make an appreciable alteration of course to allow them to attack. By 1820 they had closed in to 12,000 yards but were gaining little. At this time they started to forge ahead and this must have been due to the DUKE OF YORK's hit which reduced SCHARNHORST'S speed and has already been referred to. This was borne out by the radar plot and the fact that she ceased firing at this time.

61. As the effect of this was not apparent for some time I had already decided to turn towards the Norwegian coast, hoping the enemy would also lead round and so

give my destroyers a chance to attack. When, however, I saw the speed reduction I turned in straight at the SCHARNHORST.

62. By 1840 the first sub-division (SAVAGE and SAUMAREZ) astern of the enemy and the second sub-division (SCORPION and STORD) on her starboard beam had closed in to about 10,000 yards. At this time SCHARNHORST opened up a fairly heavy though ineffective fire on SAVAGE and SAUMAREZ which the two destroyers returned when the range closed to 7,000 yards. That both sub-divisions were not engaged by even heavier fire and considerably earlier on appears, from prisoners' statements, to have been due to the muddled handling of the SCHARNHORST'S A.A. and secondary armament. When DUKE OF YORK first engaged the enemy SCHARNHORST'S A.A. armament (4.1 in. guns' crews and below) were ordered to take cover, leaving only a skeleton crew at the guns and this order never appears to have been countermanded. The secondary armament, on the other hand, seems to have suffered from considerable disagreement between the ship's gunnery officers, resulting in a series of contradictory orders.

63. While the first sub-division to the north-westward, and still closing rapidly, was drawing the enemy's fire, the second sub-division closed in apparently unseen and certainly unengaged from the south eastward. At 1849 the enemy, his speed now definitely reduced, was illuminated by the first sub-division's starshells and was considered by SCORPION to be altering course to southward. This alteration may have been to avoid torpedoes fired by STORD who at this moment was turning to fire. SCORPION immediately turned and fired 8 torpedoes at 2,100 yards and STORD 8 at 1,800 yards, SCORPION claimed one hit, STORD none, probably due to the fact that SCHARNHORST combed the tracks. SCHARNHORST continued to alter round to starboard after this attack thus placing the first sub-division, attacking a few minutes later, in an excellent position on her starboard bow. The second sub-division was engaged by the enemy's secondary and lighter armament while retiring but the firing was wild and no damage was incurred. Both destroyers replied to the enemy's fire and scored several hits on her superstructure.

64. At 1851 SCHARNHORST was clearly seen by the first sub-division in their own starshell to be altering to a southerly and then, after the second sub-division's attack, to a south westerly course. SAVAGE with SAUMAREZ on her starboard quarter both hastily trained their tubes to starboard and turned in to attack at 1855 when on the starboard bow of SCHARNHORST; SAVAGE fired 8 torpedoes at a range of 3,500 yards and SAUMAREZ, under heavy fire and only able to train one set of tubes owing to casualties and damage, 4 torpedoes at about 1,800 yards. Both destroyers came under heavy fire from the enemy's entire armament as they attacked and both ships returned the fire as they retired to the northward. SAVAGE was undamaged but SAUMAREZ suffered damage, fortunately above the waterline, and casualties. Shells passed through her director and under her range-finder director without exploding but she suffered considerable splinter damage which reduced her speed to 10 knots on one engine only. One officer and ten ratings were killed and eleven ratings wounded. Three hits were observed from SAVAGE and one from SAUMAREZ. From subsequent analysis it seems probable that the first sub-division

scored three hits altogether though it is not possible to say from which destroyers the torpedoes were fired.

65. This gallant attack was practically unsupported and carried out, particularly in the case of the first sub-division, in the face of heavy fire from the enemy. Three heavy underwater explosions were heard in DUKE OF YORK and six in BELFAST during this time. Prisoners state that at least three hits were scored and that the ship's company were generally aghast at the relentless attack by what turned out to be four destroyers. They attributed the success of the attack mainly to the bad handling of SCHARNHORST'S secondary and A.A. armament. One torpedo appears to have hit in a boiler room and damaged a shaft which immediately reduced the enemy's speed to 22 knots; another is said to have flooded several compartments aft. After their attacks the destroyers withdrew to the northward and SCHARNHORST steadied temporarily on a southerly course, still making good about 20 knots though this speed slowly decreased as Force 2 closed in from the west to re-engage.

SECOND ENGAGEMENT BY FORCE 2.

66. During the destroyer attack Force 2 closed the enemy rapidly and as the destroyers withdrew to the northward, DUKE OF YORK and JAMAICA re-engaged at I90I at a range of I0,400 yards, the enemy still steering to the southward. Soon afterwards NORFOLK opened fire but checked after two salvos owing to difficulty in finding the right target. Hits were immediately scored while the enemy continued to fire at the retiring destroyers. After five minutes, when SCHARNHORST had been repeatedly hit and fires and flashes from exploding ammunition were flaring up, she shifted her secondary armament fire to DUKE OF YORK at a range of 8,000 yards. During this second engagement she apparently engaged DUKE OF YORK and JAMAICA only occasionally with part of her main armament.

67. After this the battle was soon over. Between I90I and I928 the enemy's speed was estimated to decrease from 20 to 5 knots. At I9I5 BELFAST opened fire on her at a range of I7,000 yards and a few minutes later she steadied on a northerly course. At I928 fire was checked in DUKE OF YORK to enable BELFAST and JAMAICA to deliver their torpedo attacks.

68. Little information is forthcoming from prisoners about this part of the action as they were not unnaturally stunned by the success of our destroyer attacks and the pounding which their ship was receiving. They have, however, been able to account for at least ten of DUKE OF YORK'S hits during this period.

69. Of the enemy's main armament, 'A' turret does not appear to have fired at all during this second engagement probably due to damage earlier on; 'B' turret, although damaged and filled with smoke, seems to have functioned intermittently until shortly before the ship sank; 'C' turret was believed by prisoners to have continued firing right up to the end. Most of the crews of the secondary and A.A. armament are thought to have been killed during this second engagement with DUKE OF YORK and by the time the final torpedo attacks came resistance was practically at an end.

Prisoners state that the Captain had sent his final signal to Hitler, assuring him that SCHARNHORST would fight to the last shell, and that the Admiral and Captain had then shot themselves on the bridge, though as regards the Captain this is not borne out by SCORPION'S evidence (paragraph 77).

TORPEDO ATTACKS BY BELFAST AND JAMAICA.

70. At 1919 I ordered JAMAICA, and at 1920 BELFAST, to close the enemy, who by this time appeared to be almost stationary, and sink her with torpedoes. Both ships at once closed. JAMAICA fired three torpedos (one of which misfired) to port at 1925 at a range of 3,500 yards but no hits were claimed, probably due to an under-estimation of the enemy's speed. BELFAST fired three torpedoes to starboard at 1927 and claimed one hit which was unobserved and considered unlikely. Both cruisers hauled round to fire their remaining tubes, JAMAICA engaging the enemy with main and secondary armament while doing so and scoring several hits. SCHARNHORST replied with wild fire from secondary armament and light weapons, causing no damage. Enemy fire had ceased before JAMAICA fired three torpedoes to starboard at 1937 at a range of 3,750 yards with the enemy broadside on and almost stopped. Two hits were claimed but were not observed as the target was completely hidden by smoke; they are considered probable as underwater explosions were felt after the correct interval. When BELFAST turned to fire her port torpedoes at 1935 she found such a melee of ships and fire round the target that she altered round to the southward to await a more favourable opportunity. She came in again for her final attack at 1948 but on firing starshell to illuminate the target it was clear from the surrounding wreckage that SCHARNHORST had by this time sunk.

TORPEDO ATTACKS BY THE 36TH DIVISION.

71. Throughout the foregoing engagement while SCHARNHORST was fleeing to the eastward the 36th Division, starting its chase well to the westward and therefore well astern of the other forces, had been tracking the enemy by radar and slowly gaining bearing on a parallel course some miles to the northward. As previously mentioned an attempt had been made to synchronise the attack with that of Force 2's screen, but unfortunately MUSKETEER never gained W/T touch with SAVAGE. Although MUSKETEER'S action in attempting to synchronise attacks was correct, SAVAGE would have been justified in proceeding with his attack as it was essential that SCHARNHORST'S speed should be reduced at the earliest possible moment.

72. When SAVAGE'S division delivered its attack the 36th Division was still a long way astern and despite the SCHARNHORST'S alteration of course to the south westward nearly forty minutes elapsed before their own attack was delivered. However, the range closed rapidly and the 71st Sub-Division (MUSKETEER and MATCHLESS) and 72nd Sub-Division (OPPORTUNE and VIRAGO) arrived in the

target area at approximately the same time that BELFAST and JAMAICA were completing their first torpedo attacks. At this time SCHARNHORST, steering an erratic course, was altering round from the north east to the south west, but by the time the two sub-divisions fired she was fairly steady on a south westerly course and almost stopped. The destroyers closed from the north and astern of SCHARNHORST on a similar course.

73. The 71st Sub-Division attacked the enemy on the port side. MUSKETEER led the sub-division in and at 1933 fired four torpedoes to starboard at a range of 1,000 yards, observing two, possibly three, hits between the funnel and the mainmast. She then withdrew to the westward. MATCHLESS followed MUSKETEER in but was less fortunate. Shortly before the attack a sea had hit her mountings while the tubes were being trained and had strained the training gear. As the attack developed the tubes had to be trained from port to starboard and before this order could be passed a heavy sea struck MATCHLESS' bridge and broke all communications with the tubes. The training gear being strained, the order to train to starboard did not reach the tubes in time to be carried out. MATCHLESS therefore hauled round without firing and came in to attack again on the enemy's port bow but by this time the SCHARNHORST had sunk and she joined SCORPION picking up survivors from the wreckage.

74. On the starboard side off SCHARNHORST the 72nd Sub-Division led by OPPORTUNE attacked at the same time. OPPORTUNE fired four torpedoes at 1931 at a range of 2,100 yards and claimed one unobserved hit; two minutes later she fired a second salvo of four torpedoes at a range of 2,500 yards and claimed a further unobserved hit. VIRAGO followed OPPORTUNE in and at 1934 fired seven torpedoes at a range of 2,800 yards and observed two hits. The Sub-Division then retired to the westward, VIRAGO opening fire on the enemy while still visible.

75. The hits scored by the 36th Division are again difficult to assess as some were not observed and as the cruisers were attacking at about the same time; five hits in all is considered the most probable assessment. Little information is available from prisoners, most of whom were engaged in abandoning ship, but SCHARNHORST seems to have taken a list to starboard and they therefore consider that most of the hits were on her starboard side. One prisoner has confirmed three hits from the same destroyer, possibly MUSKETEER or SAVAGE.

SINKING OF THE SCHARNHORST.

76. Three cruisers and eight destroyers were now in the target area and DUKE OF YORK steered to the northward to avoid the melée. All that could be seen of the SCHARNHORST was a dull glow through a dense cloud of smoke, which the starshell and searchlights of the surrounding ships could not penetrate. No ship therefore saw the enemy sink but it seems fairly certain that she sank after a heavy underwater explosion which was heard and felt in several ships at about 1945. JAMAICA, MATCHLESS and VIRAGO were the last ships to sight her at about

1938; at 1948 when BELFAST closed to deliver a second torpedo attack she had definitely sunk in approximate position 72° 16' N. 28° 41' E.

77. JAMAICA rejoined DUKE OF YORK to the northward whilst BELFAST, NORFOLK and most of the destroyers searched the area until 2040, during which time SCORPION picked up 30 survivors and MATCHLESS six. SCORPION reported subsequently that the Captain and the Commander of SCHARNHORST were seen in the water seriously wounded; the Captain was dead before he could be reached, the Commander grasped a life-line but succumbed before he could be hauled in. Soon after 2100 SHEFFIELD rejoined Force I and I ordered all forces in the area to proceed independently to Kola Inlet where they arrived without incident throughout 27th December.

78. The 36 prisoners picked up by the destroyers were transferred to DUKE OF YORK at Kola Inlet and were provisionally interrogated on board during the ship's return to Scapa. No officers survived, the most senior of the prisoners being of the equivalent rating of Acting Petty Officer.

CONDUCT OF OFFICERS AND MEN.

79. The conduct of all officers and men throughout the action was in accordance with the highest traditions of the Service.

80. Earlier in the day, the resolute attack by Force I to drive off the enemy undoubtedly saved the convoy and their subsequent shadowing was invaluable to me in my approach.

81. DUKE OF YORK fought hard and well having drawn, for over an hour and a half, the whole of the enemy's fire. She was frequently straddled with near misses, ahead, astern and on the beam. Both masts were shot through by 11 inch shell which fortunately did not explode.

82. That she was not hit was probably due to masterly handling aided by accurate advice from the plot. There is no doubt that the DUKE OF YORK was the principal factor in the battle. She fought the SCHARNHORST at night and she won.

83. This in no way detracts from the achievements of the "S" class destroyers who with great gallantry and dash pressed in unsupported, to the closest ranges, to deliver their attacks, being subjected the while to the whole fire power of the enemy. Their resolution and skill shortened the battle and ensured the sinking of the ship.

84. In general the speed of wireless communication and the exceptional performance of radar reflects the greatest credit on the personnel concerned and in this night battle contributed in great measure to its success.

85. Plotting arrangements in the Fleet Flagship worked well and were of great assistance both to me and to the ship. I myself alternated between the plot and the Admiral's bridge, the Chief of Staff remaining in the plot. I feel very strongly that the officers in the plot must always be in the closest contact with the Admiral who should obviously be on the bridge.

86. Although failings in material and personnel were few during this action it should of course be remembered that the enemy inflicted very little damage on our ships and they were not therefore extensively tested under adverse conditions.

87. I should also like to record that the accurate and concise information supplied by the Admiralty in the early stages of this operation was of great assistance.

88. I have forwarded separately my recommendations for honours and awards as a result of this action.

(Signed) BRUCE FRASER,
Admiral.

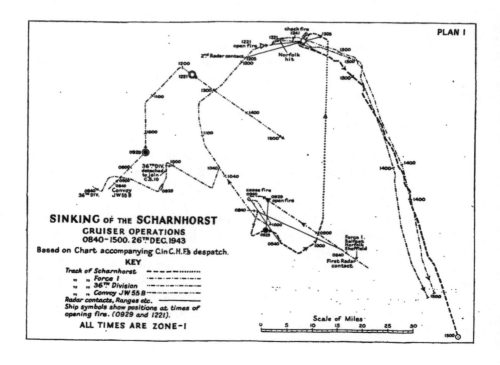

PLAN I

SINKING OF THE SCHARNHORST
CRUISER OPERATIONS
0840-1500. 26TH DEC. 1943
Based on Chart accompanying C.in C.H.F.'s despatch.

KEY

Track of Scharnhorst
   „   „   Force I
   „   „   36TH Division
   „   „   Convoy JW 55 B
Radar contacts, Ranges etc.
Ship symbols show positions at times of
opening fire. (0929 and 1221).

ALL TIMES ARE ZONE-1

Scale of Miles
0   5   10   15   20   25   30

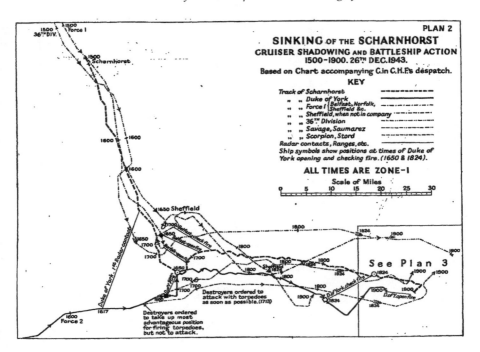

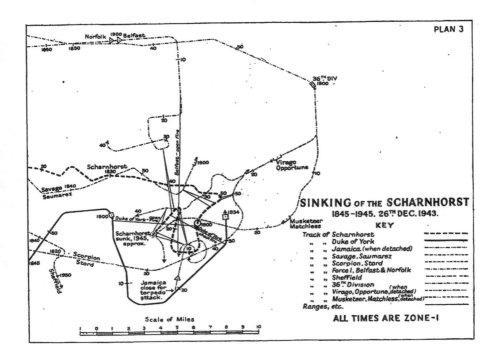

6

THE CONTRIBUTION OF THE BRITISH PACIFIC FLEET TO THE ASSAULT ON OKINAWA, 1945

The following Despatch was submitted to the Lords Commissioners of the Admiralty on the 7th June, 1945, by Admiral Sir Bruce A. Fraser, G.C.B., K.B.E.,

Commander-in-Chief, British Pacific Fleet.
Office of the Commander-in-Chief,
British Pacific Fleet.
7th June, 1945.

"ICEBERG" – REPORT.

Be pleased to lay before Their Lordships a report on the actions fought by the British Pacific Fleet during the first phases of Operation "Iceberg."

2. It is impossible yet to judge the effect of these operations on the conquest of Okinawa, but I consider that we have successfully carried out our undertakings, employing a method of sea warfare with which we were previously unfamiliar.

3. It is not less than was expected, since all had turned their minds to it, but the credit must go to Vice-Admiral Sir Bernard Rawlings, K.C.B., O.B.E., whose inspiring leadership, resolution and fine judgment were responsible.

4. Doubt as to our ability to operate in the Pacific manner was somewhat naturally in American minds. This, however, was soon changed. The toll taken by the suicide bomber of the more lightly armoured American carriers led to an increase in the proportionate effort provided by our carriers, and the evidence of American eyes that we could support ourselves logistically, relieved their anxieties on that score. We have now, I am sure, become not only welcome but necessary in Central Pacific operations.

5. Despite their doubts, the Americans put their trust in us unstintedly, and the generosity and help of all were invaluable to our success, a result which I know is most satisfactory to them.

6. We shall not, however, be able to play our full part until sufficient forces are available to form a second task group, since the effort of one, alternatively striking and re-fuelling, must necessarily be discontinuous and uneconomical of force.

7. The British Pacific Fleet have been making British naval history by operating off the enemy coast for periods up to 30 days each, but it is well to remember that similar American task groups are doing the same thing for twice as long. When we have mastered the technique of ammunitioning and storing at sea, we shall also be able to do this. These are matters receiving close attention.

8. In this connection, I wish to commend most whole-heartedly the work of Rear-Admiral D. B. Fisher, C.B., C.B.E., whose successful servicing of the Fleet at sea and in harbour has been the admiration of all.

(Signed) BRUCE FRASER,
Admiral.
Office of the Vice-Admiral,
Second-in-Command,
British Pacific Fleet,
9th May, 1945.

SIR,

I have the honour to forward for your information reports of proceedings from the ships of the British Pacific Fleet which participated in the initial stages of Operation "Iceberg" for the period from 26th March until 20th April, together with a general narrative of events for this period.* This latter duplicates inevitably many of the events and remarks made in the enclosures but is designed to present an overall and brief picture.

2. The successful capture of Okinawa, as a stepping stone on the way to the overthrow of the Japanese Empire, was appreciated as of paramount importance, and it was in consequence a matter of great satisfaction to all in the two Forces, 57 and II2, that the former was able, in however small a degree, to draw a little of the enemy fire from those American Forces destined to bear the brunt of the attack in these initial stages of the operation. It is hoped that, by their efforts in this area, any major staging of Japanese aircraft to the critical scene of operations was impeded. The resources of the Rear-Admiral, Fleet Train Task Force II2 on which we depend for logistic support are in some matters still somewhat embryonic: I have reason to believe that he stretched them considerably to keep my Force-operating.

3. Although the period under review was quiet and the enemy hard to find, those attacks which did develop gave us valuable experience and revealed several flaws in our organisation which diligence, time and additional resources will remedy. Accurate assessments of the damage inflicted by our strikes was often difficult to determine: this was in part due to the enemy's skilful use of dummy aircraft, camouflage and dispersal.

4. The difficulty of aircraft recognition when friendly and enemy planes are in the vicinity of the Fleet is an ever present problem: several proposals to obviate this confusion have been discussed, and, as remarked in the narrative, a solution to this appears of first importance. I trust we shall find one.

5. The attack by suicide aircraft on the Fleet demonstrates once again the importance of fighter interception being carried out at the maximum possible range.

6. It has been unusual, during my generation, for a British Fleet of this size to remain at sea for the length of time covered by this report and I had beforehand found myself wondering at times what shortcomings in personnel and material it would discover. Over the latter the necessary steps are in hand; as regards the former, whilst certain adjustments and additions to complement will be asked for, I am satisfied with the way in which the Fleet adapted itself to the new conditions.

7. This report, dealing as it does with an unfinished operation, is of an interim nature only. It will not, however, be out of place to remark on the helpfulness of the American authorities both at Manus and Ulithi; I trust we did not ask for their assistance until we were faced with problems which frankly seemed beyond us, but whenever we did so appeal it was responded to with the utmost vigour. I would further add that the Communication Liaison Teams in all ships have lived up to their name in its best sense, and I am very conscious both of the specialist help given me personally by the Senior Communication Officer in my Flagship, Lieutenant Commander R.F. Morris, U.S.N.R., as also in general by Captain E.C. Ewen, U.S.N. His, knowledge and views have been most valuable.

8. I have yet to find a more helpful and responsive attitude than that accorded to me by these American authorities responsible for the provision and movements of Lifeguard Submarines[†] and aircraft: I know too that what their units have accomplished is no less a source of pleasure to them than it is to us. I am very grateful for their work.

have the honour to be, Sir,
Your obedient Servant,
(Signed) BERNARD RAWLINGS,
Vice-Admiral.
The Commander,
United States Fifth Fleet.

Admiralty footnotes:-
* *Reports of proceedings of individual ships are not being reproduced.*
† *Lifeguard Submarines – submarines employed for rescue of crews of aircraft.*

INTRODUCTION TO NARRATIVE.

Allied Object.

I. The first objective of Operation "Iceberg" was to capture Okinawa Gunto and, gaining control of the Nansei Shoto area, use them to attack the main islands of Japan with their sea and air approaches.

B.P.F. Object.

2. The particular object assigned to the British Pacific Fleet was to neutralise the airfields in the Sakishima Gunto as continuously, and for as long as possible.

Assignment of B.P.F.

3. On 14th March, 1945, the British Pacific Fleet was situated as follows:-

Most of Task Force II3 (consisting of the Ist Battle Squadron, Ist Aircraft Carrier Squadron, 4th Cruiser Squadron, 25th, 4th and 27th Destroyer Flotillas) was at sea exercising from Manus, Admiralty Islands.

Task Force II2 (ships of the Fleet Train and Escort Vessels) was in harbour at Manus.

4. On the forenoon of I5th March, whilst Ist Battle Squadron and Ist Aircraft Carrier Squadron were exercising, the following signals were received:-

CTF II3 (R) CTF II2
From C.-in-C., B.P.F.

COMINCH* directs you to report Task Force II3 for duty "Iceberg" operations together with Task Force II2 to C.-in-C., Pacific.**

TF II3 (R) TF II2
From C.-in-C., B.P.F.

TF II3 and II2 must be employed in such manner that they can be reallocated on 7 days' notice from COMINCH.

   5. On receipt of these signals all exercises were cancelled and Task Force II3 ordered into harbour to top up with fuel, ammunition, stores, and to embark the aircraft squadrons which had been landed for training ashore. After considering all factors the following signal was despatched:-

C IN C PAC CTF 112. C.-in-.C., B.P.F.
From CTF 113.

Have recalled ships and am embarking air squadrons from sea and shore training exercises.

TF 113 and 112, in accordance with orders from C.-in-C., British Pacific Fleet, are hereby reported for duty. TF 113 with units of 112 will be ready to sail from Manus at 1200, 17th March and will join the United States forces under your command with feelings of great pride and pleasure.

6. The factors referred to above were:-

(*a*) Fuelling, embarkation of aircraft, stores, etc. The timetable for these was in some measure dependent upon the lack of boats and the sport of the swell.

(*b*) Final preparation of operation orders and arrangements for replenishing in the forward areas over a period of up to three weeks' continuous operations.

(*c*) The speed (9 knots in fine weather) at which the tankers could move to the first fuelling area.

(*d*) Adjustment of aircraft between the Fleet Carriers, and UNICORN, SPEAKER and SLINGER, so that the Fleet might leave fully equipped.

16th March.

7. The Fleet continued making ready.

The following signal was received from C.-in-C.; Pacific:-

The British Carrier Task Force and attached units will greatly increase our striking power and demonstrate our unity of purpose against Japan. The U.S. Pacific Fleet welcomes you.

17th March.

8. In order to have the Tanker Group in position for the Fleet to top up with fuel at the last prudent moment, Task Unit 112.2.1 and Task Unit 112.2.5† were sailed on 17th March. The former consisted of H.M. Ships STRIKER (with replacement aircraft), CRANE, FINDHORN, WHIRLWIND and the Tankers SAN AMBROSIO, CEDARDALE and SAN ADOLPHO; the latter consisted of H.M. Ships PHEASANT, SPEAKER (for CAP†† duties) and KEMPENFELT.

18th March.

9. Task Force 57 sailed from Manus a.m. on 18th March, and carrying out exercises on passage, arrived a.m. on 20th March at Ulithi where the Fleet fuelled from U.S. resources.

10. During the period 21st to 23rd March, final drafts of operation orders were

completed and distributed, intelligence material streaming in continuously. The date of sailing to commence operations, as that of sailing from Manus, was dictated by the arrival of the tankers in the fuelling area.

II. (*a*) On 22nd March the following signal was despatched:-

COM 5th Fleet‡
From CTF II3

Intend assume designation TF 57 after clearing Ulithi at 07I5, 23rd March at which time Force is ready for duty under your orders. Intend TF 57 follow directions of C IN C POA unless you direct otherwise.

(*b*) The following reply was received:-

CTF 57
From COM 5th Fleet

Welcome TF 57. Good hunting. Your message 22nd affirmative.

I2. The British Pacific Fleet, until then Task Force II3, sailed from Ulithi at 0630 on 23rd March, I945, as Task Force 57.

Composition of TF 57 on sailing from Ulithi on 23rd March, I945.

Ist Battle Squadron. TU§ I
KING GEORGE V (Flag of CTF 57),
HOWE;
Ist Aircraft Carrier Squadron TU 2
INDOMITABLE (Flag of A.C.I and Second-in-Command TF 57),
VICTORIOUS,
ILLUSTRIOUS,
INDEFATIGABLE;
4th Cruiser Squadron TU 5
SWIFTSURE (Flag of C.S.4),
GAMBIA,
BLACK PRINCE,
ARGONAUT;
Destroyers – TU 8
25th Destroyer Flotilla
EURYALUS (Flag of R.A.(D) temporarily),
GRENVILLE (Capt. D.25),
ULSTER,
UNDINE,
URANIA,
UNDAUNTED;
(Note:- URSA was docking at Manus.)

4th Destroyer Flotilla
QUICKMATCH (Capt. D.4),
QUIBERON,
QUEENBOROUGH,
QUALITY;
27th Destroyer Flotilla
WHELP,
WAGER.
(Note:- KEMPENFELT (Capt. D.27) was attached to TU II2.2.5, the group remaining in the replenishing area.

WHIRLWIND and WESSEX were attached to TU II2.2.I and TU II2.2.2 respectively, the Tanker Groups proceeding between Leyte and the replenishing area.)

Admiralty footnotes:-
* COMINCH – C.-in-C., U.S. Fleets (Admiral King, U.S.N.).
** C.-in-C., Pacific – Admiral Nimitz, U.S.N.
† Task Units II2.2.I and II2.2.5 – units of the Fleet Train.
†† CAP – Combat Air Patrol.
‡ COM 5th Fleet – Admiral Spruance, U.S.N.
§ TU – Task Unit.

NARRATIVE.

23rd March.

Task Force 57 sailed from Ulithi at 07I5 and set course for position Ant (I8° 30' N I29° 08' E), forming into cruising disposition 5D to carry out long range throw off and close range sleeve firings. Sleeve targets were towed by United States Utility Squadrons. Bombardment communication exercises were carried out by H.M. Ships KING GEORGE V, HOWE and SWIFTSURE. On completion, the Fleet formed up in Cruising Disposition 5A and proceeded at I8 knots. CAPS and ASPS* were flown during daylight hours.

25th March.

At 03I0 with H.M. Ships EURYALUS, BLACK PRINCE and ARGONAUT spread 8 miles apart, 8 miles ahead of the Fleet, radar contact was made with Task Group II2.2.5 and Task Group II2.2.I. Rendezvous was made by 0600 and the above ships with destroyers detached in turn to fuel. The Rear Admiral Commanding Destroyers, in H.M.S. EURYALUS, was made Senior Officer of the oiling force and oiling arrangements.

It had been hoped to complete this fuelling (from three tankers) by II00, but a strong north easterly wind and swell and hose troubles soon ruled out that desire. To enable the Fleet to keep this, its first appointment, on time, both battleships and STRIKER were ordered to fuel destroyers. In spite of this, of leaving one destroyer to follow later, and accepting other destroyers up to 30 per cent. short, the operation had to be stopped at I450.

CAPS were flown by SPEAKER and ASPS by the carriers while fuelling was in progress and aircraft carriers took on replenishment aircraft from H.M.S. STRIKER.

At I530 the Fleet, formed in Cruising Disposition 5B, proceeded at 23½ knots, this speed being then necessary to reach the operating area by dawn the next day. A.C.I** assumed tactical command.

H.M. Ships QUALITY and WHELP had to be left with the Tanker Group. H.M.S. WHELP, who had bearing trouble, was replaced by H.M.S. WHIRLWIND from Task Unit II2.2.I, H.M.S. QUALITY, also with defects, was replaced by H.M.S. KEMPENFELT from Task Unit II2.2.5, H.M.S. WAGER was left to continue fuelling but was able to rejoin the Fleet the following morning.

At I820 H.M.S. INDEFATIGABLE was observed to be on fire on the starboard side under the island structure. The fire, which had originated in Carley floats, was soon extinguished and no damage to the ship occurred.

26th March.

At 0605 CAPS and one ASP were flown off, whilst H.M. Ships ARGONAUT and KEMPENFELT were detached to carry out picket duties.

At sunrise (0635) strong fighter sweeps, were flown off from a position I00 miles I80° from Miyako Jima to attack the airfields at Ishigaki and Miyako; they reported little activity there.

At 0850 one aircraft was reported as having ditched 20 miles from Tarima Shima; a Walrus aircraft was flown off and subsequently rescued the pilot.

These sweeps were followed by two escorted bomber strikes and one fighter bomber strike with airfields and associated buildings as targets. Withdrawal was begun at dusk.

At 0940 a Dinah† was intercepted but not shot down by one of the Jacks†† and it was apparent that the Fleet had been reported.

Throughout the day there were frequent air raid warnings but all bogeys‡ were eventually identified as friendly except for the one Dinah.

After the last aircraft had flown on, the Fleet disengaged to the south eastward.

The night was fine and the moon bright and an enemy attack was considered likely.

27th March.

At 0245 a bogey to the eastward was contacted by radar. As it seemed that the Fleet was being shadowed course was altered in an attempt to shake off the aircraft. At

0307 H.M.S. EURYALUS was ordered to open out from the screen and fire on the enemy aircraft which then remained at a respectful distance for a time. A Hellcat was then flown off from H.M.S. INDOMITABLE to intercept, but the moon became obscured by a cloud when the pilot was about to open fire and the enemy made good his escape. At 0305 Japanese ASV‡‡ transmissions on I52 Mc/s were reported and the Fleet was ordered to commence jamming.

It is of interest to note that the fighter flown off was called by an aircraft which claimed itself to be a U.S. aircraft and warned the fighter of his approach from the south. Although there is no substantial evidence, this may have been a ruse by the Japanese aircraft to avoid inspection while closing the Fleet.

At sunrise a fighter sweep was sent in to Ishigaki only from a flying-off position I00 miles I80° from Miyako Jima. No increased activity was reported.

Two bomber strikes were directed against radio stations, barracks and airfields not covered the previous day. Coasters off the islands were also attacked. The final strike was a small fighter bomber strike. Withdrawal was begun at dusk.

At II30 H.M.S. UNDINE escorted by fighters was despatched to the rescue of an aircraft which had ditched 56 miles from the flying-off position. At I750 she rejoined the Fleet having picked up the Avenger crew and also a United States Corsair pilot who was discovered after having been adrift for 48 hours.

The American Rescue Submarine U.S.S. KINGFISH was requested to keep a good lookout for any of our ditched aircrews, but apparently she had not been fully instructed by the American authorities as she replied that "she would have to ask her boss first". The situation was soon clarified when the Commander-in-Chief, Pacific informed the submarine that Task Force 57 was operating in her vicinity and that she was to act as rescue submarine when required. At I805 American Rescue Submarine U.S.S. KINGFISH reported that she had rescued the pilot of one of H.M.S. ILLUSTRIOUS's Avengers.

It had been intended that Task Force 57 should continue operating off Sakishima Gunto the day's programme to include a bombardment of Ishigaki, but Guam reported a typhoon to the southward whose position and estimated track appeared to threaten the fuelling area. The risk of bad weather completely dislocating fuelling for some time would have precluded Task Force 57 from returning to the operating area in time to continue the strikes from L -I until L +I day§ (3Ist March to 2nd April). As it was considered that the Commander 5th Fleet attached great importance to Task Force 57 maintaining the neutralisation of Sakishima airfields during this special period, the air and bombardment programme for the next day was cancelled, and the Fleet withdrew to the fuelling area after the second day's strikes had been landed on. The necessity to withdraw was accentuated by certain ships having been short of fuel at the commencement of the operation. CTF 57 assumed tactical command.

28th March.

At 0730 made contact with Task Unit II2.2.5 and Task Unit II2.2.I in area Midge, a rectangle extending 50 miles to the south and 100 miles to the west of 19° 55' N. 129° 40' E: fuelling and transfer of aircraft were continued throughout the day.

The Fleet was divided into two groups for this operation, the non-fuelling group proceeding so as to remain within touch of the fuelling group. The Fleet disengaged from the Tanker Group for the night.

29th March.

The Rear Admiral Commanding Destroyers transferred from H.M.S. EURYALUS to H.M.S. WHIRLWIND and proceeded in the afternoon with H.M. Ships STRIKER and CRANE for Leyte. H.M.S. EURYALUS then rejoined Task Unit 5 with the remainder of the cruisers. During the day mails and correspondence brought out by the Tanker Group were distributed by destroyers around the Fleet. For the night the Fleet formed up into Cruising Disposition 5A. H.M. Ships QUALITY and WHELP rejoined Task Force 57, and H.M. Ships KEMPENFELT and WHIRLWIND rejoined the Tanker Groups.

30th March.

At 1430 fuelling was completed and the Fleet formed up in Cruising Disposition 5B. Departure was taken at 22 knots for the operating area and A.C.I assumed tactical command.

31st March.

It may be assumed in this narrative hence-forward that CAPS and ASPS were part of the normal daily flying programme. At 0530 H.M. Ships ARGONAUT and WAGER were detached to a position 300°, 30 miles from the Fleet centre to act as pickets to prevent enemy aircraft returning with our own strikes. H.M.S. ARGONAUT was chosen for this purpose as having the most suitable radar. At 0630 a fighter sweep was sent in from a flying-off position 23° 10' N. 125° 23' E. and thereafter fighter patrols were maintained over Ishigaki and Miyako. There appeared to be little activity in either island. Two bomber strikes were sent against Ishigaki airfield, installations and barracks.

U.S.S. KINGFISH again did useful service and rescued the crew of an Avenger which had ditched.

At dusk the Fleet disengaged to the south westward and CTF 57 assumed tactical command. Two fighters were kept at readiness from moonrise but the Fleet was not shadowed.

1st April.

A.C.I assumed tactical command; H.M. Ships ARGONAUT and WAGER opened out to their picket positions before the fighter sweep was sent in at 0640 from a flying-off position 23° 26' N. 125° 25' E.

At 0650 bogeys were detected by radar to the westward, height 8,000 feet, closing at 210 knots. The fighter sweep was recalled to intercept and additional fighters were flown off.

The raid split up more than 40 miles from the Fleet. The first interception was by Corsairs from H.M.S. VICTORIOUS which shot down one enemy. Seafires shot down two more close to the Fleet and a fourth was destroyed by Hellcats recalled from the fighter sweep. At 0705 the Fleet had been alerted to "Flash Red" and a few minutes later the enemy planes commenced their attacks.

One enemy single-engined aircraft machine-gunned H.M.S. INDOMITABLE in a low attack killing one rating and wounding two officers and four ratings. Still flying very low it made a similar attack on H.M.S. KING GEORGE V but without causing casualties. Considerable difficulty was experienced in identifying enemy from our own planes who were hard on the enemy heels.

At 0727 an enemy plane dived into the base of H.M.S. INDEFATIGABLE's island. Four officers and ten ratings were killed, and sixteen of her complement wounded. The flight deck was put temporarily out of action, but within a remarkably short time, and in a most creditable manner, aircraft were again being operated from this ship, although that day on a reduced scale.

At about 0755 H.M.S. ULSTER was near missed by what appeared to be a 500 Ib. bomb from an aircraft then being chased by one of our fighters. She reported that the bulkhead between the engine-room and the after boiler-room had blown, flooding both compartments, but that the ship was floating well. Casualties were two killed and one seriously wounded. She was unable to steam but her armament remained effective. H.M.A.S. QUIBERON was ordered to stand by her and as soon as the raid was over H.M.N.Z.S. GAMBIA was ordered to tow her to Leyte.

At 1215 a bombing strike was sent in against Ishigaki to bomb airfields and runways. No activity was noted. At 1430 reports were received from combat patrols over the islands that more aircraft had been sighted at Hirara and Ishigaki airfields. These were attacked by the fighter patrols and were followed by a fighter sweep. It was estimated that about 14 enemy aircraft were destroyed on the ground during this attack and others damaged.

At 1730 a low flying bogey was detected by radar to the north westward. Hellcats were sent to intercept this raid which developed into 2 plus but the enemy avoided them in cloud. Soon afterwards the Fleet sighted the enemy and opened fire, sometimes it is regretted, at friendly fighters. One enemy aircraft dived on H.M.S. VICTORIOUS; her swing under full helm was successful and the plane touched its wing only on the flight deck edge spinning harmlessly into the sea where its bomb exploded clear of the ship. The manuscript instructions to the pilot were blown on board H.M.S. VICTORIOUS; this interesting document, denoting priority of targets for suicide planes, has been translated and the contents forwarded to intelligence centre. It seems certain that VICTORIOUS's guns hit this aircraft during its dive. This matter of differentiating between our own aircraft and the enemy becomes daily of more importance. With the suicide attack and, as is inevitable, with our own fighters pursuing the enemy right on to the Fleet's guns there is only a matter of seconds in which to act. Presented at certain angles there is very little difference between the suicide-equipped Japanese single-engined aircraft and some of our own fighters. On the other hand the means of controlling, particularly of stopping, the fire of the innumerable small guns that are now scattered about ships, often with poor communications, makes the problem difficult.

At dusk the Fleet disengaged to the south eastward and CTF 57 assumed tactical command.

Admiralty footnotes:-
* *ASPS – anti-submarine patrols.*
** *A.C.I – Admiral Commanding 1st Aircraft Carrier Squadron (Admiral Vian).*
† *Dinah – Allied code name for a type of Japanese army reconnaissance aircraft.*
†† *Jack – a patrol aircraft.*
‡ *Bogey – unidentified aircraft.*
‡‡ *ASV – radar equipment in aircraft.*
§ *L day was the day of the initial sea-borne assault on Okinawa by the Americans.*

2nd April.

It was evident from experience the day before that the Japanese had started staging into the Sakishima airfields and it was therefore decided to cancel the planned bombardment in favour of air operations.

The absence of enemy activity noticed by the first fighter sweep the previous day made it appear likely that the enemy might be leaving the airfields at first light. In consequence two aircraft from H.M.S. INDOMITABLE, having been flown off by moonlight, were sent to Ishigaki at 0510. Two other aircraft flown off at the same time and destined for Miyako were unable to proceed owing to radio failures. No activity was reported from Ishigaki.

At 0630 from a flying-off position 23° 12' N. 126° 02' E. a fighter Ramrod left to attack all airfields before the Fleet withdrew. Little activity was noticed, but one airborne Zeke* was shot down over Ishigaki by Hellcats.

After landing on the fighter Ramrod at 1045 the Fleet withdrew to fuelling area Midge, maintaining a CAP of 12 aircraft until dark.

It was very disappointing to have to cancel the bombardment again, for although in so far as cratering, etc., is concerned the large bombs of the aircraft are the more effective, I particularly wished to bombard for the sake of the personnel concerned: many of these are very young and untried.

Once however enemy aircraft begin staging through or operating from an aerodrome the most profitable means of destroying them is by air and not by guns.

At 1450 H.M.S. ILLUSTRIOUS reported man overboard. Fighters of the CAP and destroyers were sent to search and the Fleet was turned 360° for a period. Unfortunately the man was not recovered.

CTF 57 resumed tactical command.

During the period 23rd March to 2nd April inclusive our losses of aircraft were 25, compared to 47 enemy destroyed or probably destroyed and 38 damaged, on the ground. Enemy vessels sunk and damaged were – I lugger sunk, I3 other small vessels probably sunk, and over 40 small craft damaged.

3rd April.

0630. There was no sign of the Tanker Group in rendezvous position Midge One I9° I2' N. I28° 00' E. Weather: heavy N.E. swell, wind north force 5.[†] Spread H.M. Ships SWIFTSURE, ARGONAUT and EURYALUS to carry out search.

0900. Made W/T contact with Tanker Group.

I320. Met Task Units II2.2.5 and II2.2.2.

Weather and cross swell were too heavy to attempt fuelling. The Fleet remained in the area throughout the day, but towards the evening meteorological information suggesting more suitable weather to the westward, the Fleet with the tankers turned west to area Mosquito.

An American Task Group of TF 58 was ordered to cover Sakishima Gunto during 3rd April.

4th April.

0630. Task Unit II2.2.3 from Leyte joined the Tanker Group making 5 tankers from which to fuel.

0730. Commenced refuelling the Fleet and transferring stores and aircraft in a heavy N.N.E. swell in position Mosquito One I9° 37' N. I24° 42' E.

I920. The Fleet disengaged from the Tanker Group for the night.

An American Task Group of TF 58 was ordered to cover Sakishima Gunto during the 4th April.

5th April.

0630. Recommenced refuelling the Fleet in position Mosquito One, the weather conditions for fuelling having considerably improved. Transferred Captain E.C. Ewen, U.S.N., Senior U.S.N. Liaison Officer, from H.M.S. INDOMITABLE to H.M.S. KING GEORGE V.

I930. The Fleet having disengaged from the Tanker Group, set course at 20 knots for the operational area. Owing to the numerous delays in fuelling, the two battleships had to proceed nearly 50 per cent. short of their full stowage and aircraft carriers had been able to embark only sufficient Avgas for the forthcoming two days' operation.

I judged it essential to leave with these shortages in order to be back at the time promised. I do not like battleships steaming about short of fuel for although they should have enough oil for the operation as planned, it leaves little in hand to meet any change of programme, and if a ship short of fuel received underwater damage her position might become embarrassing. A.C.I assumed tactical command.

An American Task Group of TF 58 was ordered to cover Sakishima Gunto during 5th April, I945.

6th April.

0450. Four fighters were flown off H.M.S. INDOMITABLE, two each to Miyako and Ishigaki airfields to attack any enemy aircraft taking off at dawn but early reports from these planes indicated little or no activity in the islands. Heavy low cloud over the islands impeded operations, but eight aircraft not previously noticed, at Ishigaki were attacked with apparent result.

0530. H.M. Ships ARGONAUT and URANIA with a CAP were detached to act as picket to the north westward.

0625. CAP and ASP for the Fleet flown off.

0635. In position 23° I6' N. I25° 36' E. flew off CAPS to cover both islands. The craters in the runway at Miyako airfield were observed to be filled in. At 0650 the picket cruiser and destroyer not being required under the circumstances were ordered to rejoin the Fleet.

At 0850 the Fleet was detected by an enemy aircraft who escaped in cloud.

Hellcats returning from Miyako in the forenoon shot down a Frances‡ after a 30 mile chase. Avengers bombed and hit Hirara runway and town, and bombed Nobara, Sukhama and Myara airstrips causing fires.

Fighters attacked radio and radar stations, sank two junks and blew up a bowser.

At about I700 bogeys were detected on the screen. Fighters intercepted them and splashed one Judy.§ One enemy aircraft out of an estimated raid of four broke through in cloud and later dived on H.M.S. ILLUSTRIOUS, who took radical avoiding action. The suicider's wingtip hit the island, spinning the aircraft into the sea where the bomb exploded. Only slight damage and no casualties were caused. Ship probably hit aircraft in dive.

One Judy and another unidentified enemy plane flying low were engaged by destroyers of 4th Destroyer Flotilla on the screen, one being hit by gunfire. Corsairs and Hellcats closed the Judy and shot it down in flames after it had jettisoned its bomb. The other plane was seen in flames on the horizon about five minutes later and is considered to have been destroyed by the 4th Destroyer Flotilla. A second Judy orbiting the Fleet at about I0 miles range was intercepted by Corsairs and Hellcats and splashed.

Most regrettably one Seafire was shot down by gunfire of the Fleet, during the raid: the pilot was not recovered.

During the day our own losses were the one Seafire shot down by the Fleet, 2 Corsairs by bomb blast and one Avenger which crashed on taking off.

Total enemy losses for the day were:-

Destroyed – airborne 4, suicide I, on ground I; total 6.

Damaged – 6.

Two junks were sunk.

Although it was judged some enemy aircraft had probably passed north of the area to join in the big attacks on the Americans at Okinawa, no use was being made of the Sakishima airfields.

After the dusk CAP had been flown on, the Fleet disengaged to the south eastward and CTF 57 assumed tactical command.

During the day the following signal was received:-

> To:- COM 5th Fleet (R) CTF 58 CTF 57 CTF 5I CTF 56 CTF I7 .
>
> From:- C IN C PAC

I share your hope we can bring enemy to decisive battle. Expect all out enemy reactions in prospect. Good luck. – Nimitz.

Admiralty footnotes:-
* *Zeke – Japanese naval fighter.*
† *Wind force 5 – fresh breeze, I6-20 knots.*
‡ *Frances – Japanese torpedo-bomber.*
§ *Judy – Japanese reconnaissance aircraft.*

7th April.

In view of Admiral Nimitz's appreciation that an all out enemy air reaction against the land and sea forces in and around Okinawa was imminent, the bombardment of Ishigaki planned to take place p.m. was cancelled in favour of air operations only, clouds over the island also influencing this decision.

A report was received that an enemy surface force had been sighted in the early hours leaving the Inland Sea and steering to the southward.

0530. A.C.I assumed tactical command.

The plan for the day was to maintain a constant CAP over the enemy airfields during daylight bombing, straffing when targets offered. The weather at dawn was good and the clouds higher than yesterday.

0530. H.M. Ships ARGONAUT and URANIA were detached to the north westward to act as picket, with orders to rejoin at 08I0.

At 06I0 CAPS for the Fleet and islands and ASP were flown off from position 23° I6' N. I25° 36' E. The island CAPS reported little activity on the islands, but noticed that bomb craters on Ishigaki had been filled in, and that Hirara and Nobara airfields appeared serviceable. It was therefore decided to send in three bomber strikes during the day to re-crater these fields. This was successfully carried out without loss.

In the afternoon H.M.S. URANIA escorted by 2 fighters was despatched to the rescue of a Corsair pilot who had lost his way and landed in the sea about 70 miles from the Fleet. An American Privateer, having reported him, dropped dinghies and remained in the vicinity until relieved by Fireflies. H.M.S. URANIA recovered the pilot, but he was unfortunately found to be dead. The afternoon strike destroyed one and damaged other aircraft found on the ground at Nobara.

Enemy search planes were again active early in the day; making intelligent use of the 9/I0 cloud cover they were not sighted by fighters sent to intercept.

By the end of the day all runways in the island were left well cratered and unserviceable. All visible aircraft had been attacked and there was no activity on any airfield.

During the day the enemy lost 3 aircraft destroyed on the ground and 4 were damaged. 4 fishing vessels and 3 luggers were damaged.

Our own losses were 2 aircraft (by flak) and 4 from other causes.

CTF 57 assumed tactical command at I930, and the Fleet set course to refuel in area Cootie, an American area closer to our operating area than areas Midge or Mosquito and which C IN C PAC had approved our using.

In the evening it was learned that aircraft of TF 58 had dealt severely with a Japanese surface force which had sallied forth from the Inland Sea. Reports, which indicated that the enemy lost I battleship, I cruiser, 4 destroyers sunk, with 2 destroyers burning, filled us with admiration and at the same time, it must be admitted, with envy.

8th April.

American Task Group 52 was instructed to cover Sakishima during the day in the absence of Task Force 57.

0600. Met Task Unit II2.2.5 and Task Unit II2.2.I in position Cootie One 2I° I2' N. I28° 44' E. and commenced to refuel the Fleet in excellent weather conditions. By dusk all ships except one battleship and one carrier had fuelled from the 5 tankers. H.M.C.S. UGANDA, H.M. Ships URCHIN and URSA, reinforcements together with H.M.N.Z.S. GAMBIA rejoining after towing the damaged H.M.S. ULSTER to Leyte, joined TF 57.

9th April.

0630. Recommenced fuelling, which was completed by I500. H.M.S. UNDAUNTED from Leyte rejoined TU II2.2.5. H.M.S. WHIRLWIND joined Task Force 57 from TU II2.2.5. H.M.S. WHELP with A/S defects was despatched to Leyte.

I3I5. SWIFTSURE, UGANDA and GAMBIA carried out independent exercises until I6I5. American Task Group 52 was instructed to cover Sakishima during the day.

At I530 Task Force 57 proceeded, setting course to carry out final strikes on Sakishima on I0th and IIth April: the programme envisaged their returning to Leyte thereafter.

At I650 the following signal was received:-

C IN C PAC (R) CTF 57
From COM 5th Fleet

On II-I2 April propose Task Force 57 strike Shinchiku and Matsuyama airfields. Request you arrange SOWESPAC AIR hit Southern Formosa fields same days. COMSUBPAC assign lifeguards to stations 9, I0 and, if possible, II on these days. TG 52.I will maintain neutralisation Sakishima Gunto.

Shortly after, the following signal was also received:-

CTF 57 and 5I.   From COM 5th Fleet

CTF 57 cancel I0th April Sakishima operations. TG 52.I continue neutralisation that day. CTF 57 advise if following not within capabilities. If approved by C IN C PAC, CTF 57 strike Shinchiku and Matsuyama airfields Formosa II-I2 April.

These were the first intimation that a change of plan was contemplated for TF 57; it looked an attractive change.

It had already been decided that, although both pilots and aircraft were beginning to feel a strain, the possibility of carrying out a fifth operational period against Sakishima Gunto was acceptable, provided it could be on a light scale. The Formosa operation, involving our maximum strength and flying 50 miles over enemy land, would, I judged, probably preclude further operations before the return of the Fleet to Leyte. These extended operational periods bring considerable strain on to the maintenance and handling crews on the carriers which, together with the operational fatigue factor of pilots, are of considerable importance. There is a great deal to be studied in respect of the personnel in this matter under conditions out here, and after further experience a comprehensive report will be forwarded.

I informed A.C.I that should we undertake the Formosa operation I would inform COM 5th Fleet that the fifth operation period would not take place. The Fleet would then arrive back at Leyte on the date as arranged between C.-in-C., B.P.F. and C IN C PAC. After receiving A.C.I's reply at I8I7 I made a signal to inform COM 5th Fleet that we were ready to attack Formosa.

Assuming that we should act in accordance with the above, the Fleet remained to the south during the night instead of proceeding back to its flying-off position from the Nansei Shoto operation, maintaining a moderate speed, the extra maintenance time being welcome.

A signal received from C IN C POA confirmed that above assumption had been correct, and approval was finally received from C IN C PAC in the early hours of the I0th April.

10th April.

The Fleet continued patrolling in the southern area during most of the day. I received an appreciation and air plan from A.C.I at an early hour; at 0845 his Chief Staff Officer was transferred to KING GEORGE V by destroyer and the various details discussed. After this discussion the following signals were made to inform all concerned of my intentions:-

COM 5th Fleet (R) C IN C POA Both H.Q.,

CT 50.5, C.-in-C., B.P.F., CTG 52.I,

CTF II2 COMAAFSWPA, CINCSWPA.

From approximate position Samson I96 deg. 30 min. from western tip Yonakuni Jima will strike Matsuyama and Shinchiku airfields II-I2 April forenoons. CTF 57 originator. Will replenish Cootie area I3th April. On I6th will arrive Leyte.

COM 5th Fleet (R) CINC PAC both H.Q.s. CTG 50.5.

From CTF 57

Request Dumbo* aircraft from 0830 to II30, II and I2 April so TF 57 can leave vicinity Formosa after strikes. Advise and indicate call signs. Fighter escort by TF 57. Rendezvous western point Yonakuni Jima 0830 for Dumbo and fighters both days.

The plan as finally evolved was to strike Matsuyama airfield from a dawn flying-off position 23° 58.5' N. I22° 46' E., retiring to the south east after strike returned. A similar strike was planned for the morning of the I2th on Shinchiku after which the Fleet would return to the oiling area. Both the above strikes were to be with the maximum available aircraft. In view of the fact that the Fleet would be operating some 50 miles from Formosa, a CAP of twenty with Jacks seemed desirable.

During these operations it would at times have been preferable to divide the Fleet in two, so that, whilst one half was sustaining air superiority over our target, the other could be away refuelling; this was however precluded *inter alia* by the fact that two carriers provide insufficient aircraft to maintain the Fleet CAP even on a lessened scale as well as to provide the strike. The position is analogous to a Fleet which, although it has enough destroyers to form a A/S screen and a striking force, cannot reasonably operate in two halves because there would then only be enough destroyers left to provide one or the other.

While the normal practice of the American air-sea rescue aircraft is to remain at call, it was felt that should aircraft ditch late in the proceedings, so much time would be required to get the aircraft from its base 265 miles away that it might entail the Fleet being delayed unnecessarily whilst destroyers were searching somewhat blindly in unhealthy waters for the casualties. This request was at once agreed to and although Dumbo was only asked to be in attendance from 0830 to II30 the reply was received that he was at our disposal until I430.

It should be noted that air-sea rescue arrangements whether carried out by an aircraft or surface ship, again reduce the fighter strength of the Fleet since a small CAP must be provided for the ship or aircraft.

At I203 in position 20° 35' N. I25° 55' E. the final signals were transmitted to Guam W/T for various authorities giving final details. At I700 with the Fleet steering for its flying-off position I handed over tactical command to A.C.I. The operation was named "Iceberg Oolong".

Admiralty footnote:-
* *Dumbo – air-sea rescue aircraft.*

IIth April.

The Fleet arrived in flying-off position 30 miles 202 degrees from Yonakumi Shima at 0600. There was a fresh N.N.E. wind, a moderate sea and short swell. Cloud base was about I,000 feet with intermittent rain and drizzle.

Course was reversed and in daylight it was soon apparent that conditions were unlikely to improve in the flying area during the day while weather reports showed that conditions over Matsuyama precluded any hope of attack. It was considered that a small fighter sweep coasting round North Formosa might find Shinchiku, but that their return journey would be a considerable gamble and surprise lost. Conditions were most unsuitable also for air-sea rescue. Operations were accordingly postponed 24 hours, and the Fleet continued to the south eastward.

At I8I3 received Commander 5th Fleet's order to all Task Group Commanders to prepare for heavy enemy air attacks on I2th April. CTF 57 assumed tactical command at 2000. Course was reversed during the night to bring the Fleet to the flying-off position at dawn.

Task Force 58 reported being under heavy air attack all the afternoon, with the enemy showing a preference to commit suicide on the decks of radar pickets.

During the night I had informed Commander 5th Fleet of the postponement and that we strike Formosa on I2th and I3th April.

12th April.

The weather had improved considerably during the night. At 0530 A.C.I assumed tactical command.

Enemy reconnaissance aircraft possibly detected the Fleet at 0555 and soon afterwards enemy air activity was detected to the northward. CAP was flown off at 06I5 and at 0704 Seafires had an inconclusive encounter with four eastbound Zekes, one of which was shot down. The main strikes, each of 24 bombers and 20 fighters, were flown off at 07I5 from position 23° 58½ ' N. I22° 46' E. and proceeded in company around the coast. Cloud prevented either strike going over the mountains.

One strike bombed Shinchiku airfields with delay fuzed bombs and attacked dispersals. There was flak but no airborne opposition. Due to cloud conditions over Matsuyama airfield the other strike attacked their alternative target Kiirun harbour where hits were observed on the chemical plant, dock area and shipping.

One flight investigated Matsuama and found little activity. A nearby railway station and factory were attacked and one Tess was destroyed on the ground. A bridge over the river south of Matsuama was destroyed and shipping at Tansui shot up.

Two Fireflies which had been sent to rendezvous with Dumbo aircraft at Yonakuni Shima shot down four out of five eastbound Sonias* at 0920 and damaged the other. As these aircraft had not been detected by radar, fighters were thereafter maintained over the island.

Corsairs attacked aircraft which had forced landed on Yonakuni Shima and set fire to a Sally.**

At 1135 a shadowing Dinah was chased by Corsairs, which, after releasing their drop tanks, caught and destroyed it.

At 1410 a Dinah escorted by two Oscars† escaped our fighters in cloud.

At 1530 Hellcats to the north westward of the Fleet shot down a Zeke.

In the evening the enemy made a sortie from Ishigaki, which was intercepted by fighters, no enemy getting within sight of the Fleet. Hellcats splashed four Oscars and two Tonies‡ and damaged two. The Corsairs splashed one Val§ and one Oscar, and damaged one. One Hellcat was badly damaged in this engagement, the pilot being killed when making a forced landing. During the day, except for the evening sortie and one shadower, all enemy air traffic appeared to have been between Formosa and Sakishima. Fighter Direction of our fighters during the day was well carried out, and some excellent interceptions were made. CTF 57 assumed tactical command at 2100.

The score for the day was:-

Enemy losses:
Destroyed – airborne 16, on ground 1; total 17.
Probably destroyed – on ground 1; total 1.
Damaged – airborne 2; total 2.

Own losses:
In combat 3, other causes 1; total 4.

After dark an enemy plane carried out an apparently unsuccessful box search for the Fleet, which had disengaged to the south eastward for the night.

It was evident from signals received that the enemy were engaging in very heavy air attacks on American forces in the Okinawa area, and that Formosa-based planes were taking part. I came to the conclusion during the evening that we must contrive to remain for a further period; even if we could do little more than occasionally strike at the Sakishima Gunto we should anyhow provide an alternative target to take some of the weight. A.C.1 had evidently come to the same conclusion, for at 2113 he informed me that, in view of the very heavy air attacks being launched against American forces on and around Okinawa, he felt that our remaining aircraft and aircrews could manage a fifth operating period provided that our losses tomorrow should remain small. In the event, and as he points out in his report, the Formosa attack days acted as tonic. I therefore made the following signal:-

COM 5th Fleet (R) CTG 52.1 C.-in-C., B.P.F. C IN C PAC CTF II2
From CTF 57

In view of current situation expect to be ready further operations I6th-I7th April. If Formosa weather bad tomorrow intend deal with Ishigaki and significant intercepted traffic between Sakishima and Formosa both ways.

Admiralty footnotes:-
* *Sonias – Japanese army light bombers.*
** *Sally – Japanese army bomber.*
† *Oscar – Japanese army fighter.*
‡ *Tonies – Japanese army fighters*
§ *Val – Japanese navy dive bomber.*

13th April.

Task Force 51 covered Sakishima Gunto.

0530. A.C.I assumed tactical command.

At 0550 four fighters were flown off. A bogey originally detected at 0540 developed into an ineffective raid by four Vals accompanied by a radar-fitted search plane probably performing the dual role of pilot plane and Gestapo. One Val dive bombed, but missed, H.M.S. INDOMITABLE. This aircraft switched on navigation lights and fired an incorrect recognition cartridge. It was engaged but probably not hit. A second was shot down by gunfire of the Fleet.

Unfortunately, gunfire also shot down one Hellcat which failed to clear the Fleet during the attack, and the pilot was killed.

At 06I5 the CAP proper was flown off in position 23° 58.5' N. I22° 46' E.

At 0640 a small group of bogeys was intercepted 25 miles to the north west of the Fleet; two Zekes were splashed by Corsairs arid the remainder retired to the northward.

At 0645 Avenger strikes were flown to attack Matsuyama and Shinchiku airfields.

The weather over Matsuyama was fair, runways, barracks and dispersal points were successfully bombed, and a petrol or ammunition dump blown up. Few aircraft were seen on the airfield. Fighters shot up about I2 aircraft on Giran airfield without apparent result.

The other Avenger force bombed Shinchiku airfield through low cloud, hitting runway intersections and installations. No aircraft were lost in either of these strikes and there was no airborne opposition.

The Firefly CAP for the Dumbo attacked the suspected radar station on Yonakuni Shima with rockets and apparently destroyed it. When relieved, they also shot up luggers and small craft in the harbour close to Iriizaki.

After these bomber strikes were flown on, the Fleet disengaged to the south eastward to refuel.

At I300 Hellcats intercepted 3 Zekes about 40 miles north of the Fleet, and Corsairs intercepted a Dinah escorted by Tojos.* All the enemy aircraft escaped in cloud.

CTF assumed tactical command at I945.

Enemy losses:
Destroyed – airborne 3.
Probably destroyed – on ground 5.
Probably damaged – on ground I.

Own losses:

In combat I.

It was with profound grief that Task Force 57 learned of the death of the President of the United States. A signal of sympathy was sent to CINCPOA on behalf of Task Forces 57 and II2.

At I840 the following signal was received, and plans for a fifth operating period were made accordingly:-

CTF 57
From COM 5th Fleet

Cover Sakishima I6th and I7th unless other orders received in interim. Affirmative your message of I2th. Appreciate your co-operation and initiative.

14th April.

0630. Made contact with Task Unit II2.2.5 and Tanker Group consisting of 5 tankers in position Cootie One 2I° I2' N. I28° 44' E.

H.M. Ships FORMIDABLE, KEMPENFELT and WESSEX were also met and joined Task Force 57.

Fuelling was commenced in fine weather and proceeded with less delays than usual.

H.M.S. ILLUSTRIOUS was sailed for Leyte at I755 screened by H.M. Ships URANIA and QUALITY.

As from today the United States Fleet was ordered to half mast colours, and I gave orders that British ships in harbour or near thereto, should conform. Since United States ships do not, I understand, fly their colours in the operation areas and the half masting of our colours at sea in war is I believe only done when convoying or burying the deceased, the position was not clear as regards TF 57. I felt it fitting, however, and in keeping with what I knew to be the feeling of the Fleet for this great leader and sincere friend of the British Empire, to mark the occasion irrespective of precedent; therefore I ordered colours to be half masted for the last hour before sunset today.

The Fleet disengaged from the Tanker Force for the night.

15th April.

0730. The Fleet joined the Tanker Group, now consisting of three tankers; fuelling and general replenishing was completed by 1400, when TF 57 disengaged, and took departure to cover the Sakishima area again. No supply of aircraft was available during this replenishment period.

16th April.

0530. A.C.I assumed tactical command.

No picket cruiser was stationed owing to the shortage of fighter aircraft.

0600. The Fleet CAP was flown off in position 23° 28' N. 125° 18' E., 17 minutes before sunrise and in excellent operating weather.

At 0622 an enemy snooper at 20,000 feet escaped before the CAP had time to gain height.

At 0630 the first strike took off to attack Ishigaki airfields. This attack, and a further one flown off at 1230, left all the runways unserviceable.

At 0930 the second strike took off to attack Miyako airfields, where previous craters were found to be filled in and every endeavour had been made to keep the airfields unserviceable. This attack, together with another flown off at 1533, left all Miyako airfields out of action. CAPS were left over both islands throughout the day; the one over Miyako being called up by a Japanese who invited our aircraft to return to base. Rocket-carrying Fireflies straffed a radar station at Miyako, and ground installations, barracks, and grounded aircraft generally were straffed. There was no airborne opposition over the targets and flak was moderate.

At 1700 bad height estimation was the cause of failure to intercept a bogey which crossed ahead of the Fleet from east to west.

At 1441 two divisions of fighters staggered in height and range got close to an erratic and fast moving bogey but were unable to find any target.

At 1505 a bogey was detected, range 9 miles, and followed from 25,000 feet to sea level where it disappeared. At about this time a large cloud of smoke was seen on the horizon and an unidentified twin was reported as sighted over the Fleet.

At 1536 fighters failed to find a 320 knot bogey closing from the westward, the bogey fading at 25 miles.

A possible explanation for these mysterious bogeys is that they were piloted flying bombs launched too far away and which failed to reach the Fleet before exhausting their fuel.

At 1722 Hellcats shot down a Myrt[†] which was apparently stalking an American Privateer search plane.

In the evening false alarms were caused by some of our fighters returning from the islands and in one case ship fire was opened on them due to an improper approach by the aircraft and faulty recognition by the ship.

In the afternoon a Seafire landing on INDEFATIGABLE bounced, cleared the barriers and crashed. The pilot was unhurt, but the plane wrecked an Avenger, damaged a Firefly, and knocked two ratings over the side. QUIBERON picked up one, but the other man was unfortunately not recovered.

In spite of having received no replenishment aircraft since 9th April and the lack of fighters consequently felt, A.C.I informed me that he considered a sixth operation period, if confined to one day, would be possible. I was happy therefore, in view of the sustained heavy enemy air attacks on our Fleetmates at and around Okinawa, to inform Commander 5th Fleet as follows:-

Continuing operations Sakishima tomorrow. Own losses light. Little enemy activity except anti-aircraft fire. If light losses continue, can strike final blow I9th April. Same Dumbo and submarine services needed.

A further signal altering the final strike date to 20th April was made to Commander 5th Fleet as A.C.I informed me that maintenance of aircraft necessitated two days' work in the fuelling area.

At dusk the Fleet disengaged to the south eastward and CTF 57 assumed tactical command at 2II0.

The score for the day was:-

Enemy:
Destroyed – airborne I, on ground I; total 2.

Own:
Destroyed in combat 2, operationally 3; total 5.

I7th April.

A.C.I assumed tactical command at 0520.

CAP was flown off at 0600 from position 23° 34' N. I25° 38' E.

In view of the apparent success of yesterday's neutralisation, the number of bombers in the main strikes was reduced, the first strike taking off at 0630. First reports showed that considerable effort had been made to fill in the runway craters at Miyako but none at Ishigaki. Consequently no bombing strike was sent to Ishigaki. Of the three strikes sent to Miyako, the first two left all airfields unserviceable and the third attacked municipal buildings and barracks.

In this last attack an Avenger was shot down and one of the crew succeeded in baling out and alighted on the water I½ miles from Hirara town. A Walrus was quickly flown off and rescued the airman, whilst a fighter escort kept down fire which was opened from the town. CAPS were maintained over both islands, but reported no activity on any airfields, all of which remained unserviceable at the end of the day. No operational aircraft could be found on the ground.

At 0609 a few bogeys were detected to the north west of the Fleet. Fighters sent to investigate splashed one Zeke.

At I627 bogeys were detected II0 miles west of the Fleet. Fighters intercepted at 55 miles and two out of 6 Zekes were shot down, the others escaping in cloud.

During the afternoon a Privateer American aircraft flying at zero feet between Ishigaki and Iriomote was momentarily mistaken for a bandit ‡ and given a short burst at extreme range by Corsairs. No damage resulted. This unfortunate incident has since been cleared up with the U.S. authorities and the question of periodical U.S. search planes approaching Task Force 57 fully discussed. It is hoped that the arrangements made will obviate such incidents in the future.

At 1750 close range weapons in KING GEORGE V suddenly opened fire on what appeared to be a blazing aircraft diving vertically on the ship. It turned out to be a dropped tank from a Corsair overhead – both parties missed.

The score for the day was:-

Enemy:
Aircraft destroyed – airborne 3.
Several small ships damaged.

Own:
Aircraft lost in combat 1.

My signal informing Commander 5th Fleet that Task Force 57 would be available to strike again on 20th April was approved by him. The following signal from CINCPAC was also received:-

CTF 57 (R) 5th Fleet C.-in-C., B.P.F.
From: CINCPAC

It was gratifying to note your message of 16th to COM 5th Fleet. Your Force is always ready to make still greater efforts whenever there is an opportunity to hit the enemy. Appreciate your offer which is traditional of British Navy.

At 1945 CTF 57 assumed tactical command and the Fleet withdrew to fuel in area Mosquito.

18th April.

0630. Commenced fuelling from Tanker Group of 5 tankers in area Mosquito. Also met Captain D.7 in NAPIER with NORMAN and NEPAL, all of whom joined Task Force 57, and UNDAUNTED who rejoined her Flotilla. Mails, stores, and correspondence were transferred but no replenishment aircraft were available; owing to the extension of operation programme none had been expected. By dusk the Fleet had completed fuelling and disengaged from the Tanker Group for the night.

Three of the five tankers, with Captain Escort Forces in PHEASANT, were detached and sailed for Leyte.

0730. The Fleet rejoined the remaining two tankers and destroyers topped up with fuel. This second day in replenishing area was necessary in order to rest aircrews, and for maintenance work on aircraft.

At I300 the Fleet disengaged and took departure for the Sakishima area, leaving Captain D.27 in KEMPENFELT in the fuelling area with 2 tankers, SPEAKER, WOODCOCK and FINDHORN, with orders to proceed to Leyte at dawn on 2Ist April.

At 0520 A.G.I assumed tactical command. CAP was flown off at 0555 in position 23° 33' N. I25° 02' E. The plan for the day followed generally the pattern of previous strikes, namely to crater the runways on all Myako and Ishigaki airfields and to maintain a CAP over them to prevent repair work, destroying any enemy airborne, and to strafe any grounded planes. In addition, 2 strikes by rocket-firing Fireflies were ordered to attack coastal shipping and ground installations.

Four bomber strikes were sent in, and found that most craters had been filled in on runways at both islands. By the end of the day all airfield runways on both islands were left unserviceable, with the exception of those, at Hirara (Myako) which were only partially cratered.

There was no enemy airborne opposition over the islands and none came near the Fleet. The several bogeys detected during the day were all found to be friendly search planes when intercepted. A lugger and some junks were rocketted and left burning, as were a possible radar station and barracks.

This was not a very fruitful day. One Avenger reported ditching I0 miles south of Ishigaki. The position was searched all the afternoon and evening without success, but the survivors were fortunately rescued the following afternoon by U.S. Naval Mariner.

The score for the day was:-

Enemy losses:
Damaged on ground I.

Own losses:
In combat I.

At I9I0 the Fleet, set course for Leyte having completed I2 strike days out of 26 days between first and last strikes. CTF 57 assumed tactical command at I930.

21st April.

H.M.S. CRANE was despatched to overtake the Tanker Group who were on their way to Leyte, to relieve H.M.S. KEMPENFELT, who was ordered to proceed at best speed to Leyte.

22nd April.

During the day, and taking advantage of the presence of Chief Staff Officer to C.-in-C., B.P.F. on board H.M.S. KING GEORGE V, Rear Admiral E.J.P. Brind, C.B., C.B.E. (Flag Officer Commanding, 4th Cruiser Squadron), and Captain J.P. Wright, D.S.O. (C.S.O. to A.C.I), were transferred by destroyer to the Fleet Flagship for conferences. C.S.4 in H.M.S. SWIFTSURE was detached at 2000 with H.M. Ships GAMBIA, UGANDA and EURYALUS to proceed ahead to Leyte. Paravanes were streamed at 1700.

23rd April.

At 0700 the Fleet formed into two groups for proceeding up Leyte Gulf.

1030. Entered the searched channel and recovered paravanes at 1115.

The Fleet was brought to anchor at 1245 in San Pedro Bay, reasonably close to the ships of the Fleet Train.

During the period under review the following aircraft losses were inflicted on the enemy and suffered by TF 57:-

Enemy aircraft:
Destroyed – in air 33, on ground 38. (Includes 2 splashed by ships' guns and 3 suiciders.)
Damaged – in air 2, on ground 50.

Own aircraft:
Losses due to enemy action 19.

Action casualties:
Pilots 16, aircrews 13.

Admiralty footnotes:-
* *Tojos – Japanese army fighters.*
† *Myrt – Japanese naval reconnaissance aircraft.*
‡ *Bandit – enemy aircraft.*

Office of Flag Officer Commanding,
1st Aircraft Carrier Squadron,
British Pacific Fleet.
26th April, 1945.

The operations now concluded have cost us 59 aircraft against which we have to set 30 enemy aircraft shot down by fighters, 3 Kamikazes* self-destroyed, and 97 destroyed or damaged on the ground; of the latter total, some few may have been non-operational or dummies.

This is an unremunerative return, but the operation was one which offered little opportunity of effecting high losses on the enemy.

Airborne opposition in the target areas – there was none, whilst airborne attack was confined to small groups of Kamikaze, who split up 30 or 40 miles from the Fleet and in their approach through cloud formed difficult targets, either for fighter interception or for gunfire.

2. On the other hand, attacks on airfields and dispersed aircraft are difficult and costly; the management of a group of airfields which are daily attacked from dawn to dusk do not display their wares. The bombers are exposed to flak concentrated in the area of attack throughout their bombing runs, whilst Ramrod sweeps are faced with dummy or unserviceable aircraft dispersed in revetments and other conspicuous places in centres of flak, whilst those serviceable are well camouflaged or concealed in woods.

The Japanese largely use smokeless, traceless and flashless ammunition; aircraft do not know they are being fired at until they are hit.

It has been a disability that cluster or fragmentation and incendiary bombs have not been available, as these would appear to be the type of missile required to destroy aircraft dispersed in the manner stated.

3. *Fighter Direction.* Whilst the number of aircraft shot down by the fighters is small, it represents, I think, a high proportion of those available for this treatment. Fighter direction, under the control and inspiration of Acting Commander E.D.G. Lewin, D.S.O., D.S.C., Royal Navy, making use of experienced teams in H.M. Ships INDOMITABLE and VICTORIOUS, has been of the highest order; the Staff Fighter Direction Officer, Fifth Fleet, Lieutenant-Commander H.A. Rowe, United States Navy, loaned for the operation, informs me that it has been as good as or better than the Fifth Fleet standard.

4. *Hellcats.* The operational efficiency of No. 5 Wing, trained and led by Acting Lieutenant-Commander (A) T.W. Harrington, R.N., has, throughout the whole course of the operation, been remarkable. Flying by day in all weathers and sometimes by night, I can recollect but one barrier crash, whilst their break-up from the landing circuit and speed of landing-on has been exceptional; whilst not so fast in the air as Corsairs, their tactical eminence has enabled them to account for their full share of what enemy aircraft have been available.

5. *Corsairs.* The Corsair Squadrons have done all that was asked of them and more, but they have not the same proved all weather propositions for landing-on purposes

as have Hellcats, and it is a grave disability that it is dangerous to land on unless their long-range tanks have been dropped or emptied. Nor can they be used for night flying.

In leading their squadrons the work of Temporary Acting Lieutenant-Commander (A) A.M. Tritton, R.N.V.R., No. 1830 Squadron, H.M.S. ILLUSTRIOUS, and Temporary Acting Lieutenant-Commander (A) C.C. Tomkinson, R.N.V.R. (since killed), No. 1836 Squadron, H.M.S. VICTORIOUS, has been outstanding.

6. *Seafires.* The Seafires have been used for CAP over the Fleet. Owing to their short endurance they have not been suitable for accompanying offensive strikes to the range at which these operations have been carried out.

7. *Fireflies.* It had been intended to use Fireflies against enemy coasters and coastal vessels, but these have been painfully few; thus with the exception of occasional rocket sorties against particular targets, such as radar stations and junks, it has been necessary to relegate them to escort duties with Lifeguard submarines and Dumbo aircraft, and to flying Jack patrols. On the only occasion on which the chance of air combat presented itself, they lost no time at all; four Sonias out of five to the guns of two Fireflies.

Acting Major V.B.G. Cheesman, D.S.O., M.B.E., D.S.C., R.M., continues to lead this Squadron with distinction and address.

8. *Avengers.* Avengers have been employed throughout as bombers and have executed this task with success; their losses to flak have been relatively high; this I attribute firstly to the determination of their leaders in coming through cloud, which has frequently been at 2,000 feet, to discharge their load, and secondly to the invisibility of the enemy flak. Four hundred tons of high explosive bombs have been unloaded on enemy airfields and installations.

The service of Acting Lieutenant-Commander (A) D.R. Foster, R.N.V.R., H.M.S. VICTORIOUS, No. 849 Squadron, has been outstanding.

9. *Air Group Leaders.* The duties have been carried out by Commander N.S. Luard, D.S.C., R.N., H.M.S. INDOMITABLE, and Acting Lieutenant-Colonel R.C. Hay, D.S.C., R.M., H.M.S. VICTORIOUS, in an able manner, particularly by the latter, and the appointments are, I think, justified. It has been their primary task to so direct the strike and fighter leaders that their offensive effort is aimed at the most profitable sections of the ordered target areas; and to redirect their effort if, for any reason, an alternative target of better value has been presented; it has been their secondary duty to make a reconnaissance each morning of the airfields and report the position of dispersed aircraft, advising me whether fighters should be sent to strafe or not.

10. *Air attack on the Fleet.* On those occasions on which hostile aircraft have penetrated the fighter defences of the Fleet the sky has been in general overcast, whilst there has been a longstop CAP essentially maintained over the Fleet under the cloud base.

There has never been a group at which to fire, not more in fact than a single aircraft; thus there has been little opportunity to use heavy artillery: gunfire has been in the main restricted to flak, and, as this is little deterred by alterations of course, and because the time between the enemy descending through the cloud base and his arrival onboard is small, it has been my practice, unless necessary to operate aircraft, to keep the Fleet almost continuously under rudder during such attacks. The U.S. Fleet, I understand, do the same.

II. *Operation of Aircraft under impending attack.* In face of the near certainty that if a hostile aircraft gets through it will hit a carrier, it has been a nice matter to decide on the chances of interception: if assessed as unfavourable, the choice has to be made between accepting the Fleet on a steady course in wind, while aircraft on deck with full tanks and loaded with bombs are flown off – to get in the way of the guns, and derange the strike programme – or to keep them on and rely on full avoiding action. The course of action selected has been based on the two factors – estimated time available and number of loaded, aircraft on deck.

I2. *Friendly aircraft shot down by fire from the Fleet.* One Seafire was shot down during a day attack and for this I could see little justification.

A Hellcat was shot down at first light. For this, although there are complementary reasons, I must accept full responsibility because I misjudged the enemy's intention, and flew off the Hellcats to attack two aircraft which I estimated then to be snoopers, but had in fact hostile intent and were upon us before one of the Hellcats was clear.

I3. *Performance of Carriers.* The carriers have, I think, stood up well to, what is for us, so extended a period of operational duty in the course of which 2,429 operational sorties have been flown. The maintenance crews, whom it has never been possible to stand down on any day throughout the operation, have done their work well: the carriers, but for shortage of pilots, bombs and stores, would be good to continue operating: that this should be so reflects credit on their Commanding Officers:

Captain M.M. Denny, C.B., C.B.E., R.N. – H.M.S. VICTORIOUS,

Captain Q.D. Graham, C.B.E., D.S.O., R.N. – H.M.S. INDEFATIGABLE,

Captain C.E. Lambe, C.B., C.V.O., R.N. – H.M.S. ILLUSTRIOUS,

Captain J.A.S. Eccles, R.N. – H.M.S. INDOMITABLE,

Captain P. Ruck-Keene, C.B.E., R.N. – H.M.S. FORMIDABLE. (This ship was brought forward from Leyte at short notice to relieve H.M.S. ILLUSTRIOUS and has operated in an admirable manner in spite of having joined the Fleet without previous experience of existing practice.)

I4. *Extension of First Operating Period.* In view of their necessities at Okinawa, and of the fact that Task Force 58 was in the field before us, it is a matter of great regret to me to have been unable to offer to continue to operate after the 20th April: having regard to the conditions set out above and to the fact that no replenishment fighter pilots have been available throughout the operation I have not felt, having regard to the future, that it was justifiable to do so: there is the consideration also that the sooner we return to replenish and relieve, the sooner we come forward.

I5. I should say in conclusion that the enemy flak positions on Hyako are unsubdued and continue to inflict casualties on our aircraft: the high explosive bombs with which we are provided have proved unsuitable for their reduction: it is believed that the positions might be neutralised by an area bombardment. Any such effort would be warmly appreciated by all our aircrews.

(Signed) PHILIP L. VIAN.
Rear Admiral.

Admiralty footnote:-
* *Kamikaze – Japanese "suicide" aircraft.*

The following Despatch was submitted to the Lords Commissioners of the Admiralty on the 10th July, 1945, by Admiral Sir Bruce A. Fraser, G.C.B., K.B.E.,

Commander-in-Chief, British Pacific Fleet.
Office of the Commander-in-Chief,
British Pacific Fleet,
10th July, 1945.

REPORT ON OPERATION "ICEBERG"

Be pleased to lay before Their Lordships a report on the second and last phase of Operation "Iceberg".

2. This covers the period from the 23rd April to 25th May, 1945, and is in continuation of my letter of 7th June, 1945.

3. I entirely endorse the remarks of the Vice-Admiral in paragraph 10 of his covering letter. The manner in which the ships of the First Aircraft Carrier Squadron remained in action, despite the damage sustained from "suicide" attacks, reflects the greatest credit on Vice Admiral Sir Philip Vian and on the Commanding Officers and ships' companies of the aircraft carriers.

(Signed) BRUCE FRASER,
Admiral.
Office of the Vice-Admiral,
Second-in-Command,
British Pacific Fleet,
6th June, 1945.

SIR,

I have the honour to forward for your information and in continuation of my letter of 9th May, 1945, the attached narrative and report of proceedings of Task Force 57 during the second phase of Operation, "Iceberg"; in so far as the British Pacific Fleet is concerned it terminates their contribution thereto.

2. The object throughout was to prevent the enemy making use of the airfields in the Sakishima Gunto group.

3. Over the whole period TF 57 was at sea for 62 days, broken by 8 days re-storing at Leyte, maintaining an intermittent neutralisation of these airfields by day. During

its absence an American Task Group took over this duty and, in the later stages, aircraft based on Okinawa also took part. Whilst the latter's contribution is not known in detail their work at night was particularly welcome.

During this time the Task Force flew 4,852 sorties, dropped 875 tons of bombs and rocket projectiles, destroyed I00 enemy aircraft and damaged 70 others; various other targets such as shipping, W/T stations, etc., were also attacked. Our own losses were 33 aircraft from enemy action; in addition 92 were lost operationally.

4. Throughout the first phase of the "Iceberg" operation and in the early part of the second phase, the position from which the Force operated was not greatly changed, except on the occasion of attacking Formosa. Since it seemed possible that the enemy might be fixing the force in daylight by shore radar on the CAP, it was decided after the attack on 9th May, I945, that it would be wiser to move the striking position further to the eastward, accepting the greater flying distance to Ishigaki. In the event, the Fleet was not seriously attacked after this was done.

5. It had been apparent since the beginning of the operation that however thoroughly the airfields were neutralised by day, the enemy was determined and able to effect repairs by night. The lack of night intruders to prevent this was keenly felt as it was evident that intermittent heckling of the airfields during the night would have slowed down the activities of the enemy working parties. Furthermore, the need for night fighters to protect the Fleet, particularly during the moonlight periods, is outstanding; so is the need for a night carrier. In this respect it was perhaps very fortunate that during our first strikes on 27th March, when the Fleet had been approached at 0245, INDOMITABLE flew off a Hellcat who successfully drove off the enemy aircraft, then remaining up till dawn. This may have given the Japanese the impression that we were night fighter equipped.

The problem of getting night fighter aircraft, including a night carrier, has been taken up separately, but the solution cannot be expected in the near future.

6. A further bombardment had been planned for the latter stages, but had to be cancelled on two successive days owing to weather. After the second cancellation on 9th May, damage to carriers and shortage of aircraft rendered any further bombardment unwise.

7. The assistance of the United States authorities at Leyte was greatly appreciated, and I must once more express my admiration and gratitude for the excellent arrangements for air-sea rescue by means of Lifeguard submarines and Dumbo aircraft.

8. The activities of the Fleet Train are the subject of a separate report. The service given in the fuelling area continued to improve throughout, and for this the Fleet owes much to Rear-Admiral Fisher. The regular delivery of mail, to take one instance, went far to maintain the general morale.

9. This operation has presented the British Fleet with several novel features; in particular it has stressed the strenuous efforts required from carriers who have no spare pilots and who could well benefit from a larger complement. They have unfortunately little extra accommodation available.

In other ships the principal problem was, perhaps, to maintain alertness and interest while engaged on less active duties.

I feel however that the Fleet as a whole kept in good heart throughout and did, I trust, what was required of it.

I0. The Vice-Admiral Commanding the First Aircraft Carrier Squadron has remarked in his report on the manner in which the carriers contrived to remain in operation in spite of damage; I wholeheartedly subscribe to his views. Their achievements, however, derived directly from the sustained determination and leadership of Vice-Admiral Sir Philip Vian himself, for to him fell the conduct and handling of the Fleet during its most active periods.

I have the honour to be, Sir,
Your obedient Servant,
(Signed) BERNARD RAWLINGS,
Vice-Admiral.
The Commander.
United States Fifth Fleet.

NARRATIVE.

On 23rd April TF 57, 32 days out from Ulithi, was brought to anchor in San Pedro Roads, Leyte, and commenced making good defects and replenishing from ships of the Fleet Train. The partial replenishment carried out at Manus in early March had been difficult due to the great distances between ships, the extreme shortage of craft and the necessity for Fleet training.

The berthing plan at Leyte giving greatly reduced distances which had been arranged by R.A.F.T. before the Fleet arrived made matters considerably easier.

The fuelling, ammunitioning, storing, etc. of the Fleet commenced p.m. on the 23rd and continued throughout the week, aided by favourable weather.

Boats were again very short and quite insufficient for libertymen to be landed. Since the libertymen could not get to the beer, I authorised the beer to be brought to them, the amount available allowing one bottle per day per head; this innovation proved immensely popular.

Every Commanding Officer reported enthusiastically on this matter, there were no "scenes," and I have no doubt whatever that it was a great and well deserved boon in a period of hard work in great heat.

Prior to their departure to refit, H.M. Ships ILLUSTRIOUS and ARGONAUT were fleeced of available stores and spare gear to meet Fleet requirements.

The heat and lethargic effect of the climate which being drier was not quite so marked as at Manus, made conditions very trying for personnel employed, between and below decks, on maintenance, boiler cleaning, etc; Much work of this type had to be done at great speed and personnel concerned did well. Office work, occasioned by the inevitable influx of correspondence after such a long period at sea, was no less trying. There was in fact, little time for rest or relaxation for officers or ratings during this period and after a day or two most of us, I feel sure, wished ourselves back at sea again.

Precautions were taken against possible attack by midget submarines, explosive motor boats, and suicide swimmers, but no suspicion of attack developed.

No air raids were experienced, although the Fleet was alerted on a few occasions at night by "Flash Red" from the shore station.

On arrival at Leyte I waited upon Admiral Kincaid, Commander 7th Fleet, and with him met Vice Admiral J.L. Kauffman, Commander Philippine Sea Frontier and Rear Admiral R.O. Davis, Commander Amphibious Group 13. They all lunched on board my Flagship. Commodore E.M. Evans-Lombe, Captain (S) J.R. Allfrey, Chief of Staff and Secretary to C.-in-C., B.P.F., after most useful discussions with Flag Officers of the Task Force, left Leyte by air for Guam: Captain E.C. Ewen, U.S.N., Liaison Officer with TF 57, travelled with them.

Uppermost in my mind during the first few days at Leyte was the question of the future employment of Task Force 57. I had been informed by C.-in-C., B.P.F. that alternative employment for the Fleet in the immediate future was under consideration as follows:-

(*a*) Continuation of Operation "Iceberg" as already planned.

(*b*) Withdrawal from "Iceberg" and engagement on an operation in Borneo with target date of leaving Leyte approximately 15th May. C.-in-C. signals made the latter appear the most probable. On 27th April a signal was received from C.-in-C. making it clear that the Fleet would not participate in the Borneo operation and C.-in-C., Pacific in a signal informed me that we should continue with Operation "Iceberg." This was very satisfactory.

In my signal I had informed Commander 5th Fleet of my intention and ability, unless otherwise ordered, to proceed from Leyte with TF 57 on 1st May to continue the neutralisation of Sakishima Gunto for a period of from three to four, weeks before requiring to withdraw for major replenishment. Operations were planned for a cycle of two days of strikes followed by two for replenishment, the first strikes to be carried out on 4th and 5th May.

By the evening of 30th April the replenishment of the Fleet was completed, thanks to the energy and foresight of the Rear Admiral Commanding Fleet Train, and those under him, the arrangements made by the Rear Admiral Commanding Destroyers greatly contributing. The Tanker Group, to top up the Fleet on their passage north, sailed from Leyte at 0700 on 30th April. H.M.S. QUILLIAM from Australia joined TF 57 on 28th April.

1st May.

Task Force 57 sailed from Leyte in groups at 0630 and consisted of the following ships:-

1st Battle Squadron

KING GEORGE V (Flag of CTF 57 – B.S.1),

HOWE;
Ist Carrier Squadron
INDOMITABLE (Flag of 2nd-in-Command TF57 – A.C.I),
VICTORIOUS,
FORMIDABLE,
INDEFATIGABLE;
4th Cruiser Squadron
SWIFTSURE (Flag of C.S.4),
UGANDA,
GAMBIA,
EURYALUS,
BLACK PRINCE;
25th Destroyer Flotilla
GRENVILLE (Capt. D.25),
URSA,
UNDINE,
URCHIN,
URANIA,
UNDAUNTED;
4th Destroyer Flotilla
QUILLIAM (Capt. D.4),
QUEENBOROUGH,
QUIBERON,
QUICKMATCH,
QUALITY;
27th Destroyer Flotilla
KEMPENFELT (Capt, D.27),
WHIRLWIND,
WESSEX.

The 7th Destroyer Flotilla, consisting of H.M. Ships NAPIER (Capt. D.7), NEPAL, NORMAN and NIZAM were, for the initial stages of the operation, assigned to Task Force II2 for duty as escorts with the Tanker Groups.

H.M. Ships ILLUSTRIOUS, ARGONAUT, WAGER and WHELP remained at Leyte to sail on 4th May for Sydney and refit. H.M.S. ARGONAUT was left with orders to put into Lae, New Guinea, on her way south.

H.M.S. ULSTER with bomb damage remained at Leyte having damage made good sufficient for her to proceed to another port for major repairs.

2nd May.

At I730 CTF 57 assumed tactical command.

3rd May.

At 0600 made rendezvous in position Mosquito (I) with the Commander, Logistic Support Group in H.M.S. CRANE, H.M. Ships AVON and WHIMBREL and R.F.A.s SAN AMBROSIO, SAN ADOLPHO and CEDARDALE.

All cruisers and destroyers topped up with fuel.

UGANDA, whilst casting off from her tanker, inadvertently lay back on one oil hose, which parted and fouled a propeller. This she was able to clear by the use of shallow water divers. By I530 fuelling was completed. The Fleet took departure for the operations area and the Tanker Group for area Cootie.

The plan for the opening of operations was:-

(*a*) To make airfields of the Sakishima Gunto unserviceable by bombing runways and air installations.

(*b*) To conduct an offensive against flak positions and to assist in cratering runways by ship bombardment.

(*c*) To maintain an offensive CAP over the islands.

The particular plan for the first day was for the bombarding force to bombard Miyako airfields and flak positions at about noon, from medium range, with the Carrier Force about 30 miles to the southward.

4th May.

At 0500 A.C.I assumed tactical command. Clouds were about 9/I0 at 6,000 feet when the CAP was flown off at 0540 in position 23° 44' N. I25° II' E.

Ten minutes later enemy air activity in the vicinity of Sakishima was detected, the general trend of traffic being to the eastward. One small group approached the Fleet and Hellcats shot down one Zeke before the others escaped in cloud.

Bomber strikes were flown off at 0605 for Miyako and at 08I5 for Ishigaki.

At Miyako the weather was good, visibility excellent and I/I0 cloud at 3,000 feet. Repair work on the airfields had apparently been proceeding by night since the day strikes by TF 52. All A.A. batteries opened fire on our aircraft. Runways at Hirara were well bombed and a direct hit on an A.A. position observed. Conditions for bombardment appeared good.

At Ishigaki one runway of Miyara airfield was found serviceable and left well cratered.

At 0800 the Dumbo aircraft provided by CTF 5I arrived, and was stationed between the target and the Carrier Force until I700.

When taking off for the Ishigaki strike, one Avenger crashed into the sea, but the crew were rescued unhurt by the safety destroyer.

At 0827 an enemy aircraft approached the Force at a great height. Our fighters could not get high enough to intercept through lack of oxygen, and the enemy entered the artillery zone. Fire was opened in blind control, but the enemy was never seen and retired to the westward. Before deciding to disengage from the carriers for bombardment I weighed up the following considerations:-

(*a*) The need for bombardment in an endeavour to reduce A.A. fire ashore.

(*b*) Conditions for bombardment near the target had been reported as excellent.

(*c*) The effect on morale of ships of the bombarding force would be most beneficial.

To be balanced against this I took into consideration the fact that the Fleet had been sighted. That in itself was nothing strange, and had happened several times before without being followed by any attack on the Fleet.

After discussing the situation with A.C.I, I detached with the bombarding force at 1000 in position 23° 54' N. 125° 10' E. and closed Miyako at 24 knots. The carriers provided an additional CAP for this force as well as aircraft for spotting.

At 1155 the bombarding force passed through position 24° 33.5' N. 125° 10' E. on the bombarding course of 070° at 15 knots. H.M. Ships KING GEORGE V and HOWE were in open order line ahead and screened by 25th Destroyer Flotilla and H.M. Ships EURYALUS and BLACK PRINCE who occupied the two port, i.e. inshore, positions on the screen. H.M.S. SWIFTSURE, H.M.N.Z.S. GAMBIA and H.M.C.S. UGANDA in open order line ahead were stationed 270° 3 miles, i.e. fire off port quarter of the Fleet Flagship. Conditions were ideal.

At 1205 fire was opened. H.M. Ships EURYALUS and BLACK PRINCE carried out a simultaneous "air burst" shoot on the A.A. defence area of Nobara airfield. H.M. Ships KING GEORGE V and HOWE bombarded Hirara airfield and the A.A. defence area to the north of the airfield, respectively. On completion of the "air burst" shoot H.M. Ships SWIFTSURE and H.M.N.Z.S. GAMBIA bombarded Nobara airfield, and H.M.C.S. UGANDA Sukama air strip.

In spite of comparatively close ranges, no form of opposition from the shore was encountered. Fire was ceased at 1250.

Photographs show that the runways at Nobara and Sukama were well hit and that all rounds from H.M.S. HOWE fell in the target area, but no photographs were obtained to show results by H.M.S. KING GEORGE V.

A few minutes after bombardment was commenced I received a signal from A.C.I to say that H.M.S. FORMIDABLE had been hit and was reduced to 18 knots. I accordingly informed the Bombarding Force and instructed ships to speed up the bombardment. As signals were corrupt and the situation not quite clear I ordered the cease fire a little earlier than planned and at 1247 turned the force to the southward and closed the carriers at 25 knots.

As soon as the Bombarding Force had disengaged, A.C.I formed the eight destroyers left with him so that two destroyers were equally spaced between each carrier and on the line joining adjacent carriers. This provided the best natural gun support and clear arcs of fire.

At about 1100 three small groups of bogeys were detected to the westward, and were soon followed up by a fourth. Probably 16 to 20 enemy aircraft were employed with some acting as decoys. Fighters engaged one group working round to the southward, but one Kamikaze group penetrated to the carriers and was first detected when a plane was seen diving on the Force. Analysis shows that this group escaped detection either because, in the absence of the Bombarding Force, too many of the reduced number of radar sets were fully engaged tracking the diversionary planes and too few acting as warning sets, or else because they made a very low approach followed by a very high climb at about I5 miles range.

There were no bandits on the screen within 20 miles when at II3I a Zeke was seen diving from a great height on to H.M.S. FORMIDABLE and engaged by gunfire. A.C.I thereupon manoeuvred his Force under wheel at high speed by successive emergency turns. Though reported hit by close range weapons from his target, the Kamikaze crashed into the flight deck of H.M.S. FORMIDABLE near the island structure and started a large fire in the deck park of aircraft. A.C.I manoeuvred the formation to keep in close touch with the damaged ship, whose speed was temporarily reduced to I8 knots.

The Kamikaze appeared to release his bomb just before the aircraft hit the deck, causing the following damage: casualties 8 killed and 47 wounded; I Corsair and I0 Avengers damaged, beyond repair; all radar except one set put out of action; both barriers damaged, the forward one irreparable; flight deck holed 2 feet square, indentation I0 feet square and 2 feet deep at the centre; armoured deck splinter passed through hangar deck, horizontal partition between down takes, escape hatch which was shut, and so to the centre boiler room where it caused slight damage and loss of steam, and finally pierced the inner bottom.

Two minutes later, at II33, 2 enemy aircraft crashed in flames ten miles to the southward, the result of our fighters.

At II34 a Zeke flying from forward to aft off the starboard bow of H.M.S. INDOMITABLE was engaged by 4.5 in. guns and temporarily disappeared in cloud. It soon reappeared diving at the ship as steeply as about 60° from the starboard beam. The Force was turning to starboard at the time and H.M.S. INDOMITABLE's wheel was increased to hard over. As the plane approached it was heavily engaged by close range weapons from the ship and set on fire; it flattened out at the last moment, deck landed on the flight deck, and bounded over the side, taking the radar arrays of the port midships directors with it. The bomb appeared to explode shortly after the plane submerged.

At II42 another Zeke dived steeply on H.M.S. INDOMITABLE whose close range weapons and those of H.M.S. QUALITY hit him hard and often. The aircraft burst into flames and crashed into the sea about I0 yards off the starboard bow of the ship.

No damage or casualties were sustained in either of these two attacks, apart from that caused to the radar arrays.

Meanwhile the fires in H.M.S. FORMIDABLE were soon under control, and by I254 the ship was capable of 24 knots. It was estimated that one barrier would be in action by I600, and that the flight deck hole would be patched by then.

At I2I5 it became necessary to turn into the wind and land on fighters, although enemy aircraft were known to be still in the vicinity. Aircraft from H.M.S. FORMIDABLE were landed on the other carriers.

At I220 a Jill* was shot down by fighters from H.M.S. INDOMITABLE and half an hour later a Val met the same fate by Seafires from H.M.S. INDEFATIGABLE. By I420 the Bombarding Force was being manoeuvred close to the Carrier Force, and the Fleet reformed in Cruising Disposition at 1450.

As the strike programme planned for the day had been completed, and as considerable reorganisation was necessary with the flight deck of H.M.S. FORMIDABLE out of action, the Fleet commenced withdrawing to the south eastward. By 1700 H.M.S. FORMIDABLE was able to receive 13 of her Corsairs – a fine recovery.

At about 1515 Corsairs from H.M.S. VICTORIOUS intercepted and shot down a Judy to the northward.

Although at various times during the afternoon there were enemy aircraft in the vicinity, it was not until 1720 that the development of another attack became evident. This was however broken up very satisfactorily by our fighters. At 1721 a Judy, believed to be the Gestapo of the Group, was shot down from 24,000 feet to the eastward by fighters. A few minutes later Seafires from H.M.S. INDEFATIGABLE intercepted 4 Zekes to the southward and shot down 3 before the other escaped to the northward.

At 1732 a Hellcat returning for an emergency landing was fired on by H.M.S. FORMIDABLE and hit. The aircraft crashed but the pilot was rescued unhurt by H.M.S. UNDAUNTED.

At 1820 Corsairs from H.M.S. VICTORIOUS were sent to intercept a bogey to the northward. They found and shot down the Zeke.

At 1945 CTF 57 assumed tactical command. A total of 14 enemy aircraft, all airborne, were destroyed during the day, 11 by fighters, 2 shot down by gunfire including one which bounded off the deck of H.M.S. INDOMITABLE, and 1 originally damaged by gunfire but which completed its suicide dive on H.M.S. FORMIDABLE. Several small vessels around the islands were damaged. Our losses totalled 15. In combat 1 Avenger. Other causes: 11 Avengers, 1 Seafire, 1 Hellcat, 1 Corsair, including 1 Corsair and 10 Avengers by bomb damage in H.M.S. FORMIDABLE.

Tonnage of bombs dropped on targets – 43¾ tons plus 50 rocket projectiles.

5th May.

As the state of affairs in H.M.S. FORMIDABLE was not clear, the programme for the day was arranged on the basis that the ship would keep 8 fighters at readiness to reinforce the CAP if required. At 0420 the ship reported that repairs to her centre boiler room were complete and that full speed was available.

A.C.1 assumed tactical command at 0500, and at 0545 the first CAP was flown off in position 23° 10' N. 125° 29' E.

Runways on Miyako and Ishigaki were well bombed again, and all of them left unserviceable by the end of the day. A CAP was maintained over each island.

Three operational aircraft were found on the ground and destroyed, and a petrol dump was left blazing. It was noteworthy that no flak at all was encountered over

Miyako, and it is hoped that the previous day's bombardment was responsible for this at least temporary change for the airmen.

The American Dumbo rescue aircraft was again maintained by CTF 5I between the Fleet and the target from 0830 till I700.

A high snooper was detected at about 0730 and a long chase of 300 miles followed. This eventually finished at 0920 when Corsairs of H.M.S. FORMIDABLE, but operating from H.M.S. VICTORIOUS, splashed the Zeke 80 miles from the Fleet and from 30,000 feet – a good result.

During the day 2 Avengers escorted by fighters were sent to Keramo Retto with press material and Comdr. A. Kimmins, Royal Navy.

Enemy losses:

Destroyed – airborne I, on ground 3; total 4.
Probably damaged – on ground 2.

Own losses:

In combat nil, operational I Corsair, 2 Seafires; total 3.

Tonnage of bombs dropped on targets – 3I tons plus 56 R/P.

At I905 the Fleet withdrew and set course for area Cootie. CTF 57 assumed tactical command at I945.

6th May.

At 0630 met in area Cootie, H.M. and H.M.A. Ships CRANE, RULER, STRIKER, NAPIER, NORMAN, NEPAL, AVON, WHIMBREL, PHEASANT, and R.F.A.s WAVE KING, WAVE MONARCH, SAN AMBROSIO, SAN ADOLPHO, CEDARDALE.

H.M.A.S. NAPIER joined TF 57 vice H.M.S. KEMPENFELT with defects.

Fuelling from the tankers and exchange of aircraft with H.M.S. STRIKER continued throughout the day.

Casualties from H.M.S. FORMIDABLE were transferred to H.M.S. STRIKER, who in company with H.M.S. KEMPENFELT, took departure at I9I5 for Leyte. The need for a hospital ship in the vicinity was considered and CTF II2 was requested to sail one as soon as ready if Admiralty instructions could by now be complied with. At I534 CAP aircraft were sent to investigate a surface radar contact to the north eastward and identified a northbound U.S. armed merchant vessel in company with a U.S. hospital ship.

At I845 the Fleet detached from the Tanker Group for the night.

U.S. Task Group 52.I covered Sakishima.

7th May.

At 0615 Cruising Disposition was formed on the tankers, and fuelling recommenced.

Fuelling and exchange of stores, mail and correspondence were completed by 1400, when the Fleet disengaged from the tankers.

H.M.A.S. NORMAN was ordered to escort R.F.A.s WAVE KING and WAVE MONARCH to Leyte, and H.M. Ships WHIMBREL and AVON similarly escorted R.F.A.s SAN AMBROSIO, SAN ADOLPHO and CEDARDALE.

During this day and yesterday H.M.S. FORMIDABLE was busy making good bomb damage, and became fully operational.

At 1400 the Fleet in Cruising Disposition took departure for the operations area.

Late this night the very satisfactory and gratifying news of the unconditional surrender of the German Armed Forces to the Allies was received. Active operations were ordered to cease at 0001B on 9th May, 1945.

U.S. Task Group 52.1 covered Sakishima.

8th May.

The plan for the day was to bomb Miyako and Ishigaki, to maintain the usual island CAPS, and also to bombard Ishigaki runways and A.A. positions with the battleships and 6 in. cruisers. The Carrier Squadron, supported by both 5.25 in. cruisers and 8 destroyers were to close Ishigaki behind the bombarding force until such time as land echoes would just not interfere with air warning.

The weather deteriorated during the night, and at 0400 as the forecast gave no hope of improvement, the plan to bombard was cancelled in favour of one to carry out four bomber strikes following previous patterns.

At 0515 A.C.I assumed tactical command, and at 0600 CAPS for the islands and Fleet were flown off in position 22° 53' N. 125° 40' E. The weather was overcast and raining at the time, and the island CAPS soon reported similar conditions with the islands difficult to locate. The first strike was therefore cancelled. It was decided to remain in the operating area to await better weather, but at 1015 the island CAPS reported no improvement and the meteorological chart showed Formosa to be shut down by similar weather.

Since it was thus evident that Sakishima could be of no use to the enemy in such conditions, at 1050 the Fleet withdrew to the south eastward, maintaining a reduced CAP.

Although the weather forecast for the following day promised deterioration rather than improvement I informed Commander 5th Fleet of the withdrawal due to weather, and of my intention to strike on 9th and 10th May. Plans for bombardment on 9th May were abandoned. At 1805, just after the last CAP for the day had been flown off, visibility shut down completely with continuous heavy rain. There were indications of clearer weather to the westward and course was shaped towards it. It was with difficulty that fighters were vectored back to the Fleet and searchlights were burned to aid them. At 1905 the fighters at sea level, having sighted the searchlights, reached the Fleet and were flown on.

CTF 57 assumed tactical command at 1920.

9th May.

At 0510 A.C.I assumed tactical command. The weather although showery was much improved and continued to do so during the day.

At 0545 the CAPS were flown off in position 23° 06' N. 126° 00' E. Weather over the targets was reported as satisfactory. All runways at Hirara were reported as serviceable.

Four bomber strikes were flown off during the day, two to each island, the first being launched at 0830 in position 23° 40' N. 125° 34' E. All runways were re-cratered, a direct hit was scored on one aircraft on the ground at Miyako. A motor transport park at Ishigaki was attacked, three vehicles being destroyed for certain.

Low flying fighters discovered a Val hidden in a cave: Firing through the entrance to the cave they destroyed the enemy in flames.

At 1145 the Fleet was sighted by a bogey which approached within 30 miles. Fighters drove it off but were unable to catch it.

At 1645 bogeys were detected very low 22 miles to the westward, coming in fast. Four Seafires intercepted at 15 miles, but allowed themselves to be all decoyed away by one aircraft which they shot down. Meanwhile four other enemy planes evaded another division of Seafires, and after climbing to about 3,000 feet penetrated to the Fleet.

From 1650 onwards the Fleet was radically manoeuvred by emergency turns at 22 knots. One minute after such a turn of 60° to starboard was executed, a suicider made a 10° angle dive onto H.M.S. VICTORIOUS from her starboard quarter. The enemy was well hit by close range weapons but crashed onto the flight deck near the forward lift. The resulting fire was quickly brought under control, but the bomb explosion holed the flight deck, put the accelerator out of action, rendered one 4.5 in., gun unserviceable, and damaged one lift hoisting motor.

At 1656 another Kamikaze made a shallow power glide from astern on H.M.S. VICTORIOUS. Though hit hard by gunfire, and well on fire, it hit the flight deck aft a glancing blow, and burning furiously passed over the side. Damage to the ship was confined to one arrester unit out of action, a 40 mm. gun director destroyed, and four Corsairs on deck damaged beyond repair.

Casualties from both these attacks were three killed, four seriously injured, and 15 wounded. At 1657 a third suicider made a pass at H.M.S. VICTORIOUS but then shifted target to H.M.S. HOWE further ahead, and approached her from the starboard quarter in a long shallow dive. This time the attacker was hit at a more reasonable range, and continued to be so until he crashed in flames 100 yards from H.M.S. HOWE after passing over the quarterdeck.

At 1705 a fourth Kamikaze approached H.M.S. FORMIDABLE and then H.M.S.

INDOMITABLE, being engaged by both ships without apparent result. It then turned and dived into the after deck park of H.M.S. FORMIDABLE.

There was a large explosion and fire and a great deal of smoke. Speed was reduced to I5 knots to aid control of the fire which was extinguished at I720. Six Corsairs and one Avenger were destroyed by fire on deck. The explosion blew out a flight deck rivet and thus allowed burning petrol to fall into the hangar which had to be sprayed. As a result a further three Avengers and eight Corsairs were damaged. The total replacements required were therefore four Avengers and I4 Corsairs, of which three Avengers and seven Corsairs were flyable duds.

Casualties were fortunately light – one killed and a few injured.

At I755 H.M.S. FORMIDABLE reported being fit to land on aircraft and that during the engagement she had definitely shot down one enemy by gunfire.

The state of the Carrier Squadron was as follows. H.M. Ships FORMIDABLE and VICTORIOUS could operate, but the former had only four bombers and II fighters serviceable, and also had two pom-pom mountings out of action. H.M.S. VICTORIOUS could operate a few aircraft at a time, but the damage to her lift seriously reduced her speed of handling. In the circumstances I concurred with a recommendation from A.C.I that the Fleet should withdraw to fuel, sort out and make good the damage, etc. and return to strike on I2th/I3th May. I informed Commander 5th Fleet of this intention, and at I950 course was set for area Cootie.

As TG 52.I had been ordered to cover Sakishima on days when TF 57 was not striking, I am afraid that the two alterations to programme, dictated first by weather and then by damage consideration, must have caused inconvenience to CTG 52.I; this is regretted.

CTF 57 assumed tactical command at 2000.

During the day 8 enemy aircraft were destroyed, 2 on the ground, 3 by suicide, 2 by gunfire and I by fighters. Also on the ground I was probably destroyed and I probably damaged. Our losses were:- in combat I Corsair; by bomb damage I0 Corsairs destroyed, 7 Corsairs, I Avenger damaged probably beyond repair.

Total tonnage of bombs dropped on targets was 7I tons plus 64 R/P. Several small craft near Ishigaki suicide boat base were damaged, and one was sunk.

10th May.

At 06I0 in position Cootie (I) met and formed on Tanker Group consisting of H.M. Ships SPEAKER, RULER, NEPAL, CRANE, PHEASANT, WHYALLA, BALLARAT, WOODCOCK, WEASEL (Tug) and R.F.A.s ARNDALE, AASE MAERSK, DINGLEDALE, SAN AMADO. The usual fuelling, exchange of mail correspondence and stores, and the replenishment of aircraft continued throughout the day.

A.C.I visited H.M. Ships VICTORIOUS and FORMIDABLE to inspect damage, and found that temporary repairs being carried out showed that both ships would be sufficiently operational to continue the programme of strikes.

A.C.I and C.S.4 then visited me to discuss measures to give better protection to the carriers, and in the light of the enemy's apparent change of tactics in attacks on this Force. The enemy appeared to have abandoned his previous practice of a high approach in favour of a low one, thereby greatly reducing the length of warning and making interception by fighters much more difficult.

To combat this, it was decided:-

(*a*) To station two radar pickets, each consisting of a 6 in. cruiser and a destroyer, 12 miles to the north west and south westward of the Fleet so as to increase the range of detection. Two fighters would be allocated to each picket, and at first contact with the enemy, other fighters would be sent to the threatened sector.

(*b*) To bring in the 5.25 in. cruisers from the screen and to station them with the main body of the Fleet to increase A.A. protection for the carriers whenever in the operation area.

(*c*) To station a destroyer astern of each carrier to afford more gun protection in what appears to be the enemy's favourite position for attacking carriers.

(*d*) To increase mutual gun support when attack threatened by bringing in the carriers to the 2,000 yards circle, and the battleships and cruisers of the main body until their distance from adjacent carriers is 2,000 yards. This new disposition was to be given a trial during the next strike period.

The question of reducing the distance between ships had been under review for some time: there are many factors to take into consideration, not least of these being the interference caused to flying in and off and forming up. Its adoption for trial now is a measure of the improvement of the pilots' skill, etc., during the present operations.

The Fleet was also instructed that in future attacks enemy aircraft must be brought under fire much earlier than has been the case recently. Commanding Officers of ships were ordered to give this matter their personal attention. At 1915 the Fleet disengaged from the Tanker Group for the night.

11th May.

At 0640 Cruising Disposition was again formed on the Tanker Group, and all fuelling and transfer of stores, aircraft, correspondence, and personnel was completed in time for the Fleet to disengage at 1640 and take departure for the operations area.

H.M.S. KEMPENFELT, having made good defects at Leyte, was met at 0630 and rejoined TF 57.

H.M.A.S. NEPAL, released from escort duty, joined TF 57. In the afternoon H.M.S. SPEAKER escorted by H.M.S. QUEENBOROUGH, who had developed shaft vibration, was sent back to Leyte, as were the R.F.A.s AASE MAERSK, SAN AMADO, escorted by H.M. Ships BALLARAT and WHYALLA.

American Task Unit 52.1.3 covered Sakishima during 10th and 11th May and reported the result of their neutralising operations there.

A.C.I assumed tactical command at 0510, and at 0520 the four counter-Kamikaze destroyers took station one close astern of each carrier.

The radar pickets, H.M. Ships SWIFTSURE with KEMPENFELT, and UGANDA with WESSEX, were stationed 12 miles 315° and 225° respectively from the Fleet centre.

Cruising Disposition was formed.

In overcast weather, the Fleet and island CAPS and the first bomber strike were flown off at 0540, twelve minutes before sunrise, from a position 23° 40' N. 126° 51' E.

Four bomber strikes were flown off during the day. One attacked Ishigaki and three Miyako; a second strike on Ishigaki had been planned but had to be cancelled owing to weather conditions. At Ishigaki, Miyara and Ishigaki runways, which were found to be serviceable, were again put out of action and A.A. and dispersal areas were straffed. No new aircraft nor activity were found. The squadron leader of 1844 Squadron was regrettably lost in his Hellcat to A.A. fire when bombing A.A. positions.

At Miyako, one runway at Hirara and both at Nobara were found to be serviceable. By the end of the first strike this position was reversed, and subsequent strikes attacked A.A. positions and installations. A large oil fire was started, a direct hit made on a 4 in. A.A. Battery, Hirara Barracks hit, and 3 aircraft found on the ground were probably damaged.

An Avenger with engine trouble ditched 75 miles west of the Fleet at 0805. The U.S.S. BLUEFISH proceeded to the position (in the Air Surface Zone), and at 1515 rescued the crew. A CAP of four Corsairs was sent to cover the submarine. The Dumbo aircraft, maintained in readiness at Keramo Retto, took off and also assisted in directing this rescue.

At 0937 another Avenger was forced to ditch, giving a position 100 miles in error from the actual position. The helio flashing of the crew at 1540 was fortunately seen by Fireflies returning to the Fleet, and H.M.S. KEMPENFELT was led to the spot by Dumbo aircraft and rescued them.

No enemy aircraft were airborne in the vicinity of the Fleet or islands during the day.

At 1915 the radar pickets rejoined. At 1930 the dusk CAP was landed on and the Fleet withdrew to the southward for the night.

CTF 57 assumed tactical command at 2010.

The score for the day was:-

3 enemy aircraft probably damaged on the ground.

65½ tons of bombs and 32 R/P directed at targets.

A 200 ton coaster damaged.

Own losses:- in combat 1 Hellcat, 1 Avenger; operationally 1 Avenger, 1 Corsair, 1 Seafire; total 5.

13th May.

At 05I0 A.C.I assumed tactical command.

Radar pickets and counter-Kamikaze destroyers were stationed, and at 0540 Fleet and Islands CAPS were flown off in position 24° 20' N. I26° 55' E. in fine weather.

The island CAPS reported that Ishigaki runways were again serviceable and a thin strip of Miyara runway had been repaired. At Miyako one runway at Hirara and both at Nobara had been made possibly serviceable.

Four bomber strikes were flown during the day, three to Miyako and one to Ishigaki.

At Miyako all runways were left unserviceable, a barracks was straffed, 8 barges were hit, and 3 major oil fires started.

The position of a new revetted dispersal area discovered at Hirara was reported to the Commander 5th Fleet and other interested U.S. authorities.

At Ishigaki camouflaged buildings and storage dumps were hit, as were two radio stations one of which was left in flames.

At 0948 a possible submarine contact was obtained close to the Fleet in position 24° 20' N. I26° 48' E. Three destroyers were detached to hunt with a CAP of 4 Corsairs.

At I203 a possible contact was attacked with depth charges, and 2 Avengers were flown off for Fleet ASP, and another armed with depth charges was sent to assist the hunt. The possible contact was later reported as stationary, and although the hunt was continued throughout the afternoon no S/M contact was found, nor is it now considered that a S/M was ever present.

An Avenger returning to land on H.M.S. FORMIDABLE was unable to lower flaps and one wheel. As it was undesirable to risk damage to the only remaining barrier in H.M.S. FORMIDABLE, the aircraft was ordered to land on H.M.S. INDOMITABLE. This the pilot did with skill and judgment and with very minor damage to his aircraft.

Again there was no enemy air activity near the Fleet or islands.

At I920 the dusk CAP was landed on and the Fleet withdrew to fuel in area Cootie. CTF 57 assumed tactical command at I950.

The score for the day was:-

Enemy aircraft destroyed and damaged, nil.

62¼ tons bombs plus 34 R/P directed at targets.
9 camouflaged barges and a few small craft damaged.

Own losses:- in combat nil;

Operationally I Seafire.

14th May.

At 0630 in area Cootie met H.M. Ships RULER, CRANE, WOODCOCK, PHEASANT, WEASEL and R.F.A.s ARNDALE and DINGLEDALE from whom fuelling commenced. The other and incoming Tanker Group were late at the rendezvous. They were found by search aircraft from the CAP and directed to the Fleet and consisted of H.M. Ships STRIKER, NIZAM and R.F.A.s WAVE KING and WAVE MONARCH. They were in station by II00.

Forty tons of bombs were transferred by H.M.S. BLACK PRINCE from H.M.S. FORMIDABLE to H.M.S. INDEFATIGABLE. This was necessary because the dimensions of American bombs supplied to ships at Leyte had prevented the full number required being stowed in H.M.S. INDEFATIGABLE. This transfer was made expeditiously, rate of embarkation rising to about one a minute as experience was gained.

During the forenoon, search aircraft were sent to direct the hospital ship TJITJALENGKA to the Fleet. This ship had been sent at my request to remain at call within 30 miles of a position 85 miles to the eastward of the normal dawn position of the Fleet in the fuelling area. Casualties by now fit to be moved, were transferred to TJITJALENGKA by destroyer in the afternoon.

During the day Sakishima was covered by TU 52.I.3.

At I9I0 the Fleet disengaged from the Tanker Group for the night.

At this stage it became necessary to consider the date on which the Fleet would leave the operations area for major storing in the rear bases. The tankers and repair ships of the Fleet Train, based at Leyte, require early notice of a firm date for redisposition, in order that with their slow speed they might reach their new stations in time to meet the Fleet and fulfil their functions.

As the Fleet was due at the storing ports early in June, and as it was evident that a considerable amount of work would be required to make good the battle damage to carriers, it appeared desirable to conclude operations with the twelfth strike day on 25th May, and so ensure the Fleet being ready to resume operations when required in July.

After consultation with A.C.I, I accordingly sent the following signal:-

Action COM 5th Fleet C IN C PAC both Info C.-in-C., B.P.F. VA(Q) FONAS(A) CTF II2

From CTF 57

Propose with your concurrence TF57 continues present strikes until 24 and 25 May then CTF57 in KING GEORGE V, 3 destroyers proceed Guam arriving I000 28th leave 0600 30th for Manus. If you concur request authority these four ships fuel with U.S. supplies Guam. Remainder TF57 to Manus after fuelling Cootie 26th arriving in forenoon 30th. Could carry out further strikes if losses remain light on 28th and 29th May which would delay above programme for four days. CTF II2 will divert slow tankers to Manus or Cootie which necessitates early decision on your needs.

15 May.

The Fleet reformed on the Tanker Group at 0630, and fuelling and exchange of stores, aircraft and correspondence was continued and completed by 1700.

H.M. Ships TROUBRIDGE and TENACIOUS joined TF 57.

H.M.A.S. NEPAL from TU 112.2.5 joined TF57.

Captain D.25 in GRENVILLE joined TU 112.2.5 to be left in the servicing area, and Captain D.4 in H.M.S. QUILLIAM assumed Senior Officer Destroyers. This was done, with the concurrence of Rear Admiral Destroyers, in order to give different Captains D experience as the Senior Officer.

The following were detached to Leyte in the afternoon:-

H.M. Ships STRIKER and NAPIER.

H.M.A.S. NIZAM with R.F.A.s WAVE KING and WAVE MONARCH.

H.M. Ships PHEASANT and WOODCOCK with R.F.A.s ARNDALE and DINGLEDALE. It had been hoped that H.M.A.S. NIZAM would join TF 57 for the next two strike periods, but she was not fit for operations owing to a small number of cases of infantile paralysis, for which she remained in quarantine.

TU 52.1.3 again covered Sakishima today.

At 1705 the Fleet disengaged from the Tanker Group and departure was taken for the operations area.

During the day the following signals were received :-

CTF 57.
From COM 5th Fleet

Not necessary, keep up coverage of Sakishima after 25th.

CTF 57.
From CINCPAC

Arrival KING GEORGE V and 3 destroyers Guam 28th May approved. Will be pleased welcome you. Guam has available fuel for topping off.

16th May.

At 0510 A.C.I assumed tactical command. Radar pickets were sent out and counter-Kamikaze destroyers closed their carriers.

At 0540 in position 23° 40' N. 126° 51' E. the Fleet and island CAPS and the first bomber strike for Miyako were flown off.

Five bomber strikes were sent to the islands during the day, three to Miyako and two to Ishigaki. As the result of these and the efforts of the CAPS, all runways were made unserviceable; four new aircraft which appeared operational were straffed but did not burn, 3 others were damaged; 10 small craft of various classes were damaged and four of them left in a sinking condition; 4 lorry loads of Japanese troops were exterminated; a large explosion was caused in Ohama town; 5 direct hits with S.A.P. bombs were made on a large cave shelter.

Several of our planes were damaged by flak.

One Avenger taking off from H.M.S. FORMIDABLE ditched; H.M.S. QUALITY rescued the crew one of whom was injured. A Corsair from H.M.S. VICTORIOUS developed engine trouble at 20,000 feet and was forced to ditch near the Fleet; H.M.S. TENACIOUS rescued the pilot.

At 1735 a Corsair from H.M.S. VICTORIOUS ditched 3 miles from Miyako; the Lifeguard submarine U.S.S. BLUEFISH was informed and made another skilful rescue by picking up this pilot during the night. The Dumbo aircraft from Kerama Retto, unaware of the rescue, as was A.C.I at the time, carried out a search the following morning. These fine efforts by the American rescue submarines and aircraft have been greatly appreciated.

The dusk CAP landed on at 1935 and the Fleet withdrew to the southward for the night. No enemy were airborne in the vicinity during the day.

CTF 57 assumed tactical Command at 1950.

Seven enemy aircraft were damaged on the ground. 77¼ tons of bombs and 112 R/P were expended on the targets, 2 suicide type boats were sunk, 2 small craft were probably sunk, and a large number of assorted types of barge and small craft were damaged, several being left in flames. Our own losses were:- in combat 1 Corsair; operationally 2 Corsairs, 1 Avenger, 1 Seafire.

17th May.

At 0510 A.C.I assumed tactical command, and the usual radar pickets and counter-Kamikaze destroyers were stationed.

The day broke with very light winds of only one or two knots, a state of affairs which persisted and proved a handicap throughout the day. The state of boiler brickwork in several ships, and the defective centre stern tube bush in H.M.S. INDOMITABLE, made high speeds most undesirable. Without high speed, little safety margin was left for operating aircraft.

At 0540 the Fleet and island CAPS were flown off from a position 85 miles 110° from Miyako. It had been planned to send in four bomber strikes, two to each island, but the second strike to Ishigaki was cancelled owing to damage to H.M.S. VICTORIOUS barriers by deck crashes, and the very light winds accentuating the defective stern bush in H.M.S. INDOMITABLE. All airfields were left unserviceable except Miyara which may not have been sufficiently cratered. Ohama and Hirara towns were bombed, and barges and small craft were well straffed.

A number of Japanese soldiers were discovered; their names will in due course be recorded in Yasakuni Shrine.

At 0742 a Corsair making an emergency landing on H.M.S. VICTORIOUS removed 2 arrester wires, crashed through both barriers, burst into flames and passed over the side. On its way it seriously damaged 2 Corsairs and I Avenger in the deck park. One officer and one rating were mortally injured, 2 ratings seriously injured and two others slightly hurt.

The ship reported that 2 jury barriers would be rigged but that it would take some time to do so. It became necessary therefore to distribute the ship's airborne aircraft to other carriers. At 1145 H.M.S. VICTORIOUS reported that 2 jury barriers were ready, and arrangements were therefore made to land on her aircraft. Though the first landed on safely, the second aircraft bounced in the gap left by the removal of the 2 arrester wires and demolished one of the jury barriers. The second jury barrier was removed 2 hours later by a similar cause.

As a result 20 aircraft from the ship, had to be accommodated in other carriers, causing congestion and offering three attractive targets of deck parked aircraft to any Kamikaze. Fortunately enemy aircraft were conspicuous by their absence throughout the day.

At 1200 a Hellcat from H.M.S. INDOMITABLE was ordered to bale out just ahead of the Fleet as the pilot was unable to release an armed bomb. The pilot was picked up by H.M.S. TROUBRIDGE.

By 1715 H.M.S. VICTORIOUS had once again rigged jury barriers and was able to accept some of her aircraft from other carriers.

CAPS were maintained until 1915, when radar pickets were recalled, and the Fleet withdrew to area Cootie to fuel.

CTF 57 assumed tactical command, at 1940.

Enemy aircraft destroyed or damaged, nil. 56 tons of bombs and 30 R/P expended on targets. Many barges and small craft damaged and several left burning. Own losses:- in combat I Corsair; operationally I Hellcat, I Corsair, I Avenger, I Seafire.

I informed British authorities concerned of the actual dates for arrival of units of the Fleet at the various ports of replenishment.

18th May.

At 0545 met in area Cootie H.M. Ships CRANE, RULER, GRENVILLE, CHASER, NORMAN, WHIMBREL, BENDIGO, PARRETT, WEASEL and R.F.A.s SAN AMBROSIO, SAN ADOLPHO, CEDARDALE. The Fleet formed on the Tanker Group and fuelling and exchange of aircraft and stores commenced.

H.M.S. BLACK PRINCE transferred bombs from H.M.S. FORMIDABLE to H.M.S. INDEFATIGABLE.

At 1103 H.M.S. FORMIDABLE was observed to be on fire, caused by a Corsair in the hangar accidentally firing her guns into an Avenger: the latter exploded. Fighting this serious fire was made difficult by the fact that the fire curtains were out of action due to earlier enemy suicide attacks. It was extinguished by drenching the hangar, but at a cost of 7 Avengers and 21 Corsairs in conditions varying from complete loss to flyable duds. By the evening the Commanding Officer reported that he considered his ship capable of operating with jury lighting in the hangar. Arrangements were therefore made to replace her damaged aircraft as far as possible, and for the ship to continue operations at any rate for the next strike period. As the repaired barriers in H.M.S. VICTORIOUS could not be guaranteed to stand up to further barrier crashes or enemy damage the availability of H.M.S. FORMIDABLE's flight deck was an important factor, and in any case, it would only lower her morale were she unable to continue in the Fleet.

At 1800 the Tanker Group were turned to the reverse course to enable them to rendezvous with the Ammunition Carrier ROBERT MAERSK expected in position Cootie (I) at 0600 the following morning. Meanwhile the transfer of bombs by cruiser continued until dark.

H.M.S. WHIMBREL was detached with mails to Leyte.

American Task Group 52.I covered Sakishima.

19th May.

At 0645 the Fleet again formed on the Tanker Group, which now included the ROBERT MAERSK with supplies of bombs, and H.M.S. CAIRNS. The transfer of bombs, fuel and stores was continued. H.M.S. VICTORIOUS and later H.M.S. INDOMITABLE went alongside ROBERT MAERSK and embarked bombs by whip and inhaul method, the rate of transfer being about 75 bombs per hour.

Continuous rain and low visibility in the afternoon prevented flying and seriously upset the numbers of replenishment aircraft to be flown in to H.M.S. FORMIDABLE and the flyable duds which were to be flown from her to H.M.S. CHASER.

Hospital ship TJITJALENGKA was contacted by aircraft and directed to the Fleet: she embarked a few sick and casualties.

H.M.A.S. NORMAN joined TF 57 replacing H.M.A.S. NEPAL. Captain D. 27 in H.M.S. KEMPENFELT assumed Senior Officer Destroyers for experience, vice Captain D. 4 in QUILLIAM who remained with the Force.

At 1800 detached H.M. Ships BENDIGO and CAIRNS with R.F.A.s SAN AMBROSIO, SAN ADOLPHO and CEDARDALE to Manus. H.M.S. PARRETT acted as additional escort to them until dusk on 2Ist, May, with orders to detach and proceed to Leyte at that time. At 1930 H.M.A.S. NEPAL was detached to Leyte to augment the escorts available to CTF II2 for the forthcoming move south of the Fleet Train.

At 1930 the Fleet took departure for the operations area.

American Task Group 52.I covered Sakishima.

20th May.

The flying-off position for the day was to be 23° 39' N. I26° 40" E.

First light was at 0458 when clouds were low and about 8/I0 and the horizon clear.

At 0500 the four "KK" destroyers including H.M.S. QUILLIAM, left the screen as previously arranged, and started to close their carriers to form astern of them. The Fleet was proceeding at 16 knots.

At 0510 A.C.I assumed tactical command. The clouds were low and rain had started. A.C.I therefore ordered the postponement of flying off aircraft for 15 minutes.

At 0515 the Fleet ran into dense fog. At 0524 H.M.S. QUILLLAM, endeavouring to form astern of H.M.S. INDOMITABLE, collided with her. Fortunately no casualties were sustained, but superficial above water damage was caused to H.M.S. INDOMITABLE, and serious damage to the bow of H.M.S. QUILLIAM. As soon as the damaged destroyer was clear of the screen, H.M.A.S. NORMAN was ordered to take her in tow. At 0615 H.M.S. BLACK PRINCE was sent to stand by both ships and escort them to area Cootie. The Commander Logistic Support Group was later ordered by signal to despatch from area Cootie H.M. Tug WEASEL to tow, and H.M.S. RULER to provide air cover.

H.M.A.S. NORMAN experienced considerable difficulty in towing H.M.S. QUILLIAM stern first, as the wrecked bow hanging in the water acted as a formidable hard over rudder. By 1300 H.M.S. BLACK PRINCE had taken over the tow, but the same difficulty restricted the towing speed to 3 and later to 5½ knots.

As the weather remained unsuitable for flying, the Fleet was manoeuvred until 0745 so as to cover the damaged destroyer.

At 0745, by which time the weather had improved slightly CAPS and the first strike were flown off. Although 4 bomber strikes were planned, weather conditions throughout the day made only one strike possible and seriously hampered its effectiveness.

Strike Able, after only finding the island with great difficulty bombed Hirara town in Miyako through a clear patch of cloud, while Fireflies rocketted ground installations.

Strikes Baker and Charlie had to be cancelled for weather, and the outlook for strike Dog was far from promising. However, in view of CTF 51's signal stressing the importance of evening strikes on Sakishima in order to reduce the weight of dusk and moonlight attacks on Okinawa, it was decided to make the attempt, and the strike took off at 1530 for Ishigaki. The weather however was so bad that the strike was unable to get through to the island and had to be brought back to the Fleet.

During the forenoon CTG 99.2's signal was received, indicating the intention of that group to strike Miyako with shore based aircraft at 1700. It was therefore decided to withdraw CAPS from that island by 1600. The strike planned for Ishigaki at 1630 was not altered. These intentions were communicated to CTF 51 and CTG 99.2. In the event, however, and presumably because of weather, CTG 99.2 cancelled his strike.

At 1210 two bogeys were detected 50 miles to the westward tracking 040°. Fighters sent to intercept found both aircraft were friendly bombers. No information of their presence nor mission was known to this Force.

At 1000 a Corsair from H.M.S. VICTORIOUS, heavily hit by flak, was reported to have ditched. Fellow Corsairs searched without success for the pilot who they consider could not have survived. At I529 a Corsair ditched on taking off from H.M.S. FORMIDABLE. The pilot was recovered unhurt by the KK destroyer.

At I845 the usual radar pickets were recalled and by I900 all CAPS had landed on; the Fleet withdrew to the southward for the night, and CTF 57 assumed tactical command at I930. At 2I00 TF 57 passed close to H.M.S. BLACK PRINCE who reported that H.M.S. QUILLIAM was satisfactorily in tow.

Enemy aircraft destroyed or damaged, nil.

I junk and 3 barges were damaged.

Bombs dropped on targets, 6½ tons plus 24 R/P.

Own losses:- in combat I Corsair; operationally I Hellcat, I Seafire.

21st May.

A.C.I assumed tactical command at 05I0. Flying-off had been planned for 0540 from a position 85 miles II0° from Miyako. The weather at dawn was similar to the previous day except that the Fleet was clear of fog patches. Flying-off was therefore postponed. Four Hellcats were flown off at 0600 to investigate the weather within a 30 mile radius. They reported clear weather to east and west, and improving weather to the northward. Acting on this information the first strike was flown off at 0655.

Five bomber strikes were sent in, three to Miyako and two to Ishigaki.

Strikes for Miyako were flown off at 0655, I2I0 and I6I0. Nobara and Hirara runways were well plastered with bombs, 2 fires started in the warehouse area of Hirara town, and a radio weather station was hit. A tented camp was straffed.

The Ishigaki strikes took off at 0855 and I440. Both runways at Ishigaki field were left unserviceable and Miyara airfield was hit.

Low cloud varying between 7/I0 and 9/I0 made bombing difficult at both islands.

At I423 a high snooper was detected approaching the Fleet from the westward. Fighters were ordered to 30,000 feet and at I442 intercepted 36 miles to the south westward at 26,000 feet. The enemy, a Myrt, was shot down 4 minutes later by Hellcats from H.M.S. INDOMITABLE.

One airborne enemy aircraft was shot down. Several barges were damaged.

55¼ tons of bombs plus 95 R/P were dropped on targets.

Own losses:- in combat nil; operationally I Avenger and 2 Seafires.

During the day Commander Third Fleet's signal was received. This indicated the nature of future operations for the British Pacific Fleet. In the light of this, and after consulting A.C.I, it was decided to release H.M.S. FORMIDABLE early for repair of battle damage. It was felt that this was necessary to ensure that 4 carriers would be available for operations on completion of the forthcoming storing period. This decision was communicated to Commander Fifth Fleet.

At I930 the dusk CAP were landed on, radar pickets were recalled, and the Fleet withdrew to area Cootie. CTF 57 assumed tactical command at I930.

22nd May.

At 0700 in position Cootie (I) the following were met:-

(*a*) H.M. Tug WEASEL towing H.M.S. QUILLIAM escorted by H.M. Ships BLACK PRINCE, GRENVILLE, NORMAN and RULER.

(*b*) Ships of the Fleet Train consisting of H.M. and H.M.A. Ships CRANE, CHASER, SPEAKER, NAPIER, AVON and FINDHORN, and R.F.A.s WAVE KING, WAVE MONARCH, AASE MAERSK, SAN AMADO, ROBERT MAERSK.

(*c*) Reinforcements H.M. Ships QUADRANT and TERMAGENT who joined TF57.

Captain D. 25 in H.M.S. GRENVILLE rejoined TF 57 as Senior Officer Destroyers, and H.M.S. WESSEX took her place as escort to TU II2.2.5.

Fuelling, and exchange of aircraft and stores and bombs, were carried out throughout the day.

After receiving mails and discharging excess complement the damaged H.M.S. QUILLIAM proceeded in tow of H.M. Tug WEASEL to Leyte, H.M.A.S. NORMAN acting as escort. CTF II2 was requested to arrange for a larger tug to meet and relieve H.M.S. WEASEL. (The American tug TURKEY was kindly sent out from Leyte, where the tow arrived safely on 28th May.)

At I800 H.M.S. FORMIDABLE was detached with orders to proceed to Manus and then Sydney to expedite repair of battle damage. She was escorted by H.M. Ships KEMPENFELT and WHIRLWIND, both of whom were due for refit.

American Task Unit 52.1.3 covered Sakishima on this day.

At I9I5 the Fleet disengaged from the Tanker Group for the night.

23rd May.

At 0745 the Fleet reformed on the Tanker Group, and fuelling and exchange of stores were continued.

H.M.N.Z.S. ACHILLES joined TF 57.

During the day 2 Hellcats from H.M.S. CHASER crashed into the sea: neither pilot was recovered.

Owing to the plummer block on the centre shaft overheating and wiping in H.M.S. INDOMITABLE, her speed had to be limited to 22 knots.

Sakishima was covered by American Task Unit 52.I.3.

At I800 H.M. and H.M.A. Ships CHASER, SPEAKER and NAPIER were detached for Manus.

At I8I5 the Fleet detached from the Tanker Group taking departure for the operations area with only 3 carriers in company. It had been hoped to bombard Miyako on the morrow, but with the reduced number of aircraft available it was judged wiser to forego this plan in favour of an entire air effort.

At 0510 A.C.I assumed tactical command. In view of the absence of H.M.S. FORMIDABLE, it was planned to send in only 4 strikes each day, the first to be flown off 2 hours later than normal so as to provide late afternoon strikes as desired by CTF 51.

At dawn visibility was low, the sky overcast with rain and drizzle. Flying-off was postponed. At 0900 four fighters flown off reported weather improving slowly in the vicinity, and at 1000 it was decided to make 3 strikes during the day, the flying-off position being 23° 40' N. 126° 52' E.

Strikes on Miyako were flown off at 1045 and 1515. Cloud over the target was 10/10 at 6,000 to 9,000 feet. Nobara runways were left unserviceable and Hirara runways were hit. Hirara town and Nishibara were hit by 12 and 4 bombs respectively. A radio station was rocketted, as were camouflaged buildings in the wooded area near Hirara where one large explosion was observed.

The Ishigaki strike took off at 1245. All runways at Ishigaki airfield were left unserviceable. Three hits with 1,600 Ib. bombs were observed on a suspected aircraft storage in a low cliff on the north side of Ishigaki east-west runway. The CAP over Ishigaki found on the ground and probably damaged 2 aircraft believed to be operational.

After a day with no enemy air activity in the vicinity the last CAP was landed on at 1907 and radar pickets were recalled. The Fleet withdrew to the southward for the night, and CTF 57 assumed tactical command at 1940.

2 enemy aircraft were probably damaged on the ground. 31 tons of bombs plus 40 R/P were dropped on targets. Own losses nil.

A.C.I assumed tactical command at 0510.

The unfavourable dawn weather cleared earlier today so that the first strike was able to be flown off at 0600 in position 23° 40' N. 126° 52' E.

3 strikes were sent to Miyako, flying off at 0600, 1115, and 1400. Results of the last strike could not be observed owing to low cloud. 26 hits were observed on Nobara runways which were left unserviceable, and 14 hits were made on Hirara runways. The Amphibious Tank Bases, a barracks, and barges at Osaki were attacked. A fire was started at Sukama town, and the suicide boat base was rocketted.

At Ishigaki 8 bomb hits were made on each of the main Ishigaki and Miyara airfields runways.

It was observed that progress was being made in levelling a new airstrip near Hegina airfield. The returning strike from Ishigaki made contact with U.S.S. BLUEFISH, who reported that during the previous night lights had been observed on Ishigaki airfield. This enterprising submarine commander had therefore bombarded the airfield.

At about 1700 a Corsair returning to the Fleet ditched near her carrier. The pilot was picked up unhurt by the attendant destroyer. There was no enemy air activity in the vicinity all day. All aircraft were flown on by 1910 and the Fleet withdrew.

CTF 57 in H.M.S. KING GEORGE V with H.M. Ships TROUBRIDGE, TENACIOUS and TERMAGENT detached at 2200 and set course for Guam.

The remainder of the Fleet, under the command of A.C.I, set course for area Cootie to top off ships with fuel as necessary for them to reach Manus, and thence to disperse to their rear bases for major storing.

The following signals were subsequently exchanged between C IN C PAC and CTF 57:-

CTF 57 Info C.-in-C., B.P.F. C IN C PAC ADV 5th Fleet

From COM 5th Fleet

I would express to you, to your officers and to your men, after two months operations as a Fifth Fleet Task Force, my appreciation of your fine work and co-operative spirit. Task Force 57 has mirrored the great traditions of the Royal Navy to the American Task Forces. – Spruance.

COM. 5th Fleet Info C IN C PAC ADV C.-in-C., B.P.F.

From CTF 57

We are proud to have been in a position to lend a hand in this crucial operation and hope we may continue so doing until Victory. Will pass your generous message with great personal pleasure, to all of the British Pacific Fleet who have been honoured by serving under you. Regret my Flagship and I were not able to greet you on your return to Guam.

Admiralty footnote:-
* *Jill – Japanese naval torpedo-aircraft.*

ABBREVIATIONS

AA	Anti-aircraft
AB	Able Seaman
AC	Admiral Commanding
ADM	Admiralty
AMC	Armed Merchant Cruiser
AOC-in-C	Air Officer Commanding-in-Chief
A/S	Anti-Submarine
Asdic	Underwater detection device (stands for Anti-Submarine Detection Investigation Committee)
ASPS	Anti-Submarine Patrols
ASV	Air to Surface Vessel
A/T	Anti-Torpedo
Bogey	Unidentified aircraft
BPF	British Pacific Fleet
C.-in-C.	Commander-in-Chief
CAP/CAPS	Combat Air Patrol(s)
CB	Companion of The Most Honourable Order of the Bath
CBE	Commander of the Most Excellent Order of the British Empire
CINCPAC	Commander in Chief, Pacific Command
COM	Commodore; Commander
COMINCH	Commander-in-Chief (US Navy)
CSO	Commander Surface Operations
CTF	Combined Task Force
CTG	Command Training Group (US Navy)
CVO	Commander of the Royal Victorian Order
D/F	Direction Finding
DR	Dead Reckoning
DSC	Distinguished Service Cross
DSEA	Davis Submerged Escape Apparatus (a form of diving equipment)
DSO	Distinguished Service Order
EF	Eastern Fleet (Royal Navy)
GCB	Knight/ Dame Grand Cross of the Most Honourable Order of the

	Bath
GCVO	Knight/Dame Grand Cross of the Royal Victorian Order
GMT	Greenwich Mean Time
HA	High Altitude; High Angle
H/F	High Frequency
H/L	High Level
HLB	High Level Bombing
HM	His Majesty
HMAS	His Majesty's Australian Ship
HMCS	His Majesty's Canadian Ship
HMNZS	His Majesty's New Zealand Ship
HMS	His Majesty's Ship
HMSAS	His Majesty's South African Ship
HMT	His Majesty's Trawler; His Majesty's Troopship
HQ	Head Quarters
HST	Higher Sound Detector
Jack	A patrol aircraft
JCS	Joint Chiefs of Staff
JW	Joint Warfare
KBE	Knight Commander of the Most Excellent Order of the British Empire
KCB	Knight Commander of the Most Honourable Order of the Bath
MBE	Member of the Order of the British Empire
Mc/s	Megacycles per second
M/F	Medium Frequency
M/L	Motor Launch
Mph	Miles per Hour
M/S	Motor Ship; Mine-Sweeping
MT	Motor Tanker
MV, M/V	Motor Vessel
MVO	Member of the Royal Victorian Order
NOIC	Naval Officer in Charge
NUC	Not Under Control
OBE	Officer of the Order of the British Empire
OC	Officer Commanding
ON	Official Number
PNTO	Principal Naval Transport Officer
POA	Pacific Ocean Areas
PR	Photo-Reconnaissance
PRU	Photo-Reconnaissance Unit
PTO	Pacific Theatre of Operations
R Nor. N	Royal Norwegian Navy
RA	Rear Admiral
RAF	Royal Air Force

RAN	Royal Australian Navy
RANVR	Royal Australian Navy Volunteer Reserve
RCN	Royal Canadian Navy
RDF	Radio Direction Finder; Range and Direction Finding; Radar
RFA	Royal Fleet Auxiliary
RFR	Royal Fleet Reserve
RM	Royal Marines
RN	Royal Navy
RNR	Royal Naval Reserve
RNVR	Royal Naval Volunteer Reserve
R/P	Rocket Projectile
SANF	South African Naval Force
SBNO	Senior British Naval Officer
SD	Anti-submarine screen formation
S/M	Submarine
SNO	Senior Naval Officer
SS	Steam Ship
SST	Submarine to Submarine Transmissions; submarine sound signalling apparatus
STU	A form of Asdic, a particular kind of hydrophone
SWPA	South-West Pacific Area
T/B	Torpedo Boat; Torpedo Bombers
TF	Task Force
TOO	Time Of Origin
TS	Tropical Scale
TU	Task Unit
UN	United Nations
USN	United States Navy
USS	Unites States Ship
V/S	Visual Signal
W/T	Wireless Telegraphy

INDEX OF PERSONS

INDEX OF AIR AND NAVAL UNITS